THE ROAD TO
ASSUNPINK CREEK

ALSO BY DAVID PRICE
Rescuing the Revolution: Unsung Patriot Heroes and the
Ten Crucial Days of America's War for Independence

The cover illustration by Graham Turner, which depicts a scene from the Battle of Assunpink Creek on January 2, 1777, originally appeared in *Trenton and Princeton 1776-77: Washington crosses the Delaware by David Bonk* (New York: Osprey Publishing, 2009).

The original spelling found in source texts has been retained throughout this work. The term [sic] is not used.

THE ROAD TO
ASSUNPINK CREEK

Liberty's Desperate Hour and the
Ten Crucial Days of the American Revolution

David Price

THE ROAD TO ASSUNPINK CREEK:
Liberty's Desperate Hour and the
Ten Crucial Days of the American Revolution
by David Price

This edition published in 2019

Published by Knox Press, an imprint of
Pike and Powder Publishing Group LLC
1 Craven Lane Box 66066
Lawrenceville, NJ 08648

ISBN 978-1-94849601-8 HC
ISBN 978-1-94849607-0 PB
LCN 2018963653

Bibliographical References and Index
1. Military 2. Colonial & Revolutionary 3. New Jersey History

twitter: @pike_powder
facebook: @PikeandPowder

Cover design by Rob Devitis

To the memory of Edward Hand
and the men he led into battle on January 2, 1777

. . . a great empire and little minds go ill together.

> — Edmund Burke, Member of Parliament, from a speech to the British House of Commons urging a policy of conciliation toward the American colonies, March 22, 1775

Those who make peaceful revolution impossible will make violent revolution inevitable.

> — President John F. Kennedy, from an Address on the first Anniversary of the Alliance for Progress, March 13, 1962

In war more than anywhere else, things do not turn out as we expect.

> — Carl von Clausewitz, from *Vom Krieg (On War)*, 1832

CONTENTS

PREFACE

This is my second exercise in writing about the period from December 25, 1776 through January 3, 1777, known as the "Ten Crucial Days" of the American Revolution. During that time, the Continental Army under the command of General George Washington won its first three significant victories of the Revolutionary War and reversed the momentum of that contest, thereby enshrining this brief period as a defining moment in America's struggle for independence.

My first foray into authorship, *Rescuing the Revolution: Unsung Patriot Heroes and the Ten Crucial Days of America's War for Independence,* concerned the exploits of a select group of largely unknown Patriot stalwarts whose heroics contributed to the legendary American triumphs that were part of this remarkable saga. The focus on their individual feats presented a different way of looking at the events that have been more famously chronicled by authors such as William Dwyer, David Hackett Fischer, Richard Ketchum, David McCullough, and William Stryker.

The work before you takes another step down the path of alternative "Ten Crucial Days" historiography by offering what many students of the period may regard as an unconventional and even contrarian approach. It does this by paying particular attention to what I believe is clearly the most unappreciated event during this vital epoch and possibly of the entire war for independence—the military action that occurred on January 2, 1777 and was associated with the Battle of Assunpink Creek. That encounter is often referred to as the Second Battle of Trenton as it followed on the heels of the initial engagement at Trenton on December 26, 1776, when Washington's army made its Christmas night crossing of the Delaware River and attacked the Hessian brigade occupying the town.

For most people, the events of the "Ten Crucial Days" are shrouded in legend and myth that to some extent have distorted the reality of how the Continental Army emerged from the brink of disaster in the waning days of 1776 to fight on against daunting odds and ultimately prevail in a war of attrition against a militarily superior foe. The Delaware crossing and ensuing defeat of the Hessians in Trenton are indelibly imprinted on our historical consciousness, but they represented only the opening act of this drama—and perhaps not even the most important one.

It may be doubted whether so small a number of men ever employed so short a space of time with greater and more lasting effects upon the history of the world.
— Sir George Otto Trevelyan, from his multi-volume work, *The American Revolution, 1899-1907*

1

A CREEK AT THE CROSSROADS

Standing in Mill Hill Park alongside the Assunpink Creek, just east of South Broad Street in New Jersey's capital city of Trenton, one is impressed by the narrowness of the stream as its waters race past this historically paramount site where the course of the American Revolution may have been decided on January 2, 1777. Here the forces of the King of England clashed with a rebel army led by George Washington, which was seeking to rebound from a string of bitter defeats at the hands of the British during a fierce and bloody encounter in which the opposing forces contended for control of the stone bridge that marked this location. In nearby Douglass Plaza, an Italian marble statue of America's foremost general stands guard just north of the creek, facing in the direction from which his adversary approached on that fateful day, with an air of steely resolve that seemingly proclaims its unyielding presence.[1]

The narrow waterway that flows beneath South Broad Street is a stream that anyone with an interest in America's war for independence should accord hallowed status. On the second day of 1777, the creek was all that stood between the opposing armies that collided at this spot. Behind it were the American defenders and behind them was a much wider body of water. "Here it would all be decided," as William Dwyer writes: "Had Washington, with the ice-choked Delaware River at his back, boxed himself into an untenable position? Was this to be another in a long series of disasters. . . . Or did the commander in chief have a surprise move in mind?"[2]

*****

At the start of the American Revolution, Trenton was a small but prosperous town with between 500 and 1,000 residents[3] living in about 100 houses, and it served as the county seat of Hunterdon (later Mercer) County.[4] Situated at the head of navigation on the Delaware River and lying along one of the principal land routes connecting Philadelphia and New York—then the two most populous cities in the American colonies, in that order—the town featured various commercial establishments, skilled artisans, inns, and taverns that catered to the needs of the many who had occasion to visit.[5] It also contained a stone barracks that was built in 1758 during the French and Indian War to house British troops quartered in this locale during that conflict, and which is open to the public today as the Old Barracks Museum.

Trenton at this time had a "long, narrow appearance" created by the wide dispersion of its houses. Most of these dwellings were wooden structures, two stories high, with a garden, well, and cellar, although some residences were built with stone. The town was a busy place in the years leading up to the Revolution. "There were some local merchants, but it was mainly a transfer point for goods going between Philadelphia and New York City. Goods arrived at Trenton by boat from Philadelphia, then were loaded onto wagons

4

to complete their journey east. The process was reversed for goods bound from New York to Philadelphia." Travelers could go by boat between Philadelphia and Trenton on the Delaware, or make the entire trip between Philadelphia and New York City by coach or stage wagon. Two busy ferries operated here—the Old Trenton Ferry or Trent's Ferry, established in 1726, located about a mile south of town, and the New Trenton Ferry, begun in 1773, situated a half-mile farther downstream.[6]

Before European immigrants arrived, the area comprising Trenton and its environs was inhabited for thousands of years by Native Americans who became known to the Europeans as "the Delaware" but who called themselves by their own name, Lenni Lenape, which means "original people." These natives, who were part of the larger Algonquian nation, referred to the Delaware River as "Lenape Wihittuck—Rapid Stream of the Lenape," and were known for "their generally peaceful demeanor and their willingness to act as arbitrators between warring tribes."[7] They maintained an agricultural lifestyle and reportedly grew beans, corn, squash, sweet potatoes, and tobacco on their land. By the time the Revolutionary War began, the Lenape had been forced out of the Delaware Valley by the European settlers, having been defrauded of their lands by dubious legal means.[8]

The initial settlement that became Trenton was established by Quakers in 1679 in the region then known as the Falls of the Delaware, which was part of the province of West Jersey.[9] They were led by Mahlon Stacy, one of a large number of Quakers who had escaped persecution in England by emigrating to North America in order to worship as they chose. By 1719, the settlement had adopted the name "Trent-towne" in honor of William Trent, a leading landholder in the area who had purchased much of the surrounding acreage from the Stacy family, and that moniker was later shortened to "Trenton." Trent established a country estate along the south bank of the Assunpink Creek, fronting on the Delaware River, which featured a brick mansion that was completed around 1719 and is open to the public today as the William Trent House Museum.

The Trenton of the 1770s was laid out in such a way that it served as a transportation hub. The town "lay astride four principal highways, which formed a shape rather like a three-pronged pitchfork, with the handle at the bottom." River Road entered from the northwest, "meandering through low ground behind the numerous ferry landings along the Delaware to carry traffic to the town's busy marketplace and mills." Stretching from the north, Pennington Road connected with the junction of King and Queen Streets, the two main roads in the village—today Warren and Broad Streets, respectively. The Princeton Road, also called the Princeton-Trenton Road, the Post Road, or the King's Highway, headed northeast from Trenton through Maidenhead (Lawrence Township today), Princeton, and over the Raritan River. The Bordentown Road, forming the handle of the pitchfork, was an extension of Queen Street. It crossed Assunpink Creek at the town's southern boundary, continued past the Blazing Star Ferry Road, "and swung off in an easy, curving arc toward Bordentown." In short, Trenton was a significant road junction.[10]

The road network that spread across town and into the surrounding countryside would play a significant role in the tide of historic events that engulfed Trenton during the waning days of 1776 and the opening hours of 1777. So too would the Assunpink Creek, which bordered Trenton on the south and marked the dividing line between Hunterdon County and the wide expanse of Burlington County below it. The latter included the towns of Bordentown, Burlington, and Mount Holly, which assumed a peripheral role in this drama. The area immediately south of the creek was known as Nottingham Township.

The Assunpink Creek derived its name from the Lenni Lenape lexicon in which "assun" meant "stony bottom," and that characterized the lower portion of this creek, while much of its upper section extended "through springy swamps and quicksand bogs." This tributary "flowed from its quiet source in Monmouth County," and its waters were utilized to operate mills at various locations along its route through Hunterdon County.[11]

The first water-powered industrial site on the creek was developed by Mahlon Stacy around 1679 in the form of a crude dam and mill. The town's first bridge over the creek, a wooden structure, was built around 1688 just west of the mill, which by the 1770s was known as Waln's Mill or the Trenton Mills.[12] In 1766, the original bridge—commonly referred to as the Trenton Bridge during the colonial era—was replaced with a span that was, according to a description from about 1787, "built with stone and lime with a high wall on each side handsomely laid."[13] It appears that the "physical layout of the bridge . . . is difficult to establish with any great certainty."[14] It was barely 16 feet wide.[15] And it was probably a double-arched structure.[16]

What can be said with certainty is that the bridge would become a strategic point of contention between two opposing armies when America's struggle for independence from the British Empire erupted almost a decade later. Little could the residents of this riverside town know that the narrow stone overpass on the Assunpink Creek had a rendezvous with history that would signify a defining moment in a momentous conflagration.

*****

As with other histories of the "Ten Crucial Days," the story set forth here is intended to be reasonably comprehensive in its coverage of that period and to convey an understanding of its context in the Revolutionary struggle. What distinguishes this work from those other chronicles is its greater emphasis on the events of January 2, 1777, when the Continental Army fought a daylong running battle against a militarily superior foe and made a successful stand with its back to the Delaware River, avoiding the very real threat of total defeat and setting the stage for a dramatic counterattack against a surprised enemy. That encounter, known as the Battle of Assunpink Creek, was the second in a chain of three victories by the Continental Army under George Washington during the 10-day period that began on December 25, 1776, which historians generally view as having dramatically altered the course of the Revolutionary War. This lightning sequence of triumphs reversed the momentum of the conflict just when it seemed that the quest for independence from Great Britain was on the verge of total defeat.

The January 2 battle has generally been given short shrift from a historiographic perspective and especially downplayed relative to the other two American successes at the time. Those other two actions bookended the Assunpink Creek fight, but the impact of that middle engagement on the outcome of the Continental Army's 10-day campaign was at least as significant as the other events.

The precursor to the battle at Assunpink was the Continentals' legendary crossing of the Delaware River on Christmas night 1776 and the next day's success against the contingent of German soldiers occupying Trenton—generally referred to as "Hessians" by Americans—who had been hired to fight for the British crown. The events of January 2—that is, the fighting that occurred during the enemy's advance from Princeton to Trenton and at the Assunpink itself on that pivotal day—segued into the Americans' overnight march around the enemy's flank early on January 3, which led to the capstone victory of the "Ten Crucial Days" at the Battle of Princeton.

It has been said of this period that the American Revolution "survived . . . in no small part because of what George Washington and his soldiers achieved against all the odds that nature and a vastly

8

superior military force could pit against them."[17] More than a century ago, the English historian George Trevelyan memorably evoked the drama and significance of these developments in the words cited at the beginning of this chapter. For both sides in this struggle, the war would never be the same. And at its end, neither would the world.

I am Imbarked on a wide Ocean, boundless in its prospect & from whence, perhaps, no safe harbor is to be found.

— George Washington, from a letter to his brother, John Augustine, upon being selected as commander-in-chief of the Continental Army by the Continental Congress, June 20, 1775

2

DURHAMS AND ENDURANCE

On December 27, 1776, Charles, Earl Cornwallis, major general in the army of His Majesty, King George III of Great Britain, sent his baggage aboard the *HMS Bristol* in New York harbor as the ship was preparing to sail from British-occupied New York back to England. General Cornwallis had been granted leave by his superior officer, Major General William Howe, commander-in-chief of the British army in North America, to return home for the winter so that he could be with his wife, Jemima, who was in frail health.

Lord Cornwallis deeply loved his wife and was very concerned about her condition. Unlike many of his peers among England's cadre of generals, he never took a mistress and was a paragon of marital fidelity. His Lordship eagerly anticipated a reprieve from the military campaign in which he had been actively engaged to suppress the American quest for independence from the British crown. The colonial rebellion appeared to be on the verge of collapse, and General Howe had issued orders to suspend the campaign until the following spring. This was consistent with the European military custom of the time that eschewed combat during the winter months.

However, as the Bristol was about to depart, Cornwallis received word of a very recent development that would preclude his voyage home and compel him to radically alter his travel plans. The rebellion that appeared moribund only a few days before had suddenly been resuscitated by an American raid at Trenton against the Hessian troops occupying the town. General Howe needed his most able and aggressive field commander to restore the military status quo ante as quickly as possible, and that meant Cornwallis would be riding south rather than sailing east.

Notwithstanding each man's personal aversion to his government's colonial laws and regulations that precipitated the crisis in America, Generals Howe and Cornwallis had agreed to oppose the Revolution in the service of His Majesty and were now determined to fulfill their sense of military duty by crushing the uprising. The rebellion had its roots in a sequence of events that reached back more than a decade. The British laws and regulations that led to war were motivated by what Prime Minister Lord North, acting as the king's faithful right hand at the helm of the House of Commons, asserted was the urge to preserve "the just rights of parliament, or in other words, of the people of Great Britain, over the dependencies of the empire."[1]

In the aftermath of a global struggle with its archenemy France, from 1756 to 1763—a conflict known as the French and Indian War on this side of the Atlantic and as the Seven Years' War in Europe—a victorious England found itself the world's foremost colonial power. However, the spoils of war included substantially larger territories won from France for the British to oversee in North America, which ministerial leadership believed "the American colonists had done very little to achieve."[2] Great Britain was now saddled with the burden of recouping the costs incurred during the prior conflict as well as the anticipated expense of defending and administering these new lands.

The new colonial policy that the imperial ministry adopted was designed to share this financial encumbrance with its subjects across the ocean and was predicated on the notion that at least a portion of the expense required to maintain some 10,000 British regulars in the colonies should be borne by the colonists. In British minds, the presence of this army was ostensibly necessary to protect against any possible threats from the French who might be spoiling for revenge or Native American tribes fearful of encroachment by colonial settlers, even though this military force was considered an unwelcome presence by many in the New World.

British policymakers concluded that the imposition of such cost-sharing requirements on the colonists was perfectly reasonable because it was their land that was to be protected, and their taxes were slight enough that it was calculated "an American paid no more than sixpence a year against the average English taxpayer's twenty-five shillings." The ministry further determined that the manner in which customs duties were collected and avoided in America must be reformed: "Smuggling must be stopped and an end put to the present disgraceful management, whereby it cost £8000 to collect £2000 worth of customs duties in American ports."[3]

British policymakers demonstrated their rejection of "colonial pretensions to a privileged place in the empire" and their intention to rule the colonists as a subservient population when they set upon a path of taxing the colonists to support "the enhanced garrisons needed for an enlarged empire." The colonists viewed these "as an unnecessary expense and a threat to their liberty."[4] The emerging stance of His Majesty's government toward its subjects across the ocean was reflected by a series of actions that commenced shortly after the end of hostilities with the French.

The first, in the form of a 1763 proclamation that prohibited colonists from moving westward into land populated by Native American tribes, was impracticable because there were simply not enough British soldiers on the continent to enforce this edict; and by 1774, some 50,000 settlers resided beyond the proclamation line. Nevertheless, this policy represented a sharp departure from England's previously understated approach to colonial oversight and governance and was widely perceived among Americans as an overbearing intrusion into their sovereignty.

Before the French and Indian War, a series of British governments had taken only sporadic interest in their expanding empire. During that period, the American colonial assemblies "attempted to assume powers which were, in the eyes of the administration in London, properly exercised by governors appointed by the Crown." The British government's new interest in America was seen by many colonists as diminishing their liberties and challenging their local assemblies, "which they regarded as American counterparts to the British Parliament." The assemblies had previously resisted "the encroachments of royal prerogative" and now saw themselves confronted by a new adversary in the British House of Commons, seemingly intent upon legislating against "their freedom and their pockets."[5]

Jon Meacham suggests that "the British demands on the colonists [for tax revenue] were hardly outrageous" given the expenses incurred by the former to defend the borders of the latter, and taking into consideration America's substantial wealth and what he contends was a "compelling case in London for 'virtual representation.'" According to this reasoning, "the king and parliament were stewards of the whole empire whether particular colonists could vote for members of the House of Commons or not."

But in this analysis, the American rebellion that denied the legitimacy of the mother country's demands stemmed from a confluence of motivating factors. These included the "intellectual and political legacy of the English Civil War" of the latter 17th century with its "liberal tradition" articulated by English philosopher John Locke and others, emphasizing individual freedom in a civic, economic, and religious context, and the "classical republican ethos" that was derived from the Renaissance and feared the corrupt exercise of power. Also contributing to the colonial unrest were the religious influence conveyed by mid-18th century preaching that "tended to focus on the centrality of the individual soul in relation to God" and the discontent of many colonists who sought to profit from their "enormous natural resources and endless economic energy" but were constantly in debt to British merchants and banks. These various elements of political, social, economic, and religious thought might be regarded "as tributaries that all helped form the larger rushing river of the American Revolution."[6]

By the time the Declaration of Independence was adopted by the Continental Congress on July 4, 1776, its adherents had determined that "the historical and affective bonds that were supposed to bind the Anglo community" had been irreparably impaired by the failure of the British government to redress their grievances. To those advocating a clean break with Great Britain, the colonists had no choice but to separate from imperial rule and assert that "these United Colonies are, and of Right ought to be FREE AND INDEPENDENT STATES."[7]

Throughout this newly declared union of republican states, animated "[c]rowds celebrated by ringing church bells, firing volleys, illuminating homes with candles, and lighting bonfires on the hills—all accompanied with lavish toasts of alcohol." And they assaulted symbols of the British monarchy, most famously an equestrian statue of George III in New York City, the lead contents of which would be melted down "to make 40,000 bullets to shoot at redcoats." This incident illustrated an ironic and pervasive aspect of the societal context in which the Revolutionary turmoil occurred, because in their zeal for liberty, the colonists utilized slaves to take down the statue.[8]

It is important to acknowledge how divided opinion was among the colonists in regard to Britain's policies toward America. What was then and is still commonly referred to as the Patriot faction—those supporting the Revolutionary agenda of initially advocating for their rights within the British Empire and then later pushing for independence from it—was "the most vocal and best organized" segment among the general public. However, it comprised no more than 45 percent of the white male population, while Loyalists—those desiring to maintain the colonists' status as subjects of the British crown and parliament—accounted for perhaps 15 to 20 percent, with the rest largely neutral.[9] Some colonists supported one side or the other in word but not deed, and some would change sides as the rebellion unfolded; however, in the eyes of ardent Patriots, anyone who did not explicitly commit to supporting their point of view "risked being branded and persecuted as an enemy of America."[10]

The use of the alternative labels, "Whig" and "Tory," as a way of designating American Patriots and Loyalists, respectively, paralleled the application of those terms to the opposing political camps in Britain during the 18th century. In the latter case, the Tories were more conservative and supportive of the monarchy and the Whigs more liberal and reform-minded. The Loyalists on this side of the Atlantic claimed to be defending "true American liberty, for they regarded Patriot committees and mobs as greater threats to freedom than the small taxes levied by Parliament," and they denounced the Patriot faction "for rupturing an empire that had long provided protection and prosperity" and for threatening "the traditional foundations of social order" through "a tyranny of the majority."[11]

16

Notwithstanding the use of the term "Patriot" in connection with the supporters of the revolution, the Loyalists' emotional attachment to America was every bit as strong as that of the Whigs; and "by strict interpretation of the word, [they] were just as much patriots." In their defense, Derek Beck explains that although "British rule had certainly become oppressive . . . and taxation without representation was indisputably unjust, Loyalists were not supporters of tyranny" but "desired only a return to the peace that had happily existed before the Stamp Act of 1765." Despite "the despotism of the English government," he contends that "the American colonies had risen to prominence in large part because of their relationship with the mother country."[12]

The developments that led to the conflagration of the 1770s stemmed from the British Parliament's multiple attempts to tax the colonists and the strenuous opposition that these actions provoked, starting with the Stamp Act in 1765 that sought to tax legal documents, newspapers, licenses, pamphlets, and bills of lading. Although Parliament rescinded these levies in 1766, it coupled that action with an assertion of its authority to impose future taxes on its American subjects by way of the Declaratory Act of 1766 and further exercised that authority through the Revenue Act of 1767 that imposed duties on tea and other items exported to the colonies by Great Britain.

An alternating sequence of American protests and British responses ensued from these imperial initiatives and led to a downward spiral that culminated in a final, irremediable break between the mother country and its New World brethren. Britain's policy had fatally affronted a deep-seated opposition to any perceived infringement of American rights, which as Parliament's great orator, Edmund Burke, noted, was anchored in "a fierce spirit of liberty [that] is stronger in the English colonies probably than in any other people of the earth."[13]

17

The milestones along the road to war included: the so-called "Boston Massacre" committed by occupying British soldiers who fired on a crowd of unruly demonstrators in March 1770; the dumping of East India Company tea into Boston Harbor in December 1773 in protest of the British tax on tea by colonists thinly disguised as Native Americans; the adoption of a series of punitive measures by Parliament, known as the "Coercive Acts" in England and as the "Intolerable Acts" in the colonies, in retribution for the "Boston Tea Party," which encompassed the abrogation of self-government in Massachusetts and the occupation of Boston by British troops who replaced those withdrawn after the Boston Massacre; and the convening of the first Continental Congress at Philadelphia in September 1774 and a second Congress in May 1775 to devise, implement, and seek support for a unified colonial response to British policy.

Tensions mounted on both sides as any hope for a peaceful resolution of the conflicting interests—the colonists' demands for political and economic self-determination versus Britain's assertion of its sovereignty over her North American subjects—gave way to a Gordian knot that made a resort to arms inevitable. The increasingly strident debate over these issues turned to battle in Massachusetts when occupying redcoats and a roused local militia exchanged fire at Lexington and Concord in April 1775.

Two months later, the Continental Army was formed with George Washington as its commander-in-chief after the costly British victory on the slopes of Bunker Hill outside Boston (actually named Breed's Hill in most accounts). Then in August, King George III issued a proclamation that declared the colonies to be in a state of rebellion; and the Continental Army subsequently laid siege to British-occupied Boston, forcing the royal army and much of the Loyalist population there to evacuate the town in March 1776. Finally, the colonies "formally severed their connection to the United Kingdom in July, by which time Britain had dispatched the largest invasion force that ever sailed from the Old World to the New, with the intent of crushing the American rebellion in one devastating blow."[14]

*****

The British ministry's determination to swiftly terminate the colonial uprising in 1776 was dramatically embodied by an armada of over 100 ships that were equipped with 1,200 cannons and carried 32,000 soldiers and 10,000 sailors across the ocean. This was the greatest "amphibious operation ever attempted by any European power, with an attack force larger than the population of Philadelphia," which exceeded that of any other city in America.[15] His Lordship, General Cornwallis had played a significant role in the successful New York campaign, in which the British and Hessian forces delivered a series of stinging defeats to Washington's army of rebellion: at Long Island on August 27, Kips Bay on September 15, White Plains on October 28, and Fort Washington on November 16. The latter was perhaps the worst defeat of the war for the Continental Army, with the loss of some 3,000 men killed, wounded, or captured.

The outcome of these contests was not surprising given the significant disadvantages under which Washington's troops were forced to contend. The rebel forces sought to counter a larger and more professional enemy land force that was supported by the mightiest navy in the world, whose warships navigated the waters around Manhattan island at will. Opposing these intruders was an improvised army of "untrained, ill-disciplined, untried, amateur soldiers, poorly armed, meagerly equipped and supplied, led by an amateur commander-in-chief, who was supported by amateur officers." They had not a single warship or transport, and their war chest "was a printing press in Philadelphia emitting issues of Continental paper dollars, worth whatever one could induce another to give for them and diminishing in value day by day."[16]

Under the circumstances, the Continentals' effort to defend Manhattan and its environs was a fool's errand from a purely military standpoint; in fact, the attempt to hold a "town [that] was, on all accounts, untenable . . . was based on political, rather than military, considerations." While some "historians say it was necessary to make the attempt, in order to fortify the American spirit of resistance," Christopher Ward contends that "if a military task is seen to be impossible of accomplishment, as this one should have been, there is little justification for an attempt to undertake it."[17]

With the New York offensive successfully concluded, Lord Cornwallis led the vanguard of General Howe's army, 5,000-strong, across the Hudson River on the night of November 19 to begin the royal invasion of New Jersey. This they did by capturing Fort Lee— named after the Continental Army's second-ranking officer after Washington, Major General Charles Lee—and its vast quantity of supplies. On November 30, General Howe and his brother, Admiral Richard Lord Howe who commanded the British fleet supporting the imperial invasion, issued a proclamation offering amnesty and protection to any colonist who swore allegiance to the crown within the next 60 days, and at least 3,000 people would respond by affirming their loyalty to the monarchy.

As more of the invaders crossed over from New York, their combined force swelled to some 10,000, and this juggernaut began a methodical but relentless push across northern and central New Jersey under Cornwallis's direction in pursuit of the beleaguered rebel troops. The weary Continentals backpedaled through Hackensack, Newark, Elizabethtown, Brunswick (New Brunswick today), and Princeton and across three rivers—the Hackensack, Passaic, and Raritan—while heading toward a fourth, the Delaware, with a view to putting that natural barrier between themselves and the enemy.

There were no bridges spanning the Delaware at this time, so Washington hastily made preparations to move his men, equipment, and supplies over to the Pennsylvania side. Anticipating the need for waterborne transportation, he dispatched orders from Brunswick to Colonel Richard Humpton in Pennsylvania and other officers to collect at Trenton "boats necessary to transport troops and baggage across the river, and to secure all other boats on the west side of the Delaware."[18] Meanwhile, the American soldiers retreating to the west were forced to endure "roads rutted knee-deep by the artillery, continuously pelted by rain that soaked and chilled to the marrow, huddling together at night because the wood they found was too wet to make a decent fire."[19]

By December 8, the Continental Army had been transported to the Pennsylvania side of the Delaware River after a crossing that took several days to complete, and these soldiers began to spread out over some 25 miles of Bucks County countryside. Washington's army had been reduced to about 10 percent of its original strength as a consequence of casualties, disease, desertions, and expired enlistments, and the Patriot cause had sustained other material damage. Over a three-month period, the British had taken 4,500 prisoners and captured almost 3,000 muskets, nearly 250 cannons, and 17,000 cannonballs.[20] Compounding these losses was the prospect of large-scale departures among Washington's remaining soldiers when their one-year enlistments expired on December 31. Many of them were suffering from having to endure the onset of winter without proper clothing, shoes, stockings, or blankets. This motley crew of amateur combatants was not only "tired and hungry and ragged" but "sullen with the knowledge that it had been badly beaten every time it had gone into battle and forced to retreat after every engagement."[21]

Furthermore, Major General Charles Lee, the English immigrant who represented the Continental Army's most experienced senior officer from his extensive service with the British army during and after the French and Indian War, was seized by British dragoons on December 13 at a tavern near Basking Ridge, New Jersey, in what was widely viewed as a significant loss to the rebel cause. And the next day, the Continental Congress fled from Philadelphia to Baltimore to elude any possible enemy attack, while thousands of the city's residents packed their belongings and fled to the countryside in search of refuge from the anticipated arrival of imperial troops.

An objective observer of these developments could hardly be blamed for sharing the prevalent conviction among British military leadership that the Continental forces were on the verge of disintegration. Captain Francis Lord Rawdon gave voice to this assumption when he opined that "their army is broken all to pieces" and "it is well nigh over with them."[22]

The grim mood among many on the rebel side reflected the military circumstances of the moment, as Ensign Peter Jaquett of the Delaware Regiment observed: "A thick cloud of darkness and gloom covered the land and despair was seen in almost every countenance."[23] Growing doubts about Washington's judgment and leadership were spreading among some of his own officers and in the Congress, which must have been especially galling to a general who "jealously guarded his reputation" while "taking care to allow others no excuse to question his conduct."[24] The most urgent matter confronting the commander-in-chief at this point was to somehow generate a flow of new recruits to what appeared a dying enterprise, as he confessed when writing to his half-brother, Augustine, on December 18: "If every nerve is not strained to recruit a new Army with all possible expedition, I think the game is pretty near up."[25]

Despite this bleak picture, the reality during these dark days for the rebellion is that Washington's troops were reeling but resilient. This was true even during their three-week-long retreat across some 80 to 90 miles of northern and central New Jersey. To be sure, the rebel army was in "sorry condition," as Mark Edward Lender characterizes it, for "enlistments were running out, desertions increased, equipment losses were serious, and the enemy had the initiative. Yet the patriot ranks never broke." Washington and his officers "called on every available resource, and in the end they did so effectively," so that the army always had "just enough transport, ammunition, food, forage, and weapons," along with "an effective artillery arm." Once the initial shock from the British and Hessian invasion subsided, "a small but steady stream of reinforcements moved toward the retreating column. Units remained intact, even if thin. In short, patriot efforts kept their battered force operational. It was a retreating army, not a fleeing mob."[26]

Still, Washington was a general with limited experience in leading an army and smarting from one defeat after another during a cruel summer and fall for the Revolutionary undertaking. And he faced the most difficult challenge of his life: to prevent the destruction of the soldiery he commanded—the most conspicuous symbol of the cause of American independence about which he felt so passionately—and to launch this force into a renewed fight against a militarily superior adversary. He would need to summon the full extent of his perseverance and resourcefulness to meet this crisis and prevail against what appeared to be very long odds.

*****

The American commander-in-chief, then 44 years old, faced the possibility of final defeat by the forces of the British lion, which he had so desperately sought to join when he was half that age. At that time, he had endeavored to secure a commission in the crown's army that would allow him to command royal troops during the French and Indian War. That contest placed an ambitious youth of fairly modest means, as compared with the larger landowners of colonial Virginia, on a path that would literally bring him fame and fortune—the former by elevating his social status and establishing his reputation as something of a military celebrity and the latter by a convenient and amicable but less-than-thoroughly-romantic marriage into wealth.

The young Washington's ancestors had lived for generations on an estate in Northhamptonshire, England, given them by King Henry VIII. Washington's great-grandfather sailed for the New World in 1657, having suffered economically after the English Civil War, and settled in Virginia. His grandson Augustine, George's father, had been sent home to receive an English education and then returned to Virginia to greatly expand the family's estates. He eventually acquired 10,000 acres and 50 slaves, as well as bearing 10 children by two wives.

George was 11 when his father died in 1743 and was not sent to school in England as his two eldest half-brothers had been, As a result, he learned less of the classics than they had but much more in the way of "practical matters" and soon took an interest in becoming a surveyor. Being "a resourceful and adventurous as well as conscientious surveyor," Washington became acutely interested in the settlement of America's western lands in the American west; and as "a speculator in various western enterprises," the young entrepreneur was naturally displeased when His Majesty's government introduced the Proclamation Line in 1763 to limit those areas in which colonial settlement would be permitted.[27]

By the time he first went to war in the 1750s, Washington was a landowner in his own right. Upon the death of his oldest half-brother, Lawrence, he had inherited 2,500 acres that included a plantation, Mount Vernon, which was named after a British admiral under whom Lawrence had served, as well as several slaves. Then hostilities with the French and their Native American allies provided the young soldier with the opportunity to become a military hero as colonel of the 1st Virginia Regiment from 1754 to

1758, during which time "he built the first professional American military force in history."[28]

As the conflict intensified between the British and their colonial subjects against the French and Native American forces in Canada, and in the Ohio Valley along the western periphery of England's North American colonies, this up-and-coming officer transformed his regiment of irregulars "from a scraggly, neglected collection of misfits" into "an efficient, well-equipped and organized little fighting machine."[29] Although Washington made the kind of battlefield mistakes that one might expect from "a young, inexperienced, and headstrong officer," the military neophyte molded his Virginia soldiers into "the best-trained and equipped provincial unit" in the 13 colonies.[30]

At the same time, Washington's "ambition for public reputation" shone brightly.[31] He wanted to be known by the qualities that were commonly associated with such repute—"[p]referment, character, credit, esteem, honor." The boyish colonel may never have explicitly voiced a yearning "to 'be talked about,' but he desired precisely that."[32]

Still, Washington never received the royal commission he very much wanted and when the British drove the French from the Ohio Valley and thereby effectively terminated Virginia's role in the war, he left behind his dreams of military glory and turned to other pursuits. Washington became a family man as the husband of widow Martha Custis and stepfather to her two young children, a planter as the owner of his sprawling Mount Vernon estate, and a politician as an elected member of the Virginia House of Burgesses.

It could be argued that the youthful Virginian was formed by his wartime experience of the 1750s, during which he endured terrible hardships and survived serious illness, while surviving enemy fire in battle; however, he could not attain what he most wished for—"to become a career officer in the British navy or army."[33] He had been spurned by the imperial military as a "mere colonial" and over time would become increasingly bitter over that rejection.[34] By the time Washington resigned his commission as a colonel at the end of 1758, he "was thoroughly disgusted not only with the British but with himself," according to Willard Sterne Randall. "In his eyes he had lost money, neglected his farms, and possibly destroyed his health," but new opportunities awaited him. The disenchanted warrior had an opportunity "to begin a new life and to prove himself adequate in his own eyes and in those of his family and friends as a husband, a stepfather, and that most revered of figures in Virginia, a planter."[35]

Over the next decade and a half, Washington became a notable figure in the life of colonial Virginia and achieved a considerable degree of wealth, acquiring along the way valuable expertise and experience that would prepare him for the challenges ahead. A rising public figure, he enhanced the managerial skills that he had already demonstrated as a colonial soldier, by successfully operating an extensive plantation, and his legislative duties in the House of Burgesses required him to "study such matters as taxation and expenditures as well as public policies from an angle of vision different from that of a soldier, to be conscious of electoral behavior and political realities—subjects often foreign to men in uniform."[36]

It was only a matter of time before events drew Washington's attention away from the prosaic routines of everyday life at his Potomac River manor. As it did for many in the planter class throughout Virginia and the other southern colonies, the imposition of British taxes represented both an infringement of his political rights and a threat to his commercial success.[37] He gradually became an ardent supporter of the Patriot movement and made clear his recognition of the need for military action to effectuate the aim of self-government among the American colonies. Upon learning of the hostilities at Lexington and Concord in the spring of 1775, which marked the point when the political debate became a shooting war, Washington wrote: "the once happy and peaceful plains of America are either to be drenched with blood or inhabited by slaves."[38]

When the Continental Congress came to appoint someone to assume direction of the new American army being assembled from the various colonial units gathering outside Boston, Washington was an obvious choice. First, he hailed from the largest colony and as a southerner would help galvanize support for the Revolution outside its New England cradle. Second, he had a highly regarded record of military experience in the earlier war and had also demonstrated as a Virginia legislator and delegate to both the first and second Continental Congresses that he was attuned to the niceties of government and politics. Finally, he projected an image of integrity and leadership that had earned him widespread public admiration and would make him an appealing figure around whom to rally support for the struggle that lay ahead. Washington looked the part of a commander and exuded an air of rectitude. He was described by contemporaries "as temperate, earnest, and prudent, with a commanding and dignified presence."[39] And the attitude of disinterest in his own personal advancement that he conveyed to others undoubtedly enhanced his stature in the Congress, notwithstanding a long-held ambition for greater public recognition that lurked within. This Virginia planter, "with his ascendance to lead the American army, had achieved what he had craved all his life: attention, honor, status."[40]

Upon assuming command of the Continental Army in July 1775, Washington confronted the challenge of bending to his will the independent-minded souls who comprised the majority of what was essentially an army of New Englanders and whose egalitarian instincts reflected a degree of "indiscipline and disorder" that was intolerable to this strict disciplinarian. These New England soldiers, in turn, had little use for what they regarded as their commander's "hierarchical attitudes," and they made up two-thirds of the army as late as June 1776. Nevertheless, the leader and led gradually found a basis for cooperation, with the southern planter learning "to listen, to reason, and to work through councils of war" attended by officers who were mostly "Yankees." At the same time, the New Englanders came to understand "that an army was not a town meeting, that somebody had to give orders, and that orders had to be obeyed." Eventually they arrived at "an untidy and unstable compromise, which allowed an army of cantankerous Yankees to operate under a gentleman of Virginia."[41]

Washington used the air of detachment or distance he projected as a way to earn the loyalty of his men, for he employed it in a way that was calculated "to reinforce his image as one who eschewed pettiness, favoritism, and partnership." This reserved demeanor added to Washington's authority, as "it elicited greater respect, enabling him to exact dutiful performance as rigorously from others as from himself." In a paradoxical way, he maintained a certain "distance from men as individuals, to avoid intimate relationships, and yet to convey . . . a spirit of togetherness."[42]

Even so, the burden that Washington was forced to shoulder as the leader of this conglomeration stretched well beyond concerns that were distinctive to soldiers from any one region. The challenges that the commanding general faced included the lack of a common national identity among his troops. The circumstances required that he "create a new army without shared traditions and composed of men almost exclusively from civilian backgrounds from all over America—frontier to seaboard, New Hampshire to Georgia." The members of this citizen army did not initially identify themselves as American nationals but rather as residents of their respective states. [43]

The essential task faced by Washington—to mold the manpower that filled the Continental ranks into an effective fighting force—was a formidable one indeed. These civilians-turned-combatants "were generally able-bodied, hardy, sufficiently courageous," and could shoot; however, they were short on military equipment, gunpowder, uniforms, experienced officers, and discipline in the ranks. Christopher Ward writes: "The need, the absolute necessity of organizing a real army, subject to centralized authority, was plainly apparent, and the Congress was prevailed upon to move toward that end, though by slow and reluctant steps." The Continental Congress adopted a series of resolutions proposing that each of the various colonies raise a specified number of soldiers to serve in the new American army, with privates under a one-year term of enlistment, to be subject "to such rules and regulations as are or shall be established for the government of said army."[44]

For his part, Washington provided the army with "a structure and organization that would remain, with certain later modernizations and reforms, throughout the war." In the process, he created a centralized staff structure and divided "his command into brigades—usually six regiments in each—and his brigades into larger units designated as divisions." In addition, the commander-in-chief brought order in substantial measure to the army and "never wavered from his long-standing conviction that discipline was the soul of any military organization."[45]

Washington had achieved one notable success in the early months of the war without actually fighting a battle, by forcing General Howe's occupying force out of Boston in March 1776 through the placement of artillery on Dorchester Heights that rendered the British position in the town untenable. However, it was a hollow triumph in the sense that Howe had been planning to evacuate Boston for months in order to find more advantageous ground on which to challenge the American forces and was only waiting for the arrival of sufficient ships to make his withdrawal. So Washington's maneuver only expedited what would have happened anyway. Beyond this symbolic but militarily insignificant development, the rebel commander's encounters with his adversary during the period leading up to December 1776 had generally yielded an unrelenting series of setbacks.

*****

William Howe, then 47, was "the third son of the 2nd Viscount Howe, an Irish peer and colonial governor," whose wife, Charlotte, was of "(illegitimate) royal blood" that "blended with her husband's aristocratic pedigree to give their offspring a privileged start in life."[46] An able and personally courageous officer who had served in the military since age 18 and made his mark during the French and Indian War, he was "already one of the most distinguished officers in the British army" when promoted to major general in 1772.[47]

In a straightforward comparison of military forces, Howe clearly had the upper hand in his confrontation with Washington. The Briton was "fortunate in coming up against an inexperienced, untrained, ill-prepared, badly equipped foe" and in addition had the advantage of leading "an army that was at least the equal, if not the superior, of any in the world."[48] Howe deployed that army in a skillful and professional manner against a militarily inferior opponent, and could be comforted by the fact that it was "more powerful than any Great Britain had ever fielded outside Europe and the largest it had assembled anywhere in the last several decades."[49]

In contrast to Washington, who was slowly and painfully learning on the job in spite of the numerous handicaps under which he labored, Howe was a "brilliant organizer and tactician" who had won impressive victories, but was without "a sense of strategic urgency" and "failed to press home attacks on the staggered enemy."[50] Competent but hardly visionary, the British commander was handicapped by a cautious approach to battlefield leadership that prevented him from going for his opponent's jugular when the opportunity presented itself.

Howe's reluctance to push the colonials harder may have been due to one or more of the following factors: an innate prudence regarding the use of military force; the shock of having witnessed the inordinate toll of British casualties at Bunker Hill; Howe's basic antipathy to British colonial policy; or his generally warm feeling toward the Americans, which manifested itself in a desire to achieve a peaceful accommodation with the colonists once he had impressed upon them the futility of militarily opposing the forces of the empire. Whatever the reason, Howe displayed obvious deficiencies as a military leader: "incredibly slow and ponderous" movements; "timorous, unimaginative, and predictable" tactics; a strategy "based on no clear conception of how the war was to be won"; and plans that were, accordingly, uninspiring and even incoherent.[51]

Howe's lack of a killer instinct accompanied a conviction, which he shared with others in the British officer corps, that the preservation of his army must be a priority. This general was not about to expose his men to what he perceived as unnecessary risks. Rather, Howe preferred a tactical approach that relied primarily on outmaneuvering his opponent and avoiding direct frontal assaults against fortified enemy positions. This was not only because he was operating at the end of a 3,000-mile supply line that made securing reinforcements problematic, but also because "it took from three to five years to train a man properly in the mysteries of precise order drill." He would not dissipate "the lives of men who could not be replaced."[52] For whatever reason, Howe pursued a dilatory course of action throughout the New York campaign and in pursuing the colonials across New Jersey in late 1776, which allowed Washington just enough time to escape the clutches of more aggressive field commanders such as Charles Cornwallis.

When the earl reached the banks of the Raritan River at Brunswick on December 1, close on the heels of the retreating Americans, he was ordered to wait for Howe's arrival from New York before proceeding further. His Lordship dutifully obeyed. It would later be reckoned "as one of the great missed opportunities of the war," but Cornwallis's troops were exhausted from their pursuit. The general had pressed them hard. An "energetic, swift moving soldier," he had nearly caught up with his prey after marching his men "20 miles over the most wretched roads in a single day."[53] These pursuers had to contend with one hindrance after another in trying to chase down the rebels: felled trees blocking roads, demolished bridges, and sniper fire. Given their extreme fatigue, Cornwallis insisted that his men were in no condition to cross the river and fight a battle.[54] In any case, by the time Howe arrived in Brunswick on December 6 and assumed command of the forces there, Washington's men had escaped immediate danger.

General Howe's troops entered Trenton on December 8, right after the last of the retreating Americans departed for the Delaware's opposite shore. The experience of Captain Enoch Anderson of the Delaware Regiment reflected that of the exhausted Continental rearguard as it scrambled to safety on the Pennsylvania side of the river: "This night we lay amongst the leaves without tents or blankets, laying down with our feet to the fire. It was very cold. We had meat, but no bread. We had nothing to cook with, but our ramrods, which we run through a piece of meat and roasted it over the fire, and to hungry soldiers it tasted sweet."[55]

Meanwhile, as with most soldiers reared in the 18th century European military tradition, General Howe "closed his mind to the possibility of winter campaigns" and with "the first frosts . . . put aside all thoughts of soldiering until spring."[56] He effectively terminated the 1776 campaign of the forces under his command several days later, returning to New York to take up quarters there for the winter and issuing the following orders:

Headquarters, December 14, 1776. The Campaign having closed with the Pursuit of the Enemies Army near ninety Miles by Lieut. Gen. Cornwallis's Corps, much to the honor of his Lordship and the Officers and Soldiers under his Command, The Approach of Winter putting a Stop to any further Progress, the Troops will immediately march into Quarters and hold themselves in readiness to assemble on the shortest Notice.[57]

Howe gave Cornwallis permission to spend the winter in England, apparently confident that Washington's army and the war would be quickly and easily terminated come spring, when Howe expected to march on the rebels' capital city of Philadelphia. He left his army in New Jersey under the command of Major General James Grant, who as a member of the British Parliament had once boasted that he could conquer the 13 American colonies with a force of no more than 5,000 men. Before his departure, Howe designated the New Jersey outposts to be garrisoned by his troops during the winter months.

At this point, Trenton represented the westernmost reach of rebel territory occupied by the forces of the British Empire. The decision was made to hold this riverside outpost with a brigade of Hessian soldiers commanded by Colonel Johann Rall, a 50-year-old officer who had been serving in the military since age 14. Being of distinctly middle-class origins, he had earned his rank by proving himself in combat rather than through social connections, unlike most other military officers from England and the various Germanic states at that time. Rall had requested the honor of having his troops occupy this front-line position, and now these German soldiers would most visibly embody the British crown's hopes for a triumphant assertion of imperial sovereignty over its insubordinate colonies.

These Teutonic combatants were in North America because the princes of seven German provinces had hired out troops to fight for George III against the colonial rebellion in early 1776. Notwithstanding the vaunted status of Britain's empire, its army was not large enough to suppress the American uprising and at the same time defend the homeland and other colonial possessions. While England's naval might was unsurpassed, its ability to project power abroad was hampered by the relatively small size of its land forces, which resulted from a long-standing British aversion to the idea of maintaining a large standing army for fear of its use "as a potential instrument of tyranny." Consequently its military successes depended on alliances with other European powers.[58] To win the war in America, His Majesty's government was compelled to contract for the services of foreign soldiers, which was then a frequent practice among nations "and, for the rulers of smaller principalities, a way to supplement their often impoverished treasuries."[59]

About two-thirds of the Germans who served in America came from the provinces of Hesse-Cassel and Hesse-Hanau, mostly the former. Although technically only the soldiers from these two provinces were "Hessians," Americans generally applied that name to all German soldiers fighting alongside the British. Strictly speaking, they were not "mercenaries," as commonly believed, because the British government paid each prince for his soldiers' services, rather than compensating the soldiers themselves. However, it should be noted that these German soldiers were generally well paid by their respective princes.

*****

At a moment when the American rebellion's fortunes appeared to have hit bottom, a combination of factors presaged a turn in the tide of war. It may have begun when the British captured General Lee, the Continental Army's second-in-command, on December 13. While this incident was thought by many at the time to be a major blow to the army's fortunes, it actually proved to be a blessing in disguise.

34

As a result of the calamitous New York campaign, Washington's tactical judgment had become increasingly subject to doubt in the minds of a growing number of skeptics in the army and without, and especially in Lee's mind. The second-in-command had lost trust in Washington's military judgment and aspired to establish his own command.[60] Indeed, he "was determined to prove that he was a better soldier and commander than Washington."[61] But now, thanks to the British having apprehended his immediate subordinate, Washington was in a position to make military decisions without looking over his shoulder for fear that Lee, with his more extensive military experience and penchant for dilatory responses to his commander-in-chief's orders, would question or undermine his authority.

With his bedraggled force arrayed along the Delaware's west bank, Washington had been waiting for Lee—and urging him with ever-increasing desperation—to bring the troops under his command across New Jersey from their previous encampment in New York and join up with Washington's dwindling contingent. Lee, however, was slow to act, believing that his troops were better off operating under what he perceived as his more-skillful military leadership. Indeed, in the eyes of many historians, he has left behind the unflattering image of someone who was "arrogant in his manner, pedantic in the use of technical military terms," and "strutted unchallenged as the one commanding officer in the army who knew what it was all about [and] . . . put himself forward as America's only hope."[62] His sudden apprehension by the enemy would greatly facilitate the Continental Army's efforts to come together in a very literal sense.

In fact, "there was an almost simultaneous demonstration of the benefit of Lee's capture." General John Sullivan, his second in command, promptly marched Lee's men to Washington's camp, arriving there on December 20, with 2,000 men. That same day, General Horatio Gates arrived from upstate New York with 500 men. Over 1,000 militia from the Philadelphia Associators led by Colonel John Cadwalader joined up with the army, although they brought no actual combat experience with them as yet. Finally, a Pennsylvania German regiment of 300 men also joined Washington's force.[63]

Many of the soldiers who were now united with Washington's units were unfit for duty because of disease, malnutrition, exposure, or wounds, but with his numbers reinforced—there were now some 6,000 soldiers available to him on paper—he was in a position to seriously contemplate an action that he had wanted to take from the moment his troops fled across the Delaware to Pennsylvania during the first week of December. That was to surprise the enemy by a sudden blow at the most vulnerable point in their chain of outposts stretching across New Jersey—the Hessian garrison occupying Trenton.

Washington's instinctive urge to take action was powerfully reinforced by two motivations. One was his fear of enemy intentions, since there was no way to know whether "the British would cross the iced-over river if the temperature stayed below freezing or construct boats for the purpose if the ice would not hold them."[64] The other was the commander's acute awareness of an impending manpower shortage that could prove fatal to his army's existence. On the latter score, the incentive to strike the enemy right away was especially urgent because of the approaching December 31 expiration date for the one-year enlistments being served by a large number of Continental soldiers.

As Washington saw it, only an immediate victory—and the promise of improved prospects for success against the European invaders that would result therefrom—could prevent his army's virtual disintegration come the last day of the year and encourage significant numbers of new recruits to join its ranks. Left with no choice but to launch an assault against what he perceived as the soft spot in the enemy's defenses, Washington confided to Colonel

Joseph Reed, the army's adjutant general or chief administrative officer: "necessity, dire necessity, will, nay must, justify my attack."[65]

Meanwhile, General Grant, the commander of the crown's forces in New Jersey who was headquartered in Brunswick, was confident, based on the intelligence reported by British spies in the American camp, that the Continental Army was on the verge of crumbling. He assumed that those rebel soldiers who were actually capable of fighting would shy away from anything so risky as entering into battle when many of them knew that they were just days away from being able to go home and leave this brutal contest behind them. Secure in this conviction, Grant spurned Colonel Rall's request for reinforcements to strengthen the position of the small Hessian contingent in Trenton.

It was at this time that Thomas Paine, a 39-year-old English immigrant who championed the Patriot cause as an editor and essayist in Philadelphia, dramatically elevated the Continentals' spirits when they desperately needed an emotional lift. His pamphlet, *Common Sense*, had roused Americans to support independence from the mother country when it first appeared in January 1776, selling more than 100,000 copies within four months. With his scathing denunciation of monarchies in general and George III in particular, combined with an eloquent plea for the North American colonies to assert their rightful place in the world as a free and prosperous people, Paine "transformed the struggle over the rights of Englishmen into a contest with meaning for all mankind."[66]

The reason for the pamphlet's success was indicated by its title, for "it was straightforward, easy to comprehend, written in clear yet striking prose which all men . . . could readily understand" and "seemed to be written from the heart, with a warmth of feeling so often lacking in publications of its kind."[67] Paine portrayed the American rebellion as a crusade for republican self-government that would be a source of universal inspiration to the masses; this evangelist for the Patriot cause "invested [it] with a global purpose that could motivate people to make the sacrifices needed to win a revolutionary war against a mighty empire."[68]

On December 19, Paine unveiled his sequel, *The American Crisis*, when it appeared in the *Pennsylvania Journal*, and it was published as a pamphlet four days later. According to legend, the initial draft was scrawled on the head of a drum while the author served as a volunteer with the Continental Army during its retreat through New Jersey.

Paine's new call to arms stirred the public to sustain the Revolutionary undertaking when its success was most in doubt. His rallying cry began with a burst of deathless rhetoric: "These are the times that try men's souls: The summer soldier and the sunshine patriot will, in this crisis, shrink from the service of his country; but he that stands it NOW, deserves the love and thanks of man and woman."[69] What followed was just as electric. The various passages in Paine's essay shouted defiance against the enemy: "I cannot see on what grounds the king of Britain can look up to heaven for help against us."[70] And he solicited his readers' support in inspirational tones: "I call not upon a few, but upon all; not on THIS State or THAT State, but on EVERY State; up and help us; lay your shoulders to the wheel; better have too much force than too little, when so great an object is at stake."[71] Paine's words were read to and by many of Washington's troops as he prepared to launch them into battle while he still had an army to command.[72]

The enemy had unwittingly planted the seeds of young America's first military comeback by leaving themselves vulnerable, both geographically and psychologically, to a winter offensive by an insurgency prepared to throw caution to the wind. At General Howe's direction, his forces were strung across New Jersey along a line of garrison posts that extended from Perth Amboy on the eastern shore to the banks of the Delaware River, with the most vulnerable being the Hessian brigade in Trenton by virtue of its geographic exposure to a potential assault.

The British commander appeared confident that the Continental Army would soon collapse and wanted "to give protection" to as many New Jersey Loyalists as possible, so he tempted providence by dispersing his troops in this manner.[73] Unfortunately for the crown's fortunes, Howe proved to be a victim of his own success when he drove Washington to pursue "a do-or-die undertaking" that Howe did not foresee—to launch what was left of the rebel army "across a swollen, ice-laden river and lead them through a blizzard to strike the sleeping enemy in Trenton."[74]

The failure of the imperial invasion force to cross the Delaware in December had given the American commander-in-chief a critically needed respite, and he took advantage of it. Washington dispatched raiding parties into New Jersey and encouraged local militia to harass the foe. They were "actively probing for weak points along Howe's lines and making life dangerous for small enemy detachments."[75] At the same time, the reprieve granted the rebel forces by the crown's military commander allowed Washington to collect reinforcements while also gathering intelligence on the disposition of enemy troops. As a result, he was able to determine that their "scattered and isolated posts were obvious attractions" as possible targets of attack.[76]

Based on the information reported to him, Washington and his generals conceived a plan, as desperate as it was daring, to assault Colonel Rall's brigade in Trenton. The Americans had never defeated the Hessians in battle, and the stakes involved in this enterprise were perhaps best encapsulated in the secret password that the commanding general devised for the operation and inscribed himself on small pieces of paper distributed to each unit of the army—"Victory or Death."[77]

Christmas night was chosen as the moment to attack, with the rebel forces scheduled to come together on the afternoon of December 25 near McConkey's Ferry on the Pennsylvania side of the river and begin crossing at about 4 p.m. The starting time was intended to ensure that the troops would be able to get over to New Jersey by midnight, thereby allowing sufficient time to arrive in Trenton while it was still dark and maximize their chances of achieving surprise. However, the actual crossing did not begin in force until closer to 6 p.m., and this delay only added to the various challenges encountered by the army in undertaking such a hazardous endeavor.

According to William Stryker, the Marbleheaders—the soldiers of the 14th Massachusetts Continental Regiment from Marblehead, known as the Marblehead Regiment and led by Colonel John Glover—were "the men on whom all relied to see the army safely landed."[78] One mid-19th century account has Glover confidently assuring Washington of success at the council of war in which the general presented his plan to cross the river to his fellow officers, promising the commander-in-chief that "my boys can manage it."[79] Glover's unit was to be joined by other mariners and seafaring types who frequented the Philadelphia waterfront before the war and local residents experienced at navigating the Delaware in the dark.

This Massachusetts regiment—comprising recruits from fishing towns on the north shore such as Beverly, Lynn, Marblehead, and Salem—was viewed as one of the best in the army.[80] Back in August, its fishermen-turned-soldiers had provided a critical assist to the Patriot cause after the defeat at Long Island. The Marbleheaders then earned plaudits by rowing some 9,500 Continental troops across the East River from Brooklyn to Manhattan with all their baggage, supplies, and artillery under the cover of night and then early morning mist, thereby saving those troops from certain destruction or capture by the enemy.

The Marblehead Regiment was notable for its ethnic diversity as well as its nautical background, as its ranks included Native American and African American soldiers. Although the latter were free men, the slave population that had been brought to America from Africa and the West Indies during the preceding decades had grown over time to where it now accounted for one fifth of the colonies' total population—the largest non-English component—estimated at about half a million people. African Americans would ultimately comprise about five percent of all those who served in the Continental Army over the course of the war—about 5,000 soldiers.[81] They filled a need that was created by the precarious nature of "white enlistment" throughout the long contest.[82] Notwithstanding the concern expressed by some officers that the presence of black soldiers might inhibit whites from enlisting, there is no indication from their diaries and correspondence that the white soldiers "who served alongside African Americans in the same companies or regiments considered their presence racially offensive. Most found it a point unworthy of comment."[83] In the process, an army led by a Virginia slaveholder became "the first integrated national institution in the United States."[84]

It may be that the Patriot leaders were mindful of "the excruciating contradiction between their revolution on behalf of liberty and American slavery."[85] Undoubtedly many Englishmen at the time concurred with their fellow countryman and celebrated essayist, Samuel Johnson, who, in voicing opposition to the protests against Britain's colonial policy by the rebellious American colonists, asked why it was "that we hear the loudest yelps for liberty among the drivers of Negroes?"[86] Indeed, "the British never tired of highlighting the hypocrisy of rebels talking the language of liberty while owning slaves."[87] Ultimately, Washington would be the only one of the republic's founding fathers to free his slaves—and only upon his death by a provision in his will that was to take effect when his wife, Martha, passed away.

The cruel irony of the Americans' failure "to resolve the contradiction between a war waged in the name of liberty and the enslavement of Africans and their descendants in America" is magnified by the sharp contrast between the British Empire's abolition of the slave trade in 1807 and slavery itself in 1834 and the entrenchment and expansion of slavery in this country.[88] This incongruity becomes even more conspicuous when one considers the number of African Americans who fought in support of the Revolution. On the other hand, the cruelty and omnipresence of bondage in North America, which was legal in every colony but especially prevalent in the South, may actually have fueled the colonial grievances that led to rebellion against the crown: "Freedom seemed all the more precious because colonists daily saw the humiliation and exploitation of the enslaved."[89]

At Washington's command, the Durham boats that were to be used in the Christmas night crossing were collected from the upper Delaware and Lehigh rivers. Daniel Bray, Jacob Gearhart, and Thomas Jones, all captains in the Hunterdon County militia, engineered this effort and reportedly concealed the boats behind Malta Island below Coryell's Ferry (today New Hope) on the Pennsylvania side of the Delaware, several miles above the site at McConkey's Ferry where the main Continental force would cross.[90] (Malta Island cannot be discerned today because of topographical changes to that area.) In addition to the Durhams, the militia gathered other boats over a 40-mile stretch of the Delaware and moored them in various creeks and behind wooded islands along the river's west bank, intending to deprive the enemy of these craft while keeping them ready for the Americans' use.

The Durham boats, which were constructed at the Durham Ironworks or Durham Furnace near Easton, Pennsylvania, typically ranged from 30 to 60 feet in length and were about eight feet wide in the beam. It is estimated that each of these boats carried between 30 and 40 soldiers, in addition to a crew of several rowers and a captain. The latter functioned as a pilot by steering the boat with a "sweep" oar, about 25 feet long and weighing some 90 pounds, protruding from the stern. The crew used oars that were about 18 feet long and weighed some 35 pounds; two men were required to operate each oar, and there were two to four oars on each side depending on the length of the boat. The Continental soldiers would have been required to stand on the Durhams; these vessels had no seats since they were not built to hold passengers but rather to transport heavy cargo such as iron ore, pig iron, produce, and timber downriver to Philadelphia.

Washington knew that the proposed crossing was a high-risk gamble that would "produce either storied success or utter calamity, and he seemed ready to pay the price."[91] According to tradition, Captain William Blackler of the Marblehead Regiment commanded the Durham boat that took Washington across the Delaware River, having been thus assigned by Colonel Glover. Colonel Henry Knox, the American artillery commander, superintended a lengthy and perilous undertaking, and his commanding general spent most of the time that it took the army to cross waiting anxiously on the New Jersey side while the weather steadily deteriorated.

The challenge of transporting the army across the river would have been formidable enough under the best climatic conditions. This maneuver involved the movement of seven brigades of infantry in the Durham boats, including 2,400 soldiers who each carried 60 rounds of ammunition and a three-day supply of rations. In addition, the army had to transport on flat-bottomed ferry boats, which were obtained from the McConkey's Ferry on the Pennsylvania side and the Johnson's Ferry on the New Jersey side, 18 artillery pieces, some 50 to 100 horses, and an unknown number of ammunition wagons. However, a full-blown northeaster descended on the area by 11 p.m.

and compounded the difficulty of carrying out Washington's battle plan. The resulting conditions turned that plan into the "first casualty of the battle." [92]

Two other American units, comprised largely of Pennsylvania militia, were supposed to cross over from the Pennsylvania side and support Washington's attack—one under General James Ewing stationed opposite the southern end of Trenton and the other under Colonel John Cadwalader in Bristol. However, they were stymied in their efforts to do so on this night by the buildup of ice on the river that was more severe in the area south of where the main rebel force crossed.

This would ultimately leave Washington's two divisions to carry out the attack against the Hessians on their own, and the elements posed a formidable set of challenges to the captain and crew responsible for conveying each boatload of soldiers across the stormy waterway. These included: poor visibility caused by cloud cover that hid a full moon; a river swollen by continuous precipitation, which meant that each boat had to be rowed an additional 50 to 80 feet beyond what would have been the case under normal weather conditions; a swift current that caused the boats to drift downstream; sheets of ice impeding the boats, which must have been unnerving to the vast majority of passengers who did not know how to swim at a time when most people (including sailors) lacked that skill; and a fierce wind blowing in the faces of the captain and crew in each boat.[93]

As a result, the crossing failed to conform to the commander-in-chief's timetable. The artillery, wagons, and horses probably caused the greatest delay. While the average crossing time is hard to ascertain, "with estimates ranging from ten to fifteen minutes," the conditions on the river could very well have increased the amount of time required for each boat to cross. It is quite possible "that loading, crossing, unloading, and returning could take an hour for each trip." Knox wrote that all the troops reached New Jersey by 2 a.m. and that the artillery was across by 3 a.m., which "means the entire crossing lasted between nine and ten hours, or three hours longer than planned."[94]

The army began its march to Trenton at about 4 a.m., some four hours behind schedule. The Continentals did not reach their objective until after daybreak, at about 7:20 a.m., after a march of almost 10 miles that was made in many cases by soldiers whose shoes were falling apart or who had to tie rags around their feet to substitute for shoes that had disintegrated. Their advance could be tracked by the trail of bloody footprints left in the snow, and at least two of the marchers froze to death along the way.[95] Each man was ordered to remain with his unit or face "instant punishment," while each officer was ordered "on no account to separate" from his unit and to carry "a piece of white paper stuck in his hat for a field mark" to guide his men.[96]

An unknown number of soldiers who crossed the Delaware under the frigid conditions that prevailed would later perish from disease, exposure, exhaustion, or malnutrition, but on this night the army could take satisfaction from the knowledge that it had made the treacherous passage without the loss of a soldier, cannon, horse, wagon, or boat.[97] The hardships suffered by these men had only begun by the time they landed on the opposite shore, given how unprepared they were for the weather, with "none of them warmly clad, many of them in threadbare summer clothing, few properly shod and many not shod at all, slogging along on the rough road made slippery by the snow," and pummeled by the wind, hail, and freezing rain.[98]

On the other hand, the elements that bedeviled this operation would actually pay dividends for the Patriot soldiers. The weather played into the hands of what European observers at the time would have regarded as the rebels' unconventional way of conducting war. The severe conditions lulled the Hessians into a false sense of security, so that they did not send patrols up the river as was part of their usual routine during less harsh weather, "and the blizzard that reached full force after the Americans had crossed the river screened their movement south." When the attacking army arrived in Trenton at about 8 a.m., it found the enemy unprepared for the assault. The Hessians were also hampered by the mindset that was prevalent among European armies at the time. They generally did not campaign during the winter, nor in inclement weather or at night. The colonial "intruders" were not encumbered by these "rules" on December 26, "and in that sense, Washington's victory at Trenton could be construed as the product of a uniquely American style of waging war in the 18th century."[99]

Colonel Rall's garrison was caught in a pincer movement between the two wings of the Continental force. These included the four brigades of the Second Division commanded by Major General Nathanael Greene of Rhode Island and accompanied by Washington, and the three brigades that comprised the First Division under Major General John Sullivan of New Hampshire.

Greene's unit, largely composed of southerners, hit Trenton from the northwest by way of the Pennington Road and then spread its men out to cover the northeast approach from the Princeton Road, while Sullivan's contingent, which included mostly New Englanders, forced its way into town from the southwest along the River Road. The two columns, each sporting nine field guns, had literally synchronized watches, and they commenced their respective assaults within a few minutes of each other.

Private Jacob Francis, a 22-year-old African American born in Amwell, New Jersey, who had been a slave to five masters in succession before earning his freedom at age 21, was now serving in the 16th Massachusetts Continental Regiment in Sullivan's division, and he recalled how the enemy was snared in the assailants' vise.

46

His regiment advanced "from the River Road into the town to the corner where it crosses the street running up towards the Scotch Road and turned up that street," where he beheld a welcome sight: "General Washington was at the head of that street coming down towards us and some of the Hessians between us and them. We had the fight."[100]

The battle scene has been sketched in grim tones that portray "the narrow village streets [as] an inferno of confusion and racket, with small clumps of Hessians here and there, firing from houses at the attacking rebels," while the Americans struck "from three sides at once, shooting from the cover of buildings, [with] smoke and snow and shouts and explosions all mixed together in the wild swirling of the storm."[101] The sense of tumult that pervaded this confrontation is reinforced by the fury with which the rebel troops "did much of their fighting—street-to-street, house-to-house—with musket butts, bayonets (short in supply), swords, and their bare hands."[102]

The sleet and snow that fell during the engagement rendered many shoulder weapons useless on both sides due to wet firing pans and enhanced the importance of artillery. Indeed, the Americans relied to a crucial degree on a decided advantage in this regard, with 18 guns compared to their foe's six three-pounder cannons (a cannon that fired a three-pound ball or shell) and their ability to concentrate their field pieces in a way that Rall never could as his guns were dispersed equally among the three Hessian regiments.

The attackers' use of their big guns was only one of a number of factors that enabled them to quickly gain the upper hand in this encounter. They had other significant advantages at Trenton: the benefit of surprise; numerical superiority, with 2,400 soldiers against 1,500 Hessians; and the state of exhaustion afflicting an enemy who had been forced to respond to a relentless series of minor but annoying attacks by New Jersey militia in recent days. In addition, the "driving snow from the ongoing northeaster reduced the visibility of the Hessian defenders, as it was blowing from behind the backs of the soldiers in Greene's division into the faces of Rall's men, while the latter had to contend with dampened cartridges and firing mechanisms on their muskets from the freezing precipitation."[103]

Captain William Washington of the 3rd Virginia Regiment, a second cousin once removed of the commander-in-chief and "a very large young man for his time,"[104] and his second-in-command, an 18-year old lieutenant named James Monroe who was recently a student at the College of William and Mary in Virginia's capital of Williamsburg, led their infantry down King Street in a furious charge that seized two Hessian cannons during a crucial moment in the battle. The 3rd Virginia was part of a brigade commanded by Brigadier General William Alexander, known to all as Lord Stirling— an ironic name for an ardent believer in the Patriot cause—because he claimed to have inherited a Scottish earldom.

During the King Street melee, Captain Washington was hit by musket fire in both hands and Monroe, who had relieved him, fell wounded as well with a musket ball in his left shoulder. He was on the verge of bleeding to death when John Riker, a young physician who had volunteered his services to the lieutenant's regiment as it passed by his house the night before, clamped the severed artery and stanched the hemorrhaging. Monroe would carry the musket ball with him for the rest of his life, but it did not impede his pursuit of a distinguished political career that culminated in his becoming President of the United States.

Overall, American casualties were extremely light: two privates died in action; at least four or five succumbed to exposure or illness; and three officers and two privates were wounded.[105] The casualties sustained by the three units in Rall's brigade—the Rall, Lossberg, and Knyphausen regiments—have been estimated as follows: 22 killed, including Colonel Rall; 84 severely wounded; and 812 taken prisoner but not severely wounded.[106] In addition, Washington's army captured six cannons, 40 horses, six wagons, a thousand muskets and bayonets, and a large quantity of ammunition.[107]

This action has been described as a raid rather than a battle, and indeed the number of soldiers involved was relatively small—fewer than 4,000 combined—but the impact on American morale was far out of proportion to the size of the engagement or its strategic significance. For an army so used to losing, any win at this point had outsized import.[108]

Generations of Americans have adhered to a popular belief that the key to the Continentals' victory was the adverse effect of excessive Christmas-related celebrating by the Hessians on their capacity to resist the American assault; however, there is no evidence to support the notion that Rall's troops were so impaired. Instead, the record indicates that the only widespread drinking in Trenton at that time was by rebel soldiers after the battle, when they discovered 40 hogsheads of rum in town. Once the commander-in-chief was apprised of this unauthorized revelry, he ordered that those casks be destroyed; however, this was after more than a few of the soldiers had partaken of the liquid refreshment. Their impaired condition was a factor of some weight in the decision that was made by Washington and his fellow generals to abandon any thought of continuing their offensive and instead withdraw to the Pennsylvania side of the river.[109]

An important side note to the December 26 victory was written by an unlikely duo whose combined efforts succeeded in diverting Hessian troops who might otherwise have been able to reinforce Colonel Rall's brigade when the Americans attacked. Colonel Samuel Griffin of Virginia had led a force of about 500 militia, mostly from the southern New Jersey counties of Cumberland, Gloucester, and Salem, in a movement toward the Mount Holly area from Haddonfield, about 30 miles below Trenton, on December 14. Their purpose was to engage the Hessian forces there, who were led by Colonel Rall's superior officer, Colonel Carl von Donop, then in overall command of the German units at Trenton, Bordentown, and Burlington.

Griffin skirmished with Donop on December 22 and 23 and was forced to pull back without seriously damaging the enemy. However, those maneuvers had the effect of luring Donop's troops in Bordentown away from their post so that on the morning of December 26 they were in Mount Holly, 18 miles from the scene of the Trenton battle rather than only six miles as would have been the case had they remained in Bordentown.

After chasing off Griffin's men, Donop did not withdraw to Bordentown but instead stationed himself in the house of a woman who, according to one of his officers, Captain Johann Ewald, was an "exceedingly beautiful young widow of a doctor."[110] Ewald reported that Donop was "exceedingly devoted to the fair sex" and accordingly quite taken with his hostess. The captain took a dim view of his colonel's interest in the widow, whose identity is unknown to this day; and he later deplored their encounter in the most strenuous terms, asserting that this "great misfortune, which surely caused the utter loss of the thirteen splendid provinces of the Crown of England, was due partly . . . to the fault of Colonel Donop, who was led by the nose to Mount Holly by Colonel Griffin, and detained there by love." Ewald grumbled that "the fate of entire Kingdoms often depends upon a few blockheads and irresolute men."[111]

Speculation about the identity of the mysterious widow has included multiple candidates. One is famed Philadelphia seamstress Betsy Ross.[112] Another is the lesser-known Mary Magdalene Valleau Bancroft.[113] Whoever she was, "the widow made a major contribution, perhaps unintentionally, to the American cause."[114] Love may or may not conquer all, but it is quite possible that it factored into the Continental Army's first significant victory of the war.

The effort made by this unknown individual, if deliberate, is emblematic of the role played by women in the struggle for independence that traditional accounts of the war largely overlook. Fortunately, recent historiography has done much to correct this deficiency. In fact, women were essential to enforcing "the American consumer boycott" of British goods and supported the insurgent forces by furnishing soldiers with clothing, as well as cooking, nursing, and washing laundry in camp; and even acting as couriers and spies.[115] And because "so many men [were] away fighting, wives and daughters had to run family farms and shops, or the economy would collapse."[116]

Perhaps no one felt more keenly than George Washington a passion for the cause of American independence, commingled though it was with a sense of despair that he strenuously sought to hide from those around him when the insurrection was floundering in late 1776. It has been said of the young nation's commanding general that even in the most difficult moments of the war, he "never doubted the cause for which he fought."[117] During the darkness that overhung the Patriot endeavor before the light cast by the first triumph at Trenton, Washington maintained this steadfast faith in the Revolutionary enterprise, and "from some deep inner source he found the determination and the will to go on, seeking the miracle that would save the cause before it was too late."[118]

On December 26, 1776, the commander-in-chief of a fledgling nation's fledgling army, whose verbal utterances were generally marked by an economy of words, summarized the importance of his dramatic coup at Trenton with characteristic brevity while perched on his horse on a snowy battlefield. When advised by General Sullivan's aide, Major James Wilkinson, that the last Hessian regiment had surrendered, Washington responded: "Major Wilkinson, this is a glorious day for our country."[119]

Even so, the significance of the attack on Trenton lay not so much in the event itself but what it ignited—an American offensive that changed the strategic equation between the two sides in this conflict in a way that the Trenton raid by itself in all probability would not have done. Had Washington merely withdrawn to Pennsylvania after the December 26 battle and remained there with his army for the balance of the winter, the impact of his brief venture across the Delaware would presumably have been fairly minimal.

Under such a hypothetical scenario, it is likely the crown's forces would have merely reoccupied Trenton with British regulars replacing the defeated Hessian brigade. In that case, Howe's army would still have maintained its grip on New Jersey and been in a position to resume its drive toward the American capital in Philadelphia in the spring in an effort to capture that city and draw Washington into an open-field battle where the rebel army could be dealt a terminal blow. In fact, given that the Delaware froze over by mid-January, Howe, having been stung by the attack on Trenton and vehemently wanting to reassert British control over the momentum of the contest, might have launched an attack across the river without waiting for warmer weather so as to smash the American army as quickly as possible and continue his push toward Philadelphia.

Fortunately for the Patriot cause, the outcome of the Trenton raid did more than justify Washington's conviction that the cause to which he was so committed was still viable from a military standpoint. It also reinforced his natural inclination to be bold and innovative in planning his next moves. The Trenton sortie "was a small victory, but for the commander of the Continental Army it changed everything." The rebel leader had probably always known that his only hope of victory against a militarily superior enemy lay in the use of creative and irregular tactics, but not until this point, "having been forced into such a strategy after so many failed attempts at classical warfare, did he take it to heart."[120] In the eight days following the catalytic event at Trenton on December 26, Washington demonstrated his adherence to this conviction in a way that would resound through the ages.

There is a tide in the affairs of men which, when taken at the flood, leads on to fortune.

— William Shakespeare, from the play, *Julius Caesar*, First Folio, 1623

3

COMING TOGETHER

On December 26, after the sudden success against Colonel Rall's brigade, Washington marched his army and its Hessian prisoners back to Pennsylvania. Most of those prisoners would spend the balance of the war working on farms in Pennsylvania and Virginia under very tolerable conditions, and a significant number chose to remain in America after the conflict ended.

The commanding general was gratified at the results of the Trenton raid but all too aware of the threadbare condition of many in his units. Even so, Washington knew that he needed a follow-up victory or the encounter at Trenton "would have no strategic consequences whatsoever," and he "was not interested in symbolic victories" for he sought to expel the enemy from New Jersey "and completely change the terms on which the campaign of 1777 would be fought."[1] Although prudence and the setbacks suffered by his troops prior to the Trenton battle might well have dictated a more cautious approach, this was a general who "could never resist a chance at fighting the decisive battle."[2]

From the standpoint of his prerogatives of command, Washington was now also a general whose determination to take the fight to the enemy was complemented by enormous latitude to do so. He was officially empowered to conduct America's war for independence as he saw fit, at least for a limited time.

The Continental Congress had invested the commander-in-chief with enhanced authority on December 12, before abandoning Philadelphia for the temporary safety of Baltimore in expectation of an enemy assault on the capital city. It expanded those powers on the day after the win at Trenton, but before learning of the engagement there. By its first resolution, Congress gave Washington "full power to order and direct all things relative to the . . . operations of war" until such time as Congress should revoke that authority, and he would employ it to proffer incentives for the recruitment and reenlistment of Continental soldiers "that normally lay outside his province."[3] On December 26, Congress followed up by granting him broad civil authority for a period of six months, subject to congressional action to rescind that grant if it so determined. This new authorization included, among its various prerogatives, the power to: appoint and discharge officers below the rank of brigadier general; raise additional regiments; and take possession of anything that the commanding general wanted for the army's use, albeit with the requirement to pay reasonable compensation if the owner refused to sell it.

"For patriots rebelling against despotism and tyranny, the decision to award what looked like supreme authority to one man was psychologically difficult, in the extreme," and the members of Congress would not have done so for anyone who had not earned their trust.[4] The man in whom they reposed such confidence responded in such a manner as to reward their faith when he wrote:

"I shall constantly bear in mind that as the sword was the last resort for the preservation of our liberties, so it ought to be the first to be laid aside when those liberties are firmly established."[5]

On December 27, Washington called a council of war with his fellow generals to discuss what course of action the army should take, as he was wont to do at difficult moments throughout the eight-year-long conflict. The commander-in-chief found that councils of war were useful because "he could hear a mixture of opinions before making his decision." Although Congress instructed Washington to hold councils of war, which were an established military practice, it is likely that he would have held them regardless.[6] He did so frequently "and encouraged a free exchange of views" in which Washington "listened more than he talked and drew freely from the best ideas that were put before him."[7]

The generals' decision-making at the December 27 council was informed by the knowledge that Colonel John Cadwalader's 1,500-man unit, largely comprising volunteer militia known as the Philadelphia Associators, had crossed the river to New Jersey that morning in its second attempt to do so. The colonel reported this unexpected development in a dispatch that arrived at army headquarters just before the council convened. A 34-year-old merchant and prominent member of the Philadelphia gentry, Cadwalader had served on the city's Committee of Safety[8] and risen to command the Philadelphia Associators, who were first organized in 1747 by Benjamin Franklin and then mustered anew in 1776. He was taken prisoner when Fort Washington fell to Howe's army on November 16 but was immediately released in consideration of favorable treatment that had been received by a British prisoner at the hands of the colonel's father in Philadelphia.

The Associators represented a cross-section of the population in Philadelphia—then the largest city in America with some 40,000 inhabitants—as well as volunteers from rural Pennsylvania counties, and among their officers was one of the most eminent artists of that era, Charles Willson Peale. These men urged Cadwalader to undertake an unplanned river crossing on December 27 and thereby created the catalyst for a critical sequence of events, without which Cadwalader inferred that the raid on the Hessians at Trenton would have limited significance. Upon traversing the Delaware, Cadwalader reported that the enemy was fleeing in panic and that the way was open to liberate the western half of New Jersey from their grip.

The imperial forces were indeed attempting to respond to the new circumstances that prevailed while coping with an atmosphere of misinformation and uncertainty. The information being reported to the British commanders "not only exaggerated rebel strength but had Washington ready to attack again at many points, from Rocky Hill in the north to Mount Holly in the south."[9]

The Hessian troops under Colonel von Donop, who had occupied Bordentown and Burlington before the assault on Rall's brigade, had quit these outposts immediately after receiving news of the debacle at Trenton and pulled back to join their redcoat allies at a safe distance from the rebels. The effect of the December 26 raid on the disposition of the German units "was instantaneous and drastic." Donop's men withdrew from Mount Holly to Allentown, and he ordered the Hessians at Bordentown to join him at once. The latter obeyed but left behind a number of sick and wounded. Burlington was also evacuated. Donop posted part of his force at Princeton and the rest at Brunswick. As a consequence, in "the shortest possible time for the movement of troops, every post in the Delaware River territory was cleared" of the invaders.[10]

With the dispatch from Cadwalader in hand, Washington realized he had a golden opportunity to follow-up the attack on December 26 with a broader offensive that could change the whole dynamic of the contest. While listening to his generals debate in council whether to take Cadwalader up on his suggestion for a renewed campaign in New Jersey, the commander-in-chief discreetly encouraged the arguments for further military action. The council slowly arrived at a consensus that the Americans could not pass up this chance to regain lost ground on the other side of the Delaware, regardless of the army's weary state and the risks involved in pursuing another offensive.

David Hackett Fischer terms this "a remarkable and very instructive success for Washington's maturing style of quiet, consultative leadership." Putting into larger context the generals' decision to cross the river one more time and attack the invader, he observes that their leader's "method was beginning to work in this army of free spirits. It was uniting cantankerous Yankees, stubborn Pennsylvanians, autonomous Jerseymen, honor-bound Virginians, and independent back countrymen in a common cause."[11]

The men gathered around Washington at this moment of fateful decision included an extraordinary collection of young talent that would earn well-deserved accolades from both their contemporaries and future historians. Two in particular stand out: Nathanael Greene and Henry Knox.

Only 34 at the beginning of the war, Greene came from a well-known Rhode Island family and had diverged from his Quaker roots to join the fighting. "Ambitious and headstrong," Greene was heavyset "with graying hair and walked with a limp caused by a stiff right knee."[12] What he lacked in prior military experience he made up for with a talent for organizational efficiency that quickly earned the commander-in-chief's attention and respect, which Washington maintained even after Greene's erroneous counsel about the feasibility of trying to defend a hopelessly indefensible Fort Washington in November 1776. Greene's failure to recognize the fort's precarious condition and the need to abandon it was his worst mistake of the war and the kind of error he never repeated, as he steadily learned on the job along with his commanding general.

This youthful major general richly deserved the degree of reliance that Washington came to place upon him as the war progressed, and he would assist the Revolutionary cause in multiple capacities, which included serving a successful stint as the Continental Army's quartermaster general and subsequently engineering a brilliant military campaign in the Carolinas as commander of the southern army. In the latter role, he famously summarized his strategy against the enemy in a way that described the Continental Army's experience in general: "We fight, get beat, rise and fight again."[13]

Henry Knox was a 26-year-old bookseller from Boston who was self-taught in the science of gunnery, having pored over various treatises on artillery while at work, and by December 1776, he was one of Washington's most trusted officers. He had created the Continentals' artillery arm from scratch, which was a remarkable achievement given that this branch of the army did not exist at the start of the war; its genesis lay almost a year before in Knox's heroic retrieval of 59 captured enemy field pieces from Fort Ticonderoga in northern New York and their delivery to Washington. The youthful artillery commander was promoted by Congress to brigadier general on Washington's recommendation on December 27, even before that body was aware of the role Knox and his artillery had played the day before.

Knox, "intelligent and highly inventive," made himself "a valued advisor on questions of management and strategy in the army." He was a "big, heavy set man with a booming voice," which proved to be a considerable asset during his successful management of the army's Christmas night river crossing and direction of the American cannons against the Hessians at Trenton. A proven leader in combat, he was also a true student of the military arts, focusing on how to "minimize losses in one's own forces while raising the cost to the enemy." From his studious pursuits, Knox knew the advantages of integrating infantry and artillery and assigned an additional artillery company to each infantry brigade. This tactic contributed significantly to the American victories on December 26 and in the days immediately following, especially in the face of a brutal winter climate. It was difficult to fire muskets in wet weather and impossible under stormy conditions, but artillery "could be protected with tampions and touchhole covers and fired using shielded slow matches."[14] The "possibilities, intricacies, and authority" of these big guns appealed to Knox."[15] He was convinced they could be made to keep pace with marching soldiers and consequently put great emphasis on building and improving their carriages to enhance the mobility of the army's cannons.[16]

Another senior officer who played an important role in the events of this period but has received far fewer accolades from both contemporaries and historians was General Greene's counterpart as divisional commander, General John Sullivan. Then a 36-year-old attorney from New Hampshire and a former delegate to the first Continental Congress, Sullivan had become a brigadier general in June 1775 and a major general in August 1776 but seems to have lacked certain skills useful to an officer. It has been observed that as "a small town country lawyer, one might expect John Sullivan to have acquired the knack of getting along well with people, but he was a contentious soul and had no trouble finding ways to irritate those about him."[17] He had been captured at the Battle of Long Island but released shortly afterwards as part of a prisoner exchange. Although Sullivan was "a heavy drinker prone to annoying his fellow officers and civilian superiors alike," he had capably led the men of his division in the strike against Rall's garrison.[18]

With the decision having been made by Washington's council of war to resume military activity, orders went out to the various army units to prepare for yet another Delaware River crossing. This would be the fourth time in December that they had made this journey.

Dispatches were sent to militia commanders in New Jersey and Pennsylvania to alert them to the impending troop movement, and on December 29 the Continental regiments and available militia units began to go across in what was a considerably larger operation than the Christmas night affair. The troops crossed at eight places: Sullivan's division at the McConkey's and Johnson's ferry landings as on December 25; Greene's division at Yardley's Ferry downstream near Trenton; and the militia at other ferry locations, including Easton, Coryell's, Trenton, and further south. It would take at least two days before all the American forces could get over due to the challenging climatic conditions. The elements were even worse than on Christmas night, although this crossing was facilitated by the fact that much of it occurred in daylight.

By December 29, six inches of snow lay on the ground and the river was half-frozen. The two Continental divisions, Greene's and Sullivan's, struggled mightily to move their troops across the Delaware in bitterly cold temperatures while finding it especially difficult to transport their artillery and wagons. The latter were part of an ample baggage train that included newly supplied tents and blankets, although the soldiers were still sorely lacking in winter clothing and shoes. Knox again superintended the movement of artillery, which included at least twice as many pieces as he had to transport on December 26 and a plentiful quantity of powder and cannon shot. Some of the newly available cannons had repaired carriages and axles, some had been captured from the Hessians, and some were obtained from Philadelphia.

*****

As his army gathered in Trenton on December 31, Washington confronted an immediate crisis. He faced the imminent loss of those Continental soldiers whose one-year enlistments would expire at midnight. Some of them were not susceptible to any appeal the commander-in-chief might make, such as Colonel Glover's now fabled Marbleheaders who were determined to return home so they could fight at sea. Still, Washington needed to find a way to reach the others before it was too late. He found inspiration in the example set by Thomas Mifflin, a 32-year-old Philadelphia Quaker and merchant who had become a brigadier general and was now stationed with Cadwalader's force at Crosswicks, New Jersey. This contingent included the Philadelphia Associators and a Continental regiment of New Englanders under Colonel Daniel Hitchcock of Rhode Island.

Most of Hitchcock's men were eligible to leave the army; however, Mifflin mustered these soldiers and made an emotional appeal to their patriotic instincts while orating on horseback. In one eyewitness's telling, Mifflin "addressed them in a very animated strain and finally desired that all who were willing to march should step forward and give three cheers."[19] He offered them each a bounty of 10 dollars in hard coin on top of their regular pay if they would continue to serve with the army for another six weeks, and almost all of them agreed to do so. His offer followed a precedent that had been set with respect to the Pennsylvania militia when officers of the Philadelphia Associators, mostly well-off Philadelphia merchants, agreed to provide such a bonus to their men as an inducement to endure several more weeks of winter campaigning.

Although Washington was dismayed at the cost of this arrangement, he would find it necessary to employ the same strategy when facing the men in Greene's and Sullivan's divisions. Emulating Mifflin, the commander-in-chief, mounted on his steed, delivered an impassioned plea to his assembled soldiers whose enlistments were about to run out. He begged them not to leave the ranks but to remain with the army for six weeks more:

My brave fellows, you have done all I have asked you to do, and more than could be reasonably expected. But your country is at stake, your wives, your houses and all that you hold dear. You have worn yourself out with fatigues and hardships, but we know not how to spare you. If you will consent to stay only one month longer, you will render service to the cause of liberty and to your country which you probably never can do under any other circumstances. The present is emphatically the crisis which is to decide our destiny.[20]

Washington demonstrated, as he would at other times throughout the war, his mastery of the theatrical gesture.[21] What the Patriot leader offered these men was a kind of nebulous quality that has been recounted as follows: "not a magnetic personality, not an ability to affect men with rhetoric, only some rather vague characteristics that might be described inadequately as the ability to inspire respect and admiration and love."[22] The image of a leader who established a singular relationship with those he led is captured by the indelible recollection of a Continental teamster who, in the narrative accompanying his military pension application almost 60 years after the war's end, reported that he saw "General Washington twice on the road with his life guard with him and will never forget while he retains his memory the polite bow that the general made to the poor wagoners as he passed them."[23] In doing so, the army's commander was conforming to an element of his 18th century sense of honor that prescribed a gentleman's code of conduct; it must be such as to have the rank he claimed respected by others, but also required that he display "appropriate respect" to both those above and below him on the social scale.[24]

In the end, the commander-in-chief persuaded a bare majority of the soldiers who heard his appeal in the waning hours of 1776 to respond affirmatively; however, their motivation to do so appears to have stemmed at least as much from his promise to reward each man as Mifflin had done with Hitchcock's regiment as it did from any personal regard for the supplicant. Washington was willing to fulfill the pledge from his own private resources, if necessary, while hoping for support from other individuals of means. Under the circumstances, he had no other choice.[25] In any case, Washington's pledge would be fulfilled by the timely efforts of his trusted partner in the Revolutionary endeavor, financier Robert Morris, known as one of the most successful merchants in Philadelphia before the war. Those efforts, along with the plea made by other officers to various units, kept the Continental Army intact to this extent: about 1,200 of the soldiers whose enlistments were up agreed to remain for the next six weeks.[26]

To meet the urgent demand for coin, Morris, according to an account steeped in legend, visited a wealthy Quaker in Philadelphia "and persuaded him to unearth a chest of hard money that Morris knew to be buried in his garden." As the story goes, those coins arrived in Trenton on New Years' Eve, barely in time to pay off the soldiers who had agreed to stay on condition of receiving this bonus.[27] It appears that Morris sent along to Washington in bulky canvas bags "all the hard money America's leading financier was able to locate in the nation's capital."[28]

*****

With his immediate manpower shortage averted, Washington was in a position to consolidate all the American forces in the Trenton area. As of January 1, these included some 2,700 veteran Continental soldiers in two divisions—about 1,200 of them serving under General Sullivan and another 1,400 under General Greene.

Sullivan's division comprised what was at this point an umbrella brigade commanded by Brigadier General Arthur St. Clair of Pennsylvania. It included the remnants of 13 New England regiments, among them the units that had been commanded by Colonel Glover and Colonel Paul Dudley Sargent of Massachusetts.

Greene's division included three brigades. One with about 350 men from Maryland, Pennsylvania, and Virginia was led by Brigadier General Hugh Mercer of Virginia. A native of Aberdeen in Scotland, Mercer had befriended Washington during their service in the French and Indian War, joined the same Masonic lodge as the Continental Army's future commander while operating an apothecary business and medical practice in Fredericksburg, and helped organize military support for the Patriot cause in 1775-1776. Another brigade with about 400 Virginians served under Brigadier General Adam Stephen, also a Scottish-born doctor from Virginia who had fought with Washington during the last war. And a Pennsylvania brigade of about 600 men was commanded by Brigadier General Matthias-Alexis de Roche Fermoy, a French enlistee in the American cause from Martinique.

Due to illness and expired enlistments, the aggregate number of soldiers in the Sullivan and Greene divisions represented a substantial reduction from the total serving before the Christmas night crossing.[29] However, these units—the army's most experienced troops—were about to receive a badly needed infusion of reinforcements. They included: a Pennsylvania militia brigade of about 600 men under Brigadier General James Ewing; a contingent of about 1,500 men under Colonel Cadwalader, which comprised a brigade of some 1,100 Philadelphia Associators and the New England brigade of about 350 Continentals under Colonel Hitchcock; and a Pennsylvania brigade of about 1,800 Continentals under General Mifflin. With these units in tow, some 7,000 American troops were assembled in Trenton by the second day of 1777.

These numbers are imprecise at best, which reflects Washington's own uncertainty as to how many men he commanded at this point. He wrote the president of the Continental Congress, John Hancock, on New Year's Day: "I have not been able to procure returns of our force owing to our situation. . . . No estimate of our force can be formed from the number of Regiments; many of 'em by reason of sickness cannot turn out more than a hundred men."[30]

Washington was equally uncertain about the fighting capacity of the new additions to his army. The reinforcements provided by Cadwalader and Mifflin "were well clothed and reasonably well fed"; however, "it was hard to say what they would be like in battle, for they had had no training whatever—they were simply farmers and mechanics . . . who knew absolutely nothing about soldiering."[31]

Washington was always an opportunist and instinctively aggressive in his choice of military tactics. Still, under the prevailing circumstances, he needed to exercise caution in deploying his forces to meet the enemy countermove that was anticipated as a response to the December 26 raid on Trenton. He could strike at the redcoats who occupied Princeton and the other British outposts that stretched beyond or wait for them to come to him. The commander-in-chief reasoned that occupying a strong defensive position would allow for the most effective utilization of his troops, who would be outnumbered and far less experienced than their foe. He had previously observed of the men he led: "Place them behind a parapet, a breast work, stone wall, or any thing that will afford them shelter, and from their knowledge of a firelock, they will give a good account of their enemy."[32]

Washington was determined to fight the invader on ground of his choosing in a way that would confer the greatest advantage on the rebel soldiers. By this calculation, he arrived at a strategic decision to confront his adversary at Trenton rather than seek a battle elsewhere; however, his thought process was as fluid as the uncertain circumstances facing his forces. Washington "was still playing things by ear" when his army arrived in Trenton on December 30. He told his officers that he expected to withdraw soon "and that they should 'hold themselves in complete readiness to advance at a moment's warning.'" At that moment, he appears "to have regarded the position as no more than a temporary bivouac, a staging area for some offensive move, but then he changed his mind and elected to stand and fight."[33]

The commander made his headquarters in a large, two-story house on Queen Street just north of the Assunpink Creek in Trenton. The house had belonged to John Barnes, the former High Sheriff of Hunterdon County and a prominent Loyalist who had vacated it in November. Washington summoned his senior officers to another council of war there on December 30 and told them of his plan to wage a defensive battle against the large enemy force believed to be gathering for a major thrust at the Continental Army.

From their attack on Trenton several days before, the American generals knew all too well how difficult it would be to shield the town from enemy assault. Its layout did not conduce to building fortifications, as Colonel Rall had apparently recognized. Even so, the opportunity to mount a formidable defense against an enemy strike presented itself, one that was recognized by the Continental officers during the December 26 engagement.

From that last fight, the Americans knew that there was a strong defensive position "on a high open knoll south of Assunpink Creek," which offered "very good ground: a deep creek in front, the Delaware River on the left flank, and impassable swamps to the right." They could easily discern that "the twisting bed of Assunpink Creek and its steep banks made a natural moat that could be crossed only at a narrow stone bridge and several fords." Furthermore, from behind this stream "a rising slope of open land made a perfect glacis, with broad fields of fire for infantry and artillery." In short, this terrain "was a natural fortress against an enemy who approached from the north."[34]

The council agreed to a plan of defense that focused on Assunpink Creek and required the rebel forces to prepare for the expected attack by entrenching themselves along a three-mile stretch on the southern bank in an area known today as the Mill Hill section of Trenton. The bridge at Queen Street, near the mouth of the creek, was the most obvious crossing point. Here the Americans' firepower could be concentrated so as to inflict maximum damage against dense formations of enemy soldiers attempting to cross the waterway. This defensive scheme envisioned that the attacking British and Hessians would file through the narrow corridor provided by the stone bridge and be hit from three sides by the defenders' musket, rifle, and artillery fire.

It appears that Washington foresaw a scenario comparable to the Battle of Bunker Hill. He anticipated that the enemy, stung by the bitter Hessian defeat at Trenton, would attempt an ill-considered attack under conditions that favored the rebels in an effort to avenge the loss of Colonel Rall's brigade. But this strategy was inherently risky, because the area that the Americans would be defending, while advantageous in some respects, was fraught with peril. "In a patch of woods to the right, two fords could be crossed by a determined enemy," and the "entire position could also be approached from the south by a long and circuitous march." An opportunistic adversary who crossed the upper fords or struck from the rear could turn the position into "a deadly trap for an unwary defender."[35]

The strategy devised by Washington and his fellow officers—to "entice a proud, aggressive, and angry enemy into a costly assault on good ground"—had not always been kind to the rebel forces, most notably in the defeat at Fort Washington in November. There were hazards inherent in this plan for an army that had little or no margin for error at this point, as suggested by Fischer: "What if the ground were not so good, or the attackers were better, or something went wrong. In many ways, a defensive battle was a greater risk than the attack on Trenton had been."[36]

In any case, orders were issued for the men to fortify the area where they were to make their stand. The Continental field guns were placed on the high ground south of the Assunpink and targeted on the bridge and the fords where the enemy might attempt to cross. The infantry were ordered to take up positions in three lines, one behind the other, 250 yards apart, while guards were posted on every road leading into Trenton, and mounted patrols were dispatched from the town in every direction.[37]

*****

Among the Continental officers who awaited the army's next action as the troops prepared their defenses along the Assunpink was an Irish immigrant who was committed heart and soul to the Patriot enterprise but had seen virtually his entire unit wither away during the previous year. Colonel John Haslet of Delaware was encamped with what was left of his regiment—the now depleted "Delaware Blues" who were named as such for the color of their uniforms.[38]

Haslet, about 49 years of age and a native of County Londonderry, was known as one of Washington's "steadiest, most reliable officers."[39] An officer in his regiment described him as one "whose integrity and quickness of perception formed him for the battle-field."[40] Haslet had worn several hats before the war: an ordained Presbyterian minister in his native land; a veteran of the French and Indian War, when he served with the Pennsylvania militia; and a practicing physician, planter, and member of the colonial assembly in Delaware. Almost a year before, Haslet had been placed in command of Delaware's Continental regiment, an elite unit whose men viewed their commanding officer as something of a father figure.[41]

The Delaware regiment, which had joined up with Washington's army at its Perth Amboy encampment the previous August, included some 750 men initially, which made it the largest regiment in the army. However, its standing was defined by its professionalism more than its size, for it had "a reputation for courage, hardihood and military efficiency second to none in the American army."[42]

The Delaware soldiers demonstrated "precision to match that of a veteran European unit" on the parade ground.[43] Serving in "the best-drilled and probably the only completely uniformed unit in the army," these men "were fiercely proud of themselves and when they went into combat they demonstrated they had every reason to be."[44] Indeed, this regiment and William Smallwood's Maryland Continental Regiment were thought to be the two best in the army.[45] They fought together for most of the protracted conflict.[46] During the failed encounter with the enemy at the Battle of Long Island in August, the Delaware and Maryland soldiers had "made a desperate stand" that held off the British advance long enough for other Americans to escape, which reportedly prompted an observing Washington to declare: "Good God! What brave fellows I must this day lose."[47]

The number of soldiers in the Delaware regiment had steadily declined throughout late 1776 due to casualties from battle and various diseases, among them "putrid fever" (typhus), smallpox, and pneumonia. By early November, only 273 reported present and fit for duty, and that number had dwindled to 92 by December 22. They were the last infantry unit to cross the Delaware on Christmas night, serving as the rearguard at McConkey's Ferry in recognition of "their discipline, toughness, and reliability."[48]

By the end of the December 25-26 expedition against the Hessians, Haslet's legs were severely swollen from an accidental tumble into the icy river, but this "unconquerable man" was not about to leave the field of combat.[49] When the enlistments of the remaining Delaware Blues ran out on December 30, all but six left its ranks, leaving behind Haslet, two other officers, a surgeon, and two privates. Washington gave the colonel a written order to return to Delaware for the winter in order to recruit new soldiers for the regiment, but he opted to postpone his departure until after the army had finished its campaign and settled in for the winter.

Haslet was still suffering the effects of his spill in the river when on New Year's Day he wrote to his fellow Delawarean, Caesar Rodney, a signatory to the Declaration of Independence. In the last letter he would ever write, Haslet reported to his friend: "On Christmas, at 3 o'clock we recrossed the river." He expressed his frustration at not being able to do more to exploit the Trenton victory on December 26: "We should have gone on, and panic-struck they would have fled before us, but the inclemency of the weather rendered it impossible." Eager to take the fight to the enemy, Haslet noted that his mishap on the river occurred during the return crossing after the fight with the Hessians but brushed aside the suffering he must have endured from his bloated legs: "no matter if we drive them to New York." However, he may have had a premonition of his imminent demise when he added: "If I return it will be to salute you; if not we shall meet in heaven."[50]

*****

In order to prepare most effectively for the expected enemy offensive, Washington needed sound intelligence as to the disposition of the crown's forces. To that end, he tasked his adjutant, Colonel Joseph Reed, with leading a mounted patrol of the Philadelphia Light Horse cavalry, a 21-member volunteer unit that had just joined the army, on a reconnaissance mission. Reed, 35, knew the area, having been born in Trenton and graduated from the College of New Jersey (today Princeton University). An attorney by profession, he had engaged in legal studies with Richard Stockton, a signer of the Declaration of Independence, as well as in London. At the beginning of the Revolution, Reed was managing a successful law practice in Philadelphia. He joined the army as a lieutenant colonel in April

1775 and was soon promoted to colonel. By late 1776, the young lawyer had become an important member of Washington's staff and a source of wise counsel to his commanding general.

Reed led the Philadelphia cavalry unit toward Princeton by an obscure route in order to scout the British troops there. On the outskirts of the village, they captured several British dragoons who were brought back to Trenton and separately questioned on the evening of December 30. From their accounts, Washington learned that the British army was indeed organizing a full-scale response to the American raid on December 26. He now knew that several thousand enemy troops were gathering in Princeton and could reasonably infer that they were preparing to launch an attack.

At the same time, Washington received additional intelligence about the disposition of British troops from Colonel Cadwalader. The latter had met with a "very intelligent young gentleman" who had been detained overnight by the redcoats in Princeton but released on the morning of December 30.[51] This youthful Patriot, whose identity is unknown to this day, informed Cadwalader of the buildup of enemy troops in Princeton and described in great detail how they were positioned.

Based on this report, Cadwalader drew a crude map of the town that indicated the strengths and weaknesses of the British alignment, which was provided to the commanding general. From this sketch, Washington could discern an opportunity to make a successful move against his adversary. The British commander in Princeton, Brigadier General Alexander Leslie, was establishing strong defenses that included artillery and breastworks to guard against a possible American incursion from the north, west, or south. But he had neglected to fortify the eastern side of the town, and so it lay open to attack from that direction. Cadwalader's map included a route from Trenton by which Washington's army could approach Princeton from the east where the enemy was most vulnerable.

Armed with the information furnished by Reed and Cadwalader, Washington held another council of war at his headquarters on the evening of January 1. He and his officers needed to consider how to respond to the large enemy force that was gathering in Princeton, presumably for an all-out assault on Trenton. Meeting with Washington were at least the following: the newly promoted brigadier general of artillery, Henry Knox; the army's two divisional commanders, Generals Greene and Sullivan; the brigade commander overseeing the 13 New England Continental regiments in Sullivan's division, Brigadier General Arthur St. Clair; and the army's adjutant general, Colonel Reed.

It was decided at this council to bring Cadwalader's force of Philadelphia Associators and their accompanying brigade of New England Continentals under Colonel Hitchcock—a total of about 1,500 men—from their encampment at Crosswicks to Trenton in order to strengthen the army's position in the coming battle. Dr. Benjamin Rush, who had been volunteering with Cadwalader's unit but was then visiting army friends in Trenton, was dispatched at once to Crosswicks to convey this directive. Rush, a native Pennsylvanian who had just turned 31, held a medical degree from the University of Edinburgh and was a professor of chemistry at the College of Philadelphia. His service on behalf of the Patriot cause made this a fitting assignment for him. Rush had been a member of the Philadelphia Sons of Liberty[52] and Pennsylvania's provincial conference to send delegates to the Continental Congress, as well as a member of Congress and a signer of the Declaration of Independence.

By the following morning, the exhausted doctor had returned from his 16-mile round trip with the eagerly awaited reinforcements from Crosswicks. He arrived at about 7 a.m. and went to General St. Clair's headquarters, where upon request he was granted "the favor of [the general's] bed for a few hours," only to be awakened by the sound of an alarm gun. When St. Clair entered the room and notified Rush that the enemy was advancing on Trenton, the doctor asked: "What do you intend to do?" A smile accompanied the general's reply: "Why, fight them."[53] As it turned out, the enemy was not as near to Trenton at that moment as the alarm suggested. But St. Clair, a 40-year-old Scottish immigrant who had served as an ensign with a British regiment in Canada during the French and Indian War, put on his sword and went out to engage the imperial army for whom he had once fought.

*****

The British and Hessians had been staggered by news of the American victory at Trenton on December 26. This development suddenly cast into doubt their hopes and expectations for a short-lived war that would culminate in a complete victory over colonial resistance by the coming spring. Hessian captain Johann Ewald would later write: "Thus had the times changed! The Americans had constantly run before us. Four weeks ago we expected to end the war . . . and now we had to render Washington the honor of thinking about our defense."[54]

General Howe, who was comfortably ensconced in New York for the winter with his Loyalist mistress, Mrs. Elizabeth Loring, now had to grapple with what had seemed like a most unlikely problem before the Americans' upset triumph over the Rall brigade. Howe, who like his brother Admiral Richard Lord Howe had agreed to fight against the colonists with great reluctance, summoned his best field commander, General Cornwallis, and gave him the task of punishing the upstart rebels for their impertinence.

A sudden sense of urgency underlay this moment for the imperial high command: "The Howes' entire premise—that America could be won back through a combination of coercion and negotiation—was dependent on the British army's completely controlling the momentum of the war," according to Nathaniel Philbrick, for if "something was not done to reverse the fiasco at Trenton, all of the British victories leading up to this point might be for naught." Prior to this unexpected turn of events, General Howe had refrained from any serious effort to destroy Washington's army because he still hoped to achieve a reconciliation with the colonials, but Britain's commanding general now assumed a more bellicose posture in his directions to Cornwallis. Under the new circumstances that prevailed, the latter "must make the Americans regret that they had ever ventured back across the Delaware by inflicting the devastating defeat that the British had so far refused to deliver."[55]

Although Cornwallis was the most aristocratic of the British generals serving in America—the sixth child and eldest son of Charles, the first Earl Cornwallis—he was "without pretension" as a soldier and devoid of "patience for pomp and fanfare."[56] He came from a family noted for its military tradition and had dedicated his life to military service since joining the Grenadier Guards at age 18. He was widely read in military matters and encouraged other British officers to do the same.[57] An Eaton College graduate and a Member of the House of Lords since his early 20s, Cornwallis was one of the few British officers to study at a military academy, having attended one of the finest such European institutions at Turin, Italy. He became a lieutenant colonel at age 23 and had seen considerable action on European battlefields prior to embarking for America in February 1776, at age 37, as a newly promoted major general.

When it came to upward mobility in Britain's army, affluence was a distinct advantage, and Cornwallis proved the rule that "wealthy officers advanced fastest."[58] Officers' commissions were controlled by the king and carried a hefty price. Still, the young general was highly regarded by the men under his command and, according to one assessment, "had done his best to master his profession, to reform the obvious abuses in the regiments he commanded, giving all the matters that came within his province the attention of an earnest and orderly if not penetrating mind."[59]

Cornwallis's service in America resulted from a preternatural devotion to duty, which overcame his distaste for the policies of His Majesty's government that had led to war with its colonial subjects. His Lordship had been one of only six members of the House of Lords to vote against the Stamp Act that imposed the first direct tax by Britain on the colonies a decade before he volunteered to fight against the rebellion in 1775. His ambivalence about the conflict was widely shared among his peers in the royal army, but most of those officers—even those opposed to their government's colonial policy—eventually obeyed when ordered to serve in America, for "loyalty to the Crown seemed to prevail over personal political preferences, at least among the largely aristocratic officer corps."[60]

Cornwallis's sympathy for the Revolution would decline after he came to America. He became convinced that a tyrannical leadership was driving the Patriot movement; however, he recognized that the prospects for British success ultimately depended on persuading the rebels that it was in their interest to cease resistance.[61]

Among the generals available to him, William Howe could not have picked one better suited for the mission he had in mind following the rebels' shocking raid against Colonel Rall's garrison—to find, attack, and destroy Washington's army without delay. Only a sudden and decisive victory would restore the sense of inevitability surrounding Britain's prospects for crushing the rebellion that the crown's soldiers had shared prior to the news of December 26. Indeed, Lord Cornwallis was a better choice than Howe himself to accomplish this task, for "certain traits not found in Howe . . . were conspicuously present in Cornwallis's make-up, namely energy and swiftness of action."[62] This warrior of noble lineage was about to display both in ample measure.

On New Year's Day 1777, one day after his 38th birthday, Cornwallis rode some 50 miles from New York to Princeton and arrived there late on a rainy night to take command of the British and Hessian forces gathering in and around the town under orders from General Howe's headquarters. His Lordship's arrival preempted the command of General Grant, until then the British commander in New Jersey. The latter had marched from his headquarters in Brunswick on the same day to join the assemblage at Princeton, leaving behind only 600 men under Brigadier General Edward Mathew at Grant's command post to guard the army's major supply depot with its military chest of about £70,000.

Cornwallis brought "an air of confidence" with him to Princeton.[63] That degree of self-assurance would appear to have been well-placed given his demonstrated record of competence as a military leader, the numerical superiority of his gathering force over the rebel army, and the elite nature of the troops who would be serving under him.

Cornwallis had at his command more than 10,000 British and Hessian soldiers with a large train of artillery that included "medium" 12-pounders—the heaviest artillery that could be deployed in the field and twice the weight of the largest cannons in Washington's army. The seven British infantry regiments that were part of the two brigades assigned to Cornwallis "included some of the best units in the army."[64] In fact, the reserve that he planned to leave behind in Princeton when he advanced against the rebels included "one of the best fighting regiments in the British army"—the 17th Foot that was part of the Fourth Brigade under Lieutenant Colonel Charles Mawhood.[65] The other part of Cornwallis's force, the Second Brigade with four regiments, was commanded by General Leslie, who had been in charge of the British force at Princeton before Cornwallis's arrival.

At this point, His Lordship was actually suffering from "an embarrassment of strengths" that would retard his move toward Trenton. His force was so large that it stretched over a five-mile area, and it would be difficult to march that many soldiers over the Princeton Road, "a narrow muddy track, broken by streams and ravines," which represented the main artery between Princeton and Trenton.[66]

Upon arriving in Princeton on the night of January 1, Cornwallis called his generals into council to advise them of his plans. They met at the commanding general's headquarters at Morven, the abandoned home of Richard Stockton on the outskirts of town. These gatherings by Cornwallis, and other British commanders for that matter, were generally not consultative in nature, as were Washington's councils of war with his senior officers. Instead they were an opportunity for the commanding general to inform his senior officers of his decision.

As befitted his style of action, His Lordship intended to advance without delay and deploy his troops in the most aggressive manner possible. There was no subtlety to his plan, for he proposed to march on Trenton the next morning and "commit all his strength to a single thrust" down the Princeton Road directly toward the opposing army.[67] Cornwallis refused to be dissuaded from this strategy by the urging of Carl von Donop, the Hessian colonel who was more familiar than his superior with the local geography and the recently demonstrated mobility of Washington's army.

Donop argued for a two-pronged advance by which one column would take the Princeton Road as Cornwallis planned and the other proceed through Cranbury and Allentown along a route that would flank the Americans on their right. This would, he asserted, force the rebels to abandon Trenton and retreat into the countryside, where they would be in a less secure position without supplies and open to attack by their pursuers. But Cornwallis rejected this advice, presumably because he believed his force was superior to Washington's numerically and qualitatively and should therefore pursue a direct and concentrated thrust at his weaker opponent. Hessian captain Johann Ewald later observed: "The enemy was despised and as usual we had to pay for it."[68]

On the other hand, Cornwallis's inflexibility in this matter may have been owing more to an ingrained deficiency in leadership style than a low regard for his opponent, stemming from his being "a better battlefield commander than a planner of grand strategy."[69] The earl's chief fault may have been the reverse of William Howe's—that is, being too aggressive for his own good—and throughout the war, his strategic approach often manifested itself in an excess of audacity over caution. Ironically enough, Cornwallis's major weakness was possibly "his excellent military background," according to Hugh Rankin, for "his troop dispositions in battle were more in the classic textbook tradition when the situation called for a more fluid arrangement," and he never, in any battle in which he commanded an army, utilized "the flanking movements that had proved so successful for Howe, and in which Cornwallis had taken part," such as at Long Island and Brandywine Creek.[70]

Whatever the motives behind Cornwallis's plan of action, this boldest of British generals would be foiled by a small contingent of American soldiers whose efforts to thwart his attack along the road to Assunpink Creek were as audacious as anything His Lordship could have envisioned. As a consequence, events conspired to prevent him from employing the very type of flanking maneuver that might have earned Charles Cornwallis the most decisive victory of the war.

Audentis Fortuna luvat.

> — Latin proverb cited by the Roman poet Virgil in the epic poem,
> *Aeneid*, 19 B.C., which translates to "fortune favors the bold"
> or "fortune favors the brave."

4

HAND'S HEROICS

Before daylight on January 2, 1777, the British and Hessian troops under General Cornwallis's command had a meal of biscuits and brandy, and at about 8 a.m. their vanguard began leading the march from Princeton to Trenton. These soldiers were the cream of His Majesty's armed might and if things went according to plan, they would subdue the rebel army—and thereby extinguish the insurgency's best hope—within the next 24 to 48 hours.

Cornwallis would advance on Trenton with about 8,000 troops, including 60 cavalry and 28 cannons. For the moment, he would leave in reserve some 2,700 men. These included about 1,200 under Colonel Mawhood, who was ordered to remain in Princeton with his three regiments—the 17th, 40th, and 55th Foot—and a scattering of soldiers from other units. Another 1,500 under General Leslie were to be posted to Maidenhead as the crown's forces passed through that village en route to their objective.

Colonel von Donop was at the helm of Cornwallis's vanguard as a seemingly endless column of imperial troops began to wend its way southward. Two companies of jägers, one mounted and one on foot, supported by a company of Hessian grenadiers and two troops of the British 16th Light Dragoons, spearheaded the advance, followed by British light infantry, artillery and British and Hessian grenadiers.[1] Donop was eager to pay back the Americans for the defeat of Rall's brigade. He and the other Hessian officers were "spoiling for revenge against the rebels" after the humiliation at Trenton, and the colonel ordered his Germans to take no prisoners "on pain of severe corporal punishment."[2]

Cornwallis was anxious for his troops to reach Trenton early enough to complete their work—to put the rebels to rout while there was sunlight enough for that purpose on this short January day. European armies of the 18th century did not generally fight at night, and even if they did, the fact that His Lordship did not know the ground on which his opponent was situated would have made a nighttime operation especially problematic. Cornwallis "was determined to hit the Americans at midday and potentially finish them by nightfall."[3]

The pastoral scene through which this extended formation marched belied the violent nature of what would soon transpire along that route. The road they took "ran nearly straight southwest and the soft, gentle country" surrounding Princeton became "almost dead flat—a plain tilted ever so slightly downward in the direction of the Delaware River," with "no sharp features in this terrain, only some low-lying hills," as well as patches of red clay in the nearby fields showing through old snow and expanses of woodland that prevented one from seeing very far in any direction.[4]

Given the logistical demands of the contestants in this conflict, thoroughfares such as this were central to the action generally and no less so than on this particular day. Almost every battle of the

Revolution was fought along a road because virtually everything that an army needed was transported on wagons that could only travel on roads. While a small unit of soldiers could operate independently for a brief time by carrying their food or foraging for it, the movement of an army with its horse-drawn cannons and cavalry was dependent on a train of wagons that could carry sufficient provisions on a daily basis to feed the troops and horses, as well as "ammunition, tents, medical supplies, entrenching tools, and an array of services including a portable blacksmith shop complete with anvils and bellows."[5]

As was the case generally with the combined imperial forces throughout the war, the infantry comprising Cornwallis's attack force included three discrete and specialized categories of foot soldiers that operated in separate units within both the British and Hessian contingents apart from the regular line infantry—light infantry, grenadiers, and Jägers.

The British light infantry were known "for their physical ability and fighting qualities, hardihood, vigor and alacrity in combat" and were primarily utilized in "reconnaissance, skirmishing and outpost work" like their American counterparts. By contrast, the grenadiers, both British and Hessian, were the tallest and strongest men in both armies in keeping with the mission for which they were first organized, to throw explosive hand grenades for a long distance, and each wore a tall, mite-like head piece that enhanced "his apparent height and thus his fearsome appearance."[6] Finally, the jägers were "an element in the German forces in America, few in number, perhaps about 600, but active and efficient in combat." They functioned in a manner similar to the British light infantry and were equipped with short, heavy, large-bore rifles that carried no bayonets.[7] The jägers, who were the elite troops among the German units fighting with the British, had been recruited "from hunters, gamekeepers, and other marksmen [and] were famous for their skills as riflemen and skirmishers, as well as for discipline and bravery under arms in the most trying of circumstances."[8]

Cornwallis's army was a fearsome aggregation of the most proficient fighting men that the Old World could have sent to America's shores. But on this day, they were forced to contend with both the forces of nature and rebellion, and these proved to be a potent combination. Unusually warm temperatures had prevailed the day before and lasted into the night, reaching 51 degrees on New Year's Day and 39 on the morning and afternoon of the 2nd, accompanied by overnight rain and melting snow.

The elements rendered the road conditions inhospitable for marching troops, no matter how skilled they might be. The road that lay before them was a veritable quagmire, "a morass of mud and slush so deep that men sank to their knees and thighs," and "every step was a struggle." The soldiers turned off "the highway and marched through fields that became as muddy as the roads." Horses and artillery sank into "a thick sucking ooze." It "was heavy labor to advance a few miles," and even worse for the troops at the rear of the column.[9] As a result, large gaps opened up between the various units in this long-drawn-out procession.[10]

And if the mud was not bad enough, there came the New World's sharpshooters. As the vanguard of Cornwallis's column passed through the area held by British troops north of Maidenhead, they began to encounter scattered fire from rebel pickets who constituted the most forward deployed of their skirmishers stationed along the route. That long stretch of road would soon seem interminable for the forces of the crown; for them, it would be "slow going all the way."[11]

*****

The opening act in the drama that unfolded on January 2 had actually occurred two days before when Washington decided to deploy forward units as a first line of defense against the anticipated enemy advance to Trenton. This move presaged what would prove to be an elaborate and persistent effort to delay the crown's forces from reaching the main body of Washington's army as long as possible. Doing so was designed to forestall any attempt at a quick strike by Cornwallis and thereby frustrate the intent of Britain's most dynamic senior field commander to smash the rebels in one sudden, massive blow.

Washington dispatched a body of soldiers halfway up the road to Princeton on New Year's Eve in order to impede the enemy's movement toward Trenton. He knew he could not defeat the large force that Cornwallis would be bringing down from Princeton. The defenders in Trenton would be outnumbered, even with the reinforcements supplied by the soldiers from the Cadwalader and Hitchcock brigades, but Washington hoped to make the enemy pay dearly for any success they achieved. He sought "to delay and punish the British for as long as he could and then make them pay a heavy price to attack him on Mill Hill," in other words to "make it another Bunker Hill."[12]

The forward deployment of rebel units on December 31 included about a thousand men and was commanded by the Frenchman, General Fermoy. This contingent comprised the following: the 1st Pennsylvania Regiment led by Colonel Edward Hand; the German Regiment under Colonel Nicholas Haussegger, which was the only American regiment named after the ethnic identity of its soldiers; a brigade of Virginia Continentals led by Colonel Charles Scott; and a pair of field guns manned by the 2nd Company of the Pennsylvania State Artillery under Captain Thomas Forrest.[13]

Before sunrise on New Year's Day, the troops under Fermoy's command occupied a position called Eight Mile Run—known as Shipetaukin Creek today—about six miles south of Nassau Hall in Princeton, which housed the College of New Jersey. This site featured a stream with steep banks crossing the Princeton Road and hills on both sides of the road. There the American pickets skirmished with British and Hessian patrols on January 1, and the rebels' stiff resistance forced the enemy to bring up reinforcements in the form of several battalions who finally pushed the outnumbered Americans back but at a heavy cost. This action should have been viewed as a warning by Cornwallis and his officers, for these skirmishers were "fighting well on good ground, holding their positions, inflicting casualties on picked troops, and taking few losses in return."[14] Their efforts were the precursor to a far more extended action the next day.

*****

January 2 was to bring with it a severe test of the Americans' ability to make the enemy's forward progress toward Trenton as painful and prolonged as possible. Whether or not they passed that test would rest in large measure on the leadership provided by an Irish-born rifle commander who had turned 32 just two days before, and in retrospect it might seem as if his men were about to mark that occasion by extending an animated greeting to His Majesty's forces. Edward Hand had come a long way from his birthplace in Clyduff, King's County (now County Offaly) to this rural Hunterdon County setting where he and the soldiers he led were about to contend with a large and imposing foe.

The son of John and Dorothy Hand was the descendent of English ancestors who probably came to Ireland in the 16th or 17th centuries. Little is known about his formative years. While in his early twenties, he had pursued medical studies at nearby Trinity College in Dublin—"the great Irish university, which was serious enough educationally to rival Cambridge and Oxford"[15]—although there is no record of his being a matriculated student there.[16] Hand enlisted as a surgeon's mate (assistant physician) in the 18th Royal Irish Regiment of Foot with the rank of warrant officer in 1767.

For someone who aspired to be a physician in Ireland, this type of military service apparently represented a preferred alternative to the other route available for medical training, that of serving a five-year apprenticeship with a Dublin physician; and in the 18th century, Trinity College graduates often occupied positions in the medical department of the British Army.[17]

Hand sailed with his regiment for the New World on May 19, 1767 and arrived in Philadelphia in July. The young soldier would find himself investigating Native American medical practices and horticulture while serving frontier duty at Fort Pitt (the future site of Pittsburgh) and profitably engaging in a number of land transactions. The latter provided Hand with the means to purchase an ensign's commission in 1772, and he became a supply officer at Fort Pitt.

However, this enterprising emigrant was becoming disenchanted with British colonial policy, which reminded him of what the Irish generally regarded as England's overbearing posture toward Hand's native land. Many of his fellow 18th century migrants from the British Isles—Scotch-Irish and Irish—came to these shores bitterly resentful of the British government, for they "had been pushed around and persecuted" by the government and landlords to the point where "they could no longer feel much loyalty to the English crown."[18] Hand's sympathy for the Patriot cause led him to sell his officer's commission and resign from the army in 1774. He settled in Lancaster, Pennsylvania—a community of about 3,000 people—where he practiced medicine and met Katherine Ewing, whom he married in 1775. (They eventually had three daughters, only one of whom lived to adulthood, and a son.) The former soldier "established himself as a capable physician, industrious vestryman, and active and responsible man of public affairs."[19]

As the colonies' dispute with Britain intensified, Hand was exposed to opinions in newspapers and various tracts in support of the Patriot cause that he could understand in terms of his own experience. The views expressed were similar to "those put forward by his fellow Anglo-Irishmen in their dispute with Parliament and Britain" during Hand's time as a student in Dublin and presumably resonated with him.[20]

At the Revolution's outbreak, this soldier-turned-doctor helped organize a local militia unit known as the Lancaster County Associators, and he was subsequently commissioned a lieutenant colonel in command of a rifle unit known as the 1st Pennsylvania Continental Regiment. As someone with both military and medical experience, Hand was an attractive commodity to rebel organizers when he enlisted in the cause. He joined the other Continental soldiers of Irish and Scotch-Irish origin who constituted about 40 percent of Washington's army and would become known as the "shock troops of Independence."[21]

In mid-1775, after Hand's promotion to colonel, his regiment marched some 400 miles to join the newly designated Continental Army encamped in Cambridge, Massachusetts, just outside Boston, where the occupying British army under General Howe was still reeling from its costly victory at the June 17 bloodbath on the slopes of Bunker Hill. Hand's men represented the first detachment of soldiers to join the rebel army from beyond the boundaries of New England, and he and the other officers whose active duty began during the siege of Boston that summer would form the nucleus of the Continental Army's officer corps for the balance of the war.[22]

*****

The members of Hand's 1st Pennsylvania Regiment "were backwoodsmen—tall, lean men who wore hunting shirts, leather leggings, and Indian moccasins," and they carried a deadly long rifle that became "a thing of terror to the British and Hessians."[23] Their colonel made a considerable effort to properly equip his men and instill in them "a sense of esprit de corps." He ordered a silk standard or color for the regiment—made in Philadelphia and delivered to his unit by the fall of 1776—which he described as "a deep green ground, the device a tiger partly enclosed by toils, attempting the pass, defended by a hunter armed with a spear . . . on a crimson field the motto Domari nolo," a Latin expression for refusing to yield or be subdued.[24]

Hand's skilled marksmen would become known for the death-dealing manner in which they employed their American-made long rifles against the human targets they encountered in battle. And these soldiers from the backcountry were also noted for their utility, as they could be employed effectively in a variety of tactical operations, "as snipers, on scouting patrols, in joint operations with regular troops," and in the same manner as light infantry units in European armies.[25]

Anecdotal information about the rifle's accuracy was spread far and wide, as "American riflemen loved to give demonstrations, aiming at a small mark the size of a man's eye or the tip of his nose, and hitting it repeatedly from a distance of 250 yards."[26] A British spy with the rebel army outside Boston in the summer of 1775 reported to General Howe on the prowess of the rifle companies from Pennsylvania and Virginia, noting that there was "scarcely a regiment in Camp but can produce men that can best them at shooting."[27] These potent weapons were "a backcountry tool, made mostly in Pennsylvania and used there and in the Chesapeake colonies by men who hunted for much of their fresh meat." The rifle's long barrel was etched or "rifled" with seven or eight internal grooves, unlike the smooth-bore muskets, and the effect was to make it accurate at a range of about 200 and perhaps even 300 yards, which was several times the range of a musket.[28]

The singular nature of these instruments was recognized by the Continental Congress when it established the Continental Army in June 1775 in support of New England's uprising against the British troops in Boston. Rifles were scarce in the colonies and, while popular in the more rural areas, were largely unknown around Boston. John Adams eagerly expounded on them to his wife, Abigail, informing her that the Continental Congress in which he served "is really in earnest in defending the Country. They have voted ten companies of Rifle Men to be sent from Pennsylvania, Maryland and Virginia, to join the Army before Boston. These are an excellent Species of Light Infantry." He explained that they "use a peculiar kind of Musket call'd a Rifle" that "carries a Ball, with great Exactness to great Distances," and commended these sharpshooters as "the most accurate Marksmen in the World."[29]

Despite its far greater range over the musket, the rifle had certain disadvantages. It took longer to reload than a musket "because the shot had to be forcefully rammed in for a snug fit." In addition, because the rifle was designed for hunting rather than fighting, it had no bayonet mount, which rendered its owner defenseless during combat at close quarters. Consequently, riflemen had to be escorted by soldiers with muskets; and, notwithstanding the increased role played by the rifle throughout the war, the musket remained "the workhorse" of the American troops.[30]

As for their adversary, His Majesty's army had never adapted to the use of rifles. To the British command, the length of time required to load and fire a rifle and its failure to accommodate a bayonet were critical deficiencies. Reflecting the methods of warfare that were utilized by most European armies in the 18th century, in which regiments fired in blocks rather than aiming individually, many officers regarded rifles as "an unnecessary and wasteful expense."[31] Instead, the British relied on the same Brown Bess musket that was carried by American soldiers in units that were not rifle companies. The use of this weapon, although highly unreliable because its effectiveness was limited to a range of 80 to 100 yards, facilitated the redcoats' use of their favorite tactic—the bayonet charge that was sure to have "a fearsome effect on an enemy, no matter how experienced he might be."[32]

The bayonet's prominent role in British infantry tactics—having primacy over firepower—was predicated on the conviction that "a well-disciplined soldier could outrun the range of a musket in the time it took an enemy to reload."[33] Few rebel combatants, "even when properly formed and encouraged by their commander, could ever stand against the cold steel of the bayonet."[34] They understood that with "the full force of a soldier's body behind it, a bayonet could cause terrible damage to tissue, arteries, and bones."[35] On Revolutionary War battlefields, the British "object in almost every case was to close with the Americans, absorbing casualties until they could charge with bayonets." These instruments of cold steel probably accounted for most of the combat deaths that occurred among Patriot soldiers during the conflict. Because musket fire was generally inaccurate and caused relatively few casualties, even when used against dense formations of troops advancing at a deliberate pace, the bayonet charge "made good tactical sense so long as the defenders were not too well entrenched."[36]

By the end of 1776, Colonel Hand's 1st Pennsylvania regiment had fought in nearly every important engagement since joining Washington's army.[37] These men were at the Battle of Long Island in August and endured the subsequent New York campaign and long retreat across New Jersey. Serving in the brigade commanded by General Fermoy, Hand's soldiers combined with the German Continental Regiment under Colonel Haussegger when they engaged the Hessians at Trenton on December 26. Their charge toward the Princeton Road northeast of the town curtailed an attempt by Colonel Rall's regiment to escape toward Princeton by circumventing the Continentals' left flank and thereby helped seal the fate of a doomed enemy garrison.

Well before the advent of the rebel army's 1776-1777 winter campaign, these rural warriors had demonstrated in dramatic fashion what their long rifles could do in the face of overwhelming enemy numbers. On October 12, General Howe landed 4,000 troops at Throg's Neck above Manhattan in an effort to trap Washington's force on the New York island by cutting off the main crossing to the mainland; however, a small group of Hand's men "stopped the British army in their tracks, then held them while another 1,500 American infantry hurried to their support," forcing the redcoats to abandon the effort and look for a better place to land—which they found at Pell's Point a few days later, but not in time to prevent Washington's escape from Manhattan.[38]

Describing the encounter between the advance guard of this sizable landing party and the Pennsylvanians, Christopher Ward reports that "under orders of General [William] Heath, Colonel Hand and a detachment of riflemen had torn up the planking of the bridge [connecting Throg's Neck to the mainland] and concealed themselves behind a long pile of cord wood near its western end. When the enemy advanced nearer the gap, a sudden, well-aimed fire blazed in their faces." Thrown into confusion, the British fell back to the top of the nearest hill and dug in there, forsaking their objective. To put it dramatically, if not hyperbolically, some 25 "American riflemen behind a wood-pile had stopped the British army."[39]

*****

On the morning of January 2, 1777, the lead elements of General Cornwallis's column—the Hessian jägers—began to encounter scattered resistance before they had ventured far from Princeton, as small parties of rebel skirmishers "took positions in patches of woodland along the road and began a harassing fire."[40] The vanguard of imperial soldiers encountered their initial resistance at Eight Mile Run, and when they paused at the village of Maidenhead to allow their main body to come up, a jäger who gave chase to a civilian on horseback was shot from his saddle by hidden riflemen. By mid-

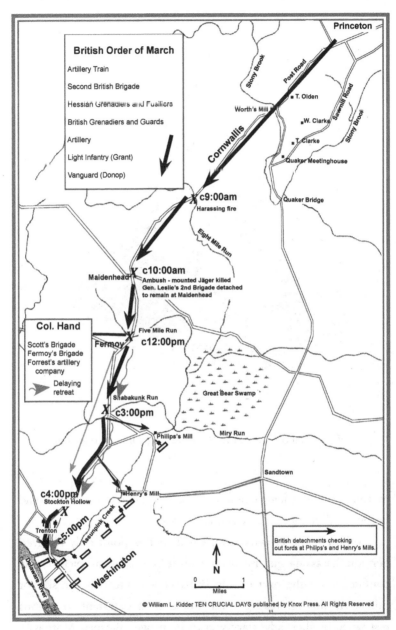

British Order of March

Artillery Train

Second British Brigade

Hessian Grenadiers and Fusiliers

British Grenadiers and Guards

Artillery

Light Infantry (Grant)

Vanguard (Donop)

Princeton

Stony Brook

Post Road

Worth's Mill

■ T. Olden

Sawmill Road

■ W. Clarke

■ T. Clarke

Stony Brook

■ Quaker Meetinghouse

Cornwallis

X c9:00am
Harassing fire

Quaker Bridge

Eight Mile Run

Y c10:00am
Ambush - mounted Jäger killed
Gen. Leslie's 2nd Brigade detached
to remain at Maidenhead

Maidenhead

Five Mile Run

Fermoy   c12:00pm

Col. Hand

Scott's Brigade
Fermoy's Brigade
Forrest's artillery
company

Delaying
retreat

Great Bear Swamp

Shabakunk Run

X c3:00pm

Philips's Mill

Miry Run

Sandtown

c4:00pm
Stockton Hollow

X

■ Henry's Mill

Assunpink Creek

c5:00pm

Trenton

Delaware River

Washington

British detachments checking
out fords at Philips's and Henry's Mills.

N

0   1
Miles

© William L. Kidder TEN CRUCIAL DAYS published by Knox Press. All Rights Reserved.

Delaying Actions, January 2, 1777

Edward Hand - New York Public Library Digital Collection

morning, the advancing column had begun to enter into what would become a daylong series of running battles.

Although the crown's troops had to this point only received periodic harassing gunfire from a dispersed cadre of pickets, any confidence on the part of the British command that the size or caliber of this impressive force would be a deterrent to serious resistance by their adversary was to be proven illusory. Moreover, time was slipping away. Trenton was five miles distant and less than five hours of daylight remained.[41]

94

A mile below Maidenhead, the Princeton Road crossed a stream called Five Mile Run, known as Little Shabakunk Creek today, where only token resistance was offered by rebel pickets. A mile beyond that was a larger waterway known as Big Shabakunk Creek. In the woods behind this larger stream, some three miles north of Trenton, lay the bulk of the American regiments who had exchanged fire with the enemy at Eight Mile Run the day before. As they awaited the enemy approach, the officer commanding them, General Fermoy, apparently "lost his nerve," suddenly mounted his horse without speaking a word to anyone, and fled to the rear in the direction of Trenton—thereby ceding his command to Colonel Hand as the next senior officer present.[42] It is not entirely clear why Fermoy acted as he did, but he appears to have had a drinking problem and would eventually be separated from the Continental Army under discreditable circumstances.

Fortunately for Hand and the American cause, his "tough and undisciplined backcountry riflemen were devoted to him" and as ready as he was to meet the daunting challenge before them. Their colonel "looked the part of a soldier . . . tall, lean, and leathery, a natural leader."[43] He "was an amiable, soft-spoken fellow who had the unlimited confidence of his men and his superior officers." And his immediate ascension to command "was the best possible thing that could have happened under the circumstances."[44] The affinity that the members of his regiment had for Hand "was based on his fairness, zeal, energy, and decisiveness."[45]

To confront Cornwallis's army, Hand had available the thousand or so men who had deployed at Eight Mile Run two days before. These included: his regiment, the 1st Pennsylvania; the German Regiment led by Colonel Haussegger; the Virginians under Colonel Scott; and Captain Forrest's artillery battery. Major Henry Miller of Hand's regiment—"a very able officer from Baltimore" known for his bravery—would act as the colonel's second-in-command during the extended skirmishing that followed.[46] Miller was positioned on the left and Hand on the right among the defenders hidden in the woods behind the Big Shabakunk Creek. In addition to the men in Hand's regiment, others would distinguish themselves during this day's fighting as well, both on the road to Trenton and at Assunpink Creek, including Charles Scott and Thomas Forrest in particular.

Colonel Scott, 37, had been a 16 year old orphan when he enlisted in a Virginia regiment commanded by Colonel George Washington, then 23 years of age, at the beginning of the French and Indian War. He served as a noncommissioned officer in the disastrous 1755 campaign waged by British Major General Edward Braddock, to whom Washington was attached as an aide-de-camp. Braddock's enterprise ended ingloriously during the battle at the Monongahela River where two-thirds of his force became casualties and Washington very narrowly missed being one himself. Scott's subsequent promotion to captain reflected Colonel Washington's recognition of Scott's performance as "the finest scout, woodsman, and sergeant of the First Virginia Regiment."[47]

When peace came, the young Virginian turned to farming on land left to him by his late father but would re-enter military service as soon as the Revolution erupted, first with the militia and then the Continental Army. In May 1776, Scott took command of the 5th Virginia Regiment that had been formed the previous February in Richmond County. He was promoted to colonel in August and reunited with Washington in November when his Virginians joined up with the rest of the army during its retreat across New Jersey.

Captain Forrest, 29, commanded a Pennsylvania battery that was part of the Philadelphia Associators. He had been commissioned a captain when his artillery unit was formed in October 1776 to help defend Philadelphia. He and his crew joined up with Washington's army at the beginning of December and were in better condition than the other artillery units by virtue of having missed the punishing New York campaign. Forrest was a "resourceful, dependable commander" whose well-trained battery was positioned by Washington near the head of Nathanael Greene's Second Division column during the early morning march to Trenton following the Christmas night crossing.[48] At Trenton on December 26, Forrest's crew joined with two New York batteries in assaulting the Hessians from the high ground at the juncture of King and Queen Streets.

Hand knew that the opposing force bearing down on his position was much larger, better trained, and more experienced in military operations than his skirmishers. At this moment, one imagines that the colonel's feelings reflected a firmness of purpose suited to the occasion as well as a yearning for the kind of tranquility that he would express in a letter from Fort Pitt to his wife, Katherine, later that year, after being promoted to brigadier general. It was addressed to "My Dearest Kitty," employing the nickname with which Hand's correspondence customarily greeted her: "Every thing is quiet here now. God grant it may continue so, and that I may soon have the Happiness to fold you & our Dear little Babes in my longing arms."[49]

From his previous service with the 18th Royal Irish Regiment, Hand was well-acquainted with the discipline of the British regulars and the advantage it afforded them in combat; however, he also knew that it rendered them vulnerable to his marksmen. The enemy's "linear tactics of standing shoulder to shoulder in two or three ranks would make ideal targets." The riflemen knew the drill by now: "Shoot low and look for the gorgets marking the officers. . . . Concealment, patience, and accuracy were the ingredients of Hand's message to his men."[50]

The Big Shabakunk Creek in front of the Americans was fordable in several places; however, the defenders were well hidden in a wood that was a mile in depth, and they had dismantled the wooden bridge over the creek. In addition, their foe was approaching from open fields on the north side of this waterway, and the redcoats labored under some disadvantages peculiar to their attire and accoutrements. It was the 18th century British foot soldier's lot to go into action under adverse conditions, and Richard Ketchum explains why:

The brilliant scarlet coats made ideal targets, knee breaches were so tight they often cut off the circulation in the legs, the wide white belt from which the bayonet hung was worn as tight as possible, a stiff collar and high leather stock restricted movement of the head, and none of the cumbersome hats—some of them heavy bearskins— had a visor or brim to shield the face and eyes. On one side the foot soldier carried an ammunition pouch, on the other his cartridge box, and into the haversack on his back went extra clothing, provisions, a canteen, and various camp tools. When fully dressed and equipped, the British private bore a weight computed at approximately 125 pounds, and with this burden added to his constricting uniform, he was expected to march into battle and fight efficiently.[51]

On top of this, the defenders who sought to hinder Cornwallis's advance brought to the fight some considerable assets of their own—courage, tenacity, and marksmanship. What the Continentals lacked in numbers, they made up for in the lethal accuracy of their long rifles. These weapons, when deployed from behind the protective cover of the surrounding woods, would make the road ahead a precarious one for the oncoming enemy column. The rebel rustics were about to demonstrate the particular skill that provided many American soldiers a noteworthy advantage over their Old World adversary.

A sharp difference in styles of combat manifested itself on this day and indeed throughout the war. Taking aim at a specific target was not emphasized in British army tactics, for in traditional European warfare, large formations faced each other across open terrain, "needing only to point their muskets in the direction of enemy formations to achieve effective fire." By contrast, their opponents "were superior marksmen, being accustomed to firearms and hunting from childhood." They had adopted a style of guerrilla warfare learned from contending with Native Americans over many years. As a result, the Patriot soldiers "fought best in wooded terrain where they could engage in fighting retreats and make the most of the familiar ground to find cover and take careful aim."[52]

As the flank and advance guards of Cornwallis's force approached the Big Shabakunk Creek, the rebel snipers unleashed a deadly fire that broke the enemy vanguard and sent it reeling backwards into their main body, creating great confusion among these troops. The defenders fired their volleys at nearly point-plank range as the redcoats crossed the stream.[53] Moreover, the effects of the heavy, accurate rifle fire were enhanced by Forrest's artillery.[54] Cornwallis was now forced to propel his main body into this unexpected confrontation and to deploy his artillery against the skirmishers who were blasting away from their concealed positions in the dense woods behind the creek.

The backwoodsmen employed a brutal style of combat that often dispensed with what their European adversaries regarded as proper etiquette; it mixed cunning, courage, and cruelty—as Hessian Lieutenant Friedrich Wilhelm von Grothausen discovered at his peril. In the skirmishing by the Big Shabakunk, "a group of Hand's riflemen had come out of the brush and signaled to the Germans, as if they intended to surrender," but when Grothausen and several others approached the Americans, the lieutenant was shot in the chest and mortally wounded "before the riflemen disappeared again into the woods."[55]

This type of subterfuge typified what the imperial troops regarded as contemptible behavior by an unmannerly opponent.

From the beginning of the conflict, "the rebels' fighting methods had been portrayed as an insult to any professional soldier serving His Britannic Majesty." To the royal forces, the methods employed by the Americans—shooting "from hidden emplacements, making feigned requests for quarter, picking off sentries, pickets, messengers, even officers, with snipers—these were all tactics more worthy of frontier savages than the soldiers of civilized nations."[56] In the eyes of British and Hessian soldiers, the colonials' practice of deliberately aiming at those who led the crown's men into battle was especially barbaric; however, officers—identifiable by their shoulder epaulets, swords, and uniform buttons and trim—made inviting targets for the riflemen from Pennsylvania and Virginia. In so doing, these sharpshooters emulated Native American warriors who used this tactic to sow confusion and panic among their adversary.[57]

The time required for Cornwallis's forces to rearrange their formations in order to deal with the rebel nuisance before them was of incalculable value to the Patriot cause, for the longer it took the British commander to get to Trenton, the less time he would have to attack Washington's army before his limited window of opportunity snapped shut. Once His Lordship arrived at Trenton, he would have to reconnoiter the unfamiliar terrain and the layout of enemy troops, devise a strategy to counter Washington's defensive alignment, and initiate an assault that would cripple his opponent or at least set a fatal trap for him. And he hoped to do all this before darkness interrupted his offensive; however, the invaders were continually frustrated by their opponent's dilatory maneuvers, which consumed Cornwallis's precious time.

The backwoods riflemen used to their advantage "every kind of cover—woods, ravines, bends in the road"—as they took aim at the oncoming foe and forced the main body to halt repeatedly while troops from the advance guard were deployed to drive off the unseen rebels. Whenever the British formed a new battle line, the

Americans would disappear into the woods, "falling back to another position and firing from cover as they were accustomed to do on the frontier."[58]

This New World manner of waging war, and the geographic setting in which it occurred, generally reflected the image portrayed by British Major General John Burgoyne in a paper entitled "Reflections on the War in America" that he submitted to his government in early 1776. In his analysis, the general predicted how the insurgents would resist His Majesty's forces and described the colonials' defensive approach to combat, whether fighting from behind trees and stone walls as they had during the British retreat from Concord, Massachusetts, in April 1775 or from behind earthworks as at the Battle of Bunker Hill two months later. Burgoyne wrote:

> Composed as the American army is, together with the strength of the country, full of woods, swamps, stone walls, and other enclosures and hiding places, it may be said of it that every private man will in action be his own general, who will turn every tree and bush into a temporary fortress, from whence, when he hath fired his shot with all the deliberation, coolness, and certainty which hidden safety inspires, he will skip as it were to the next, and so on for a long time.[59]

Under unrelenting pressure from the imperial troops' advance, Colonel Hand "stood tall and demonstrated his tactical ability."[60] In order to effectively contest the enemy forces with his much smaller contingent, he was required to use the utmost skill in coordinating the deployment of his riflemen, supporting artillery, and regular infantry with their muskets.[61] The soldiers under his command fell back in the face of superior numbers but fought a stubborn and adroit delaying action for most of the afternoon.

Various accounts of the fighting convey its intensity: "Every place which would even for a few moments give shelter from which to take a steady aim was taken advantage of, and every part of the road was disputed in all possible ways."[62] The defenders "waylaid their foe with a lethal fire from concealed positions in the untidy dark brown forests" and engaged in a series of "time-consuming firefights before melting away to take up new positions further down the road, from which they opened up yet again on their prey."[63]

Hand interspersed his withdrawal with occasional advances toward the enemy, which forced the attackers "into formations in which they could (and did) fend off such American tactical thrusts." In their effort to contest "almost every inch of ground" between the advancing imperial troops and the main American force at Trenton, Hand's men threw everything they had at the enemy—artillery fire, ambushes, irregular warfare, and regular infantry tactics.[64] Writing in his bygone narrative style, William Stryker reports that "the gallant little American force, somewhat protected by the dense woods, harassed the redcoats and continually thinned their ranks with musketry and artillery." He observes of their effort: "Right well did they carry out the plan of General Washington to consume the entire day, if possible, in skirmishing and so retard the enemy's advance toward Trenton."[65]

At one point, a detachment of British troops launched a probe to their left toward the upper fords of the Assunpink Creek in an effort to outflank Hand's skirmishers on their right; however, the New England brigades from the main body of Washington's army that were posted there came forward and, according to one British officer, made "a Demonstration of Passing the Creek at two Different places in their Possession where it was fordable, so that by that means to turn our left Flank if we advanced towards Trenton."[66] This caused the British to abort their flanking maneuver and rejoin their main column.

Under his determined leadership, Hand's small force held off the enemy until almost 3 p.m.[67] Then, facing continued heavy pressure and outnumbered by more than six to one, they began a slow withdrawal through the woods toward Trenton "in good order with all their equipment."[68] Being "under increasingly devastating fire, the defenders began their planned retreat, grudgingly giving up ground—firing, falling back, reloading, and firing again."[69] The rebels had been sparring with the British and Hessians for about five hours and had impeded their progress as long as they could. The imperial troops were frustrated by the slow pace of their advance, being forced to contend with an elusive enemy who was often invisible yet posed a deadly hindrance to their advance. In the accounts of Cornwallis's redcoats, "one senses the pressure that they felt, caught between the impatience of their commander and the resolve of their American opponents."[70]

At a ravine called Stockton Hollow, about half a mile above Trenton, the rebel skirmishers made their final stand with about 600 men. Hand's regiment was positioned on the left with Forrest's guns behind the ravine and Scott's Virginia regiments on the right between the Princeton Road and the upper fords of the Assunpink.

Washington, accompanied by Generals Greene and Knox, rode out from town to personally encourage the skirmishers' continued resistance and to emphasize the importance of delaying the enemy until nightfall, as he had devised a plan to foil Cornwallis that required holding off the latter as long as possible. The commander-in-chief thanked the defenders for their efforts, "gave orders for as obstinate a stand as could be made on that ground, without hazarding the [artillery] pieces," and "retired to marshal his troops for action beyond the Assunpink."[71]

Washington "was well pleased with the all-day running fight, and begged the little party not to yield until compelled to," according to Stryker. A "battery of British artillery was soon after brought into position and made every effort to dislodge the American advance force," but almost an hour passed before Hand's men, "unable any longer to sustain themselves, began again to yield the ground and retreat . . . into the village, having captured some twenty-five or thirty men during the day."[72]

In Stryker's account, Stockton Hollow—the site of the final skirmish by Hand's contingent—marked the point at the northern edge of town where "some little earthworks had been hastily thrown up at a ravine which led down to the Assunpink Creek" and where Forrest's artillery had been positioned. Here the retreating defenders "made another post of resistance, and the Virginia troops distinguished themselves, as the Pennsylvania riflemen had done for several hours previous."[73]

When the full weight of the imperial force was brought to bear on this last point of resistance, Hand and Forrest were forced to yield ground to avoid being outflanked. Daylight was already fading. Some of Scott's Virginians withdrew toward the upper fords of the Assunpink on their right. Scott's 5th Virginia Regiment, supported by Colonel Mordecai Buckner's 6th Virginia Regiment, retreated southwest toward the Assunpink in an effort to prevent Hessian Lieutenant Colonel Friedrich von Minnigerode's composite grenadier battalion, with its remnants of the Rall brigade, from flanking Hand's riflemen and the Continental Army's German battalion. However, "Scott and Buckner were unable to stop the enemy flanking movement, and Hand ordered the artillery withdrawn and slowly retreated with his infantry."[74] The colonel's "tactic was to load and fire, retreat while reloading, then fire again."[75]

By 4 p.m., as the shadows lengthened and the British and Hessians entered Trenton, Hand's men were falling back through the embattled town. They continued to level a steady fire at their pursuing foe from behind the houses they passed while heading toward the Assunpink Creek bridge held by Washington's main body.

The principal part of Cornwallis's column lagged some distance behind when its forward attackers penetrated Trenton's perimeter. According to Stryker, this advance guard of about 1,500 men "entered Trenton at the head of King and Queen streets, at the same place where the guns of Captains Forrest and Hamilton had opened fire on Rall's brigade" on December 26. On their way down Queen street, they took rebel "fire from behind houses [that] was continuous and galling," and when "they reached Tucker's Corner, where Queen street is crossed by Second street, they first began to receive the shots from the batteries of the main American army posted on the high ground on the south side of the Assunpink Creek."[76]

The enemy advance gathered momentum as British and Hessian troops rushed into the side streets. They poured fire into the flanks of the retreating rebels, as well as the soldiers in Colonel Hitchcock's Rhode Island brigade whom Washington had dispatched across the bridge to support Hand's withdrawal. The Americans on the north side of the creek began running toward the waterway, most heading for the bridge but some swimming across at the lower fords near the Delaware River.

Hitchcock's soldiers advanced up Queen Street to Fourth Street, where the men and artillery in Hand's detachment passed through them in their retreat. Private John Howland of Hitchcock's brigade recalled that the Rhode Islanders opened ranks as Hand's men raced through in their dash to the bridge: "We then closed in a compact and rather solid column as the street through which we were to retreat to the bridge was rather narrow."[77] Under the protective fire provided by Hitchcock's Continentals, as well as American artillery below the creek, Hand and his weary cohort crossed the bridge. There Washington sat astride his horse and observed the movement of Cornwallis's troops coming his way.

At one point, the attackers attempted to cut off the retreat of Hand's men "by leaving the road and marching directly toward the bridge" but were stalled by American artillery fire from behind the creek that poured "into the heads and flanks" of their columns.[78] The enemy was following so closely in pursuit, according to one New Jersey militiaman, that before the rebels crossed the bridge to the southern side, "some of our troops on the Trenton side of the creek, with a field piece, motioned for us to get out of the street while they fired at the British at the upper end of it."[79] As the American field guns below the creek began to make their presence felt, the charge of the enemy vanguard stalled and the latter pulled back to a safer position to await further orders.

*****

Those Trenton residents who had not abandoned their homes prior to the Hessian occupation in December could hear the firing coming ever closer as the imperial troops pursued Hand's force, and they urgently "sought cover" from the returning invaders.[80] With the enemy infiltrating Trenton, any American soldiers who were conducting business or otherwise spending time in town, away from the main body of the army, joined the retreating skirmishers in a frantic dash to the relative safety of their lines below the creek. Not everyone made it.

One who did not escape was John Rosbrugh, a 62-year-old Presbyterian minister from Northampton County, Pennsylvania, serving as chaplain of the Third Battalion of the Northampton County militia. A native of Ireland and a graduate of the College of New Jersey, he had left behind a young wife and five children upon answering the call to service. Rosbrugh was sitting in the Blazing Star Tavern when he heard the sounds of battle and ran into the street, only to discover that someone had made off with his horse. He tried to run for the creek but was captured by several Hessian soldiers who took to heart Colonel von Donop's order to take no prisoners.

According to a deposition that Reverend George Duffield later made to a justice of the peace, Rosbrugh surrendered and begged for mercy but was struck in the head with a sword or cutlass and bayoneted by a Hessian who denounced him as a "damn'd rebel minister," while enemy officers "highly applauded the perpetrator for what he had done."[81] Rosbrugh became the first United States Army chaplain killed in battle.[82] His naked body would be "found in an open field with thirteen bayonet wounds and many saber cuts to the head."[83]

Stryker reports that during the enemy advance through town, the commander of the German Regiment in General Fermoy's brigade, Colonel Haussegger, was taken prisoner on Queen Street, but that the "the capture was made in so suspicious a manner" that the colonel's "devotion to the cause of liberty has ever since been doubted."[84] In this account, Haussegger was taken by the British light infantry, along with other members of his regiment, near the lower fords of the Assunpink, and was given quarter—as Colonel von Donop order to the contrary applied only to the Hessian soldiers under his command. However, more recent research indicates that the colonel actually deserted or allowed himself to be apprehended by the British at Princeton, either before, during, or after the battle there on January 3.[85] Indeed, Haussegger's later correspondence with Washington (after being paroled by the British) supports this latter interpretation, although the colonel vigorously defended his actions in that letter.[86] In any case, according to Fischer, "Haussegger was regarded with deep suspicion in the American army and was openly critical of its commanders. Even his friends were convinced that he was not captured" but turned traitor.[87] Still, it appears that evidence credible enough to bring Haussegger to trial never materialized.[88]

Jacob Bottomer, a private in Hand's regiment who was wounded in the skirmishing against the British and Hessians along the road to Trenton, barely escaped to the other side of the Assunpink.

Drawing of the Battle of Assunpink Creek by George A. Bradshaw

Bottomer's lieutenant ordered some soldiers to "bring him along," but when they had almost reached the bridge, the injured private collapsed and was trampled by some 50 soldiers. After Bottomer's unit crossed the bridge, he crawled to safety despite being "very weak from loss of blood." Although it appeared that he was mortally wounded, Bottomer "was placed under the care of army surgeons and survived."[89]

Private Isaiah Crandall, 17 years old, was another fortunate Continental. As his Rhode Island regiment, led by Colonel Christopher Lippitt, retreated through town, the young private was felled by British musket fire that struck him in the back. However, the musket ball hit his knapsack and pierced a folded blanket only to have its force spent by "a hard lump of bread" that probably saved Crandall's life.[90]

The first act of this day's drama was over, and the second was about to begin. It was now past 4 p.m., and the sun would set at 4:46.

Colonel Hand's men had bought Washington the time he needed if he was to have any hope of fending off the enemy attack against the American troops below the creek, because there was not enough daylight left for Cornwallis's intended all-out strike.

All the British commander could do, before it became too dark to fight, was to initiate a series of probing actions that might detect any weakness in the Continentals' defensive alignment, in preparation for a later and larger assault. He would employ the forward part of his army in an effort to find and exploit any such opportunity while the rest of his long column, stretching over several miles, continued to file into Trenton. Cornwallis's immediate objective was to establish a foothold on the Americans' side of the Assunpink. Then the rest of his troops could use their larger numbers to widen the salient and shove the outnumbered rebels back toward the Delaware River, ejecting them from their entrenched positions overlooking the creek and foreclosing any possibility of escape.

If any general in the crown's service had the competence and drive to deliver a knockout blow to Washington's army, it was Lord Cornwallis. He had been confident of accomplishing his mission when his troops began their early morning march to Trenton, and he felt no less assured of victory as the shadows lengthened across the battlefield.

Washington's force had eluded Cornwallis a month earlier when the rebel army fled across the Delaware to Pennsylvania, but this time the British general resolved that the outcome would be different. From his perspective, the Americans had returned to New Jersey and fallen into a trap of their own making that would spring shut when the crown's troops forded the Assunpink. Washington had no boats, and the southern New Jersey interior could not support his army. Cornwallis would press him to the limit, no longer shackled by the constraints imposed by General Howe during the rebels' retreat across New Jersey back in November and early December. With a mandate to swiftly punish the rebels for their raid on the Rall brigade, Cornwallis had the benefit of clear-cut orders that perfectly suited his style of command: to track down the American army and finish it off. His Lordship had done the former, and now he quickly developed a plan to accomplish the latter.

19th century rendition of the Battle of Assunpink Creek

Let it be told to the future world, that in the depth of winter, when nothing but hope and virtue could survive, that the city and the country, alarmed at one common danger, came forth to meet and to repulse it.

— Thomas Paine, from *The American Crisis*, Number I, December 19, 1776

5

THE DESPERATE HOUR

As the vanguard of His Majesty's forces moved through Trenton toward the Assunpink Creek at day's end on January 2, Washington and his troops could easily discern the immediacy and gravity of the threat looming before them. The defenders were united in the intensity of the moment and their physical proximity to each other.

These men later spoke of their leader's "composure" at this critical time and how they rallied to "his quiet leadership." Many of them would be physically near the commander-in-chief in the course of the upcoming battle and even speak with him. "They felt that they were one with him and were inspired by his example," according to David Hackett Fischer, who noted that their feelings for the general included "not only trust and loyalty but also confidence and complete approval."[1] As the American soldiers above the creek

111

retreated across the bridge, Washington directed them to defensive positions that conformed to his battle plan.

The Americans had before them a natural barrier against the king's troops. The stream was running "high and swift" after the recent rain and melting snow, and Henry Knox reported that it "could be crossed only at a few points."[2] The bridge over the creek "was an arched span made of stone and barely wide enough for the passage of a horse and carriage." On the east side of the bridge, the Assunpink formed an extensive millpond, and to the west it ran its course for about a quarter of a mile to the Delaware River.[3]

As the oncoming British and Hessian attackers pushed their way in his direction, Washington calmly eyed their movements from behind the stone overpass. Private John Howland of Rhode Island remembered that the "noble horse of General Washington stood with his breast pressed close against the end of the west rail of the bridge, and the firm, composed, and majestic countenance of the General inspired confidence and assurance in a moment so important and critical." Howland proudly noted that it was his good fortune "to be next to the west rail and, arriving at the end of the bridge rail," he "pressed against the shoulder of the General's horse and in contact with the boot of the General." He observed that the "horse stood as firm as the rider, and seemed to understand that he must not quit his post and station."[4]

Knowing how consequential the stakes were in the upcoming fight, Washington had configured the defensive alignment of the Continental units and supporting militia near the creek with extreme care. They were spread out for nearly three miles along the southern bank of the Assunpink, which Washington called "Mill Creek." Their left stretched to the mouth of the creek at the Delaware River. Further to the east, the rebel troops "had thrown up a series of small earthworks on the ridge and across the road below the Queen street bridge." Behind this front line of battle, the commanding general placed his reserve units.

General Mercer's brigade was located on the extreme right of the army, two miles above the bridge to the east, and would thereby avoid the brunt of the impending action. The Philadelphia Associators under Colonel Cadwalader, equipped with five cannons, were initially stationed in a field on the right about a mile from the town; however, as the enemy assault unfolded, they would be repositioned closer to the bridge on Washington's orders in order to reinforce the defenders at that most critical point.[5]

In attempting to safeguard such an extended position against the veteran European troops approaching the creek, Washington needed to focus primarily on the three most feasible crossing points. These included: a lower ford on his left near the Delaware; "the sturdy stone bridge, strong but very narrow" in the center of his alignment; and the upper fords, one at Philips's Mill that was "easily passable that day" and the other at Henry's Mill, which was "reported so deep and swift that it was barely usable for horses and nearly impassable for all but strong swimmers."[6]

Washington assigned the most experienced Continental Army units to guard these crossing points. Colonel Hitchcock's Rhode Island brigade was to protect the lower ford on the left. General St. Clair's New England brigade was posted on the high bank just east of the bridge, from where those men were to defend the army's position on the right, especially at Philips's Ford. The three Virginia regiments under Colonel Scott would be front and center, immediately behind the bridge, with two militia units posted on either side of the Virginians—General Ewing's Pennsylvanians on their left and Colonel Silas Newcomb's New Jerseyans to their right. The militia were purposely interspersed between the Continentals. Behind Scott's Virginians, Washington placed the deadliest sharpshooters in his army—Colonel Hand's Pennsylvania riflemen—along with Colonel Haussegger's German Regiment. And behind this second line of defense were more Pennsylvania troops under General Mifflin.

*****

The bridge was where the fiercest fighting was likely to occur, given its status as the only span across the creek in the area of contention between the two armies. The Virginians whom Washington had posted directly behind it knew they would be severely tested in the coming attack.

In Charles Scott, the colonel of the 5th Virginia Regiment who had fought with Colonel Hand's riflemen along the Princeton Road for much of the day, Washington had "a rough diamond from the Virginia frontier with little schooling and less polish." The men in Scott's regiment referred to him as "Charley." Reputed to be "the most profane and disorderly" soldiers in the army, they were also "hard and tough and fought tenaciously." Scott "led from the front and was tougher and more profane than his men."[7] From their long acquaintance dating back to the French and Indian War, the colonel was in the habit of "affectionately" referring to his commander-in-chief as "the old boss," and his use of that title delighted his unpolished soldiers.[8] This plain-spoken frontiersman "could take pride in his family heritage," as his ancestors had been living in Virginia since the mid-17th century.[9]

Ensign Robert Beale of the 5th Virginia reported that the brigade led by Scott, which comprised Beale's regiment plus the 4th and 6th Virginia Regiments, "was ordered to form in column at the bridge and George Washington came and, in the presence of us all, told Colonel Scott to defend the bridge to the last extremity." And he noted the colonel's response, punctuated by an "oath"—"Yes, General, as long as there is a man alive."[10]

As the soldiers in his brigade awaited the approaching enemy, Scott offered some words of encouragement and practical advice:

> Well boys, you know the old boss has put us here to defend this bridge; and by God it must be done, let what will come.

Now I want to tell you one thing. You're all in the habit of shooting too high. You waste your powder and lead, and I have cursed you about it a hundred times. Now I tell you what it is, nothing must be wasted, every crack must count. For that reason boys, whenever you see them fellows first begin to put their feet upon this bridge do you shin 'em. Take care now and fire low. Bring down your pieces, fire at their legs, one man Wounded in the leg is better [than] a dead one for it takes two more to carry him off and there is three gone. Leg them dam 'em I say leg them.[11]

Washington had placed the regiments under Scott at the bridge because he knew them better than any other in the army. He knew where they came from, his native Virginia; he knew the caliber of their leader, Colonel Scott, from their time together in the last war; and he knew from experience that he had no better fighting men to deploy on this most vital ground. When the commander-in-chief told one of the Virginians, Captain Richard Parker, that they must defend the bridge "to the last extremity," Parker responded that they intended "to sleep on it."[12] In short, Washington chose the toughest men he had to defend the toughest spot on the field, and it proved an astute decision—perhaps as much as any he made throughout the war.

Scott's brigade would "be tested by professional European soldiers who ranked among the best that the Old World could send against the New," but Washington "knew the temper of his fellow Virginians and had good reason to repose such confidence in these soldiers." Indeed, he "paid them the highest compliment possible by positioning them directly behind the bridge as the Continentals' first line of defense, knowing that they would do as he had ordered, whatever the consequences."[13]

*****

At this point, the size of the American army along the creek was almost three times as large as the one that had assaulted Trenton on December 26.[14] Although this force totaled about 7,000 men, the reserves that Washington was counting on to support the Continental soldiers against the approaching attackers were militia units with little if any combat experience. They had left behind the relative comforts of civilian life to face enemy troops who had made a career of soldiering and in many cases had extensive battlefield experience in European wars.

The militia in America embodied a concept of citizen soldier that had existed for generations. Ever since the earliest settlements, the colonists had been compelled to provide for their own defense against hostile natives and European adversaries. With few exceptions, every able-bodied adult male was required to participate in militia training exercises in his community as required by local ordinance.

When they enlisted, militia conscripts generally signed a covenant stipulating the conduct, responsibilities, and rights expected of them, and because "few towns had enough resources to provide their militias with any sort of equipment, it was usually expected that each man avail himself of a good firelock and prescribed quantities of gunpowder and lead." Subsistence farmers and laborers comprised the bulk of the militia, as they "represented the lowest and most numerous classes." In addition, "craftsmen, artisans, shopkeepers, gentlemen farmers, and other members of the middle class" were obligated to serve, while clergymen, doctors, jurists, and others "whose role was deemed critical to the welfare of the community" were generally exempt. Slaves were excluded from service, and the very wealthy could avoid conscription by hiring substitutes. The effectiveness and preparedness of each militia unit was determined by "the fitness of the conscripts and the professionalism and zeal of the officers, who were generally elected by their own troops."[15]

Notwithstanding Washington's often-cited remarks about the shortcomings of militia, the latter provided an important supporting role on occasions such as the one at Assunpink Creek. While he had

116

written, shortly after assuming command of the Continentals in 1775, "that no Dependence can be put on the Militia for a continuance in Camp, or Regularity and Discipline during the short time they may stay," the commanding general did concede that the regular army and militia could act in distinct but mutually supporting capacities.

Washington envisioned that militia units would provide internal security on the home front against Loyalists and Native American tribes, but that in an emergency situation such as the regular army found itself facing during the "Ten Crucial Days" and in particular on January 2, 1777, the various militias would also "be pressed into service with the main army to play a supporting role, although they should never be considered an adequate substitute for Continentals."[16] Notwithstanding Washington's less-than-enthusiastic comments about the militia in his correspondence, "the ways he employed it indicate he had a better opinion than he expressed outwardly, or at least he was savvy enough, or desperate enough, to bow to pragmatic necessity."[17]

*****

More and more of the imperial troops appeared before the rebel defenders in the waning January daylight of this Thursday afternoon. The British and Hessians sensed that they had their opponent on the run until the creek came into view and they could see the Americans were dug in for a fight. A royal engineer, Captain-Lieutenant Archibald Robertson, observed that Washington's forces were positioned where Colonel Rall's Hessian brigade should have been when it was attacked on December 26.[18] He and his fellow officers "were studying the American position through their field telescopes in the deepening twilight."[19] A British captain named Hall (first name unknown) recalled that the "enemy abandoned Trenton on our approach, after a faint resistance, in which a few were killed on both sides," and that this "happened . . . late in the day when the rebels, on evacuating the town, withdrew their whole force over

117

a rivulet, the Assunpink, which runs by the place, and took their position on some high ground near it, with a seeming determined countenance to defend them."[20]

Washington's troops had a clear view of the opposing forces from their position on the heights south of the stream. As Cornwallis's troops occupied the high ground above Trenton, then fully visible from the other side of the creek, the British commander "formed his men into long lines in 'battalion order' along the crest of the rising ground where they would be most visible," while his marching columns of infantry in the town pushed forward toward the creek. The "Americans could see the strength of attacking British and Hessian forces, who outnumbered the defenders."[21] And the rebels' numerical inferiority was compounded by their reliance on inexperienced militia to support the Continental regulars.

*****

Although the Patriot troops along the Assunpink were fewer than Cornwallis's total force, they were able to deploy more artillery— some 40 field pieces to the enemy's 28—and these were arranged so as to create overlapping fields of fire. They were the "vital element" in the American defenses. Washington positioned 18 or 19 guns in the center of his alignment, all to cover the bridge—some within 40 yards of it—while placing 12 guns by the upper fords and the rest to cover the lower ford.[22]

Where the commander-in-chief had counted on his big guns to play a decisive role during the attack against the Hessians the week before, now he needed them to anchor his defensive strategy. Henry Knox's batteries would again be depended on to magnify the army's destructive force, and they met the challenge in impressive fashion. In the late afternoon and early evening of January 2, the rebel gun crews arrayed along the southern edge of the Assunpink greeted their unwelcome visitors with "the heaviest fire ever delivered on any field in the Western Hemisphere up to this time."[23] Knox recounted to his wife, Lucy, in a letter from Morristown, New Jersey, five days after the battle, that when "the enemy advanced within reach of our cannon," those guns "saluted them with great vociferation and some execution."[24]

It has been argued that "Knox's gunners saved the army from what would have been a disastrous defeat" at the Assunpink.[25] Their display of firepower reflected a remarkable ability by the army's artillery chief to overcome significant technical challenges in the effective use of his heavy guns. Throughout the war, Knox struggled with a medley of "ill-assorted cannon of various caliber"—captured British cannons, French field pieces, and "guns cast in crude American foundries"—and never achieved uniformity in the army's artillery. In addition, his guns employed different types of ammunition—some solid cast-iron shot, some grapeshot, and others canister—and the size of those guns varied to such an extent "that ammunition usually was not interchangeable." In spite of these complications, the young officer assembled a potent force "and rightfully deserves his reputation as 'father of the American Army artillery.'"[26]

Knox's gunners were "a new breed of warrior" employing a weapon that displayed "the most unprecedented power." They "fought indirectly, servicing a machine that killed and destroyed at a distance" by "accelerating projectiles to speeds that surpassed the limits of human vision."[27] The Continental artillerists at Assunpink were led by a motley assortment of captains who skillfully directed a fierce barrage against their adversary. Four in particular stand out from this period of the war.

Alexander Hamilton, 21, commanded the New York State Artillery Company. An emigrant from the British island colony of Nevis, where he was born out of wedlock, he had been a student at King's College in New York (Columbia University today) until dropping out to engage in the Patriot insurgency. Hamilton wrote

119

essays in support of the rebellion and was appointed captain of his artillery company in March 1776. He had come to Washington's attention during the Americans' retreat across New Jersey, in particular on the banks of the Raritan River at Brunswick on December 1. The artillery battery that Hamilton commanded dueled with Cornwallis's field guns while the Continental Army made its getaway under the protective fire of this rearguard action; and Washington's stepgrandson (who became his adopted son), George Washington Parke Custis, later wrote that the commander-in-chief had been "charmed by the brilliant courage and admirable skill" of the young captain.[28]

At Trenton on December 26, Hamilton's battery was positioned with Nathanael Greene's division on the strategic high ground at the head of King and Queen Streets, which dominated the battlefield. By the following March, he would be promoted to lieutenant colonel and serving as an aide-de-camp to the commanding general. From there his role grew dramatically in importance as he became Washington's secretary and right-hand man throughout the war years. In Hamilton, the general "found an aide whose meticulousness, intelligence and zeal made him indispensable."[29]

Sebastian Baumann, 37, led the New York Company of the Continental Artillery that had been authorized by the Continental Congress in late 1775 and organized between December 1775 and May 1776. Like Hamilton's battery, Baumann's company supported General Greene's division during the earlier fighting at Trenton.

Thomas Forrest, 29, headed up the Pennsylvania battery supporting Colonel Hand's contingent in their prolonged delaying action against the enemy that consumed most of January 2.

Joseph Moulder, 62, commanded the 2nd Company of Artillery, Philadelphia Associators. A sailmaker and schooner owner from Philadelphia who had served as a delegate to his colony's provincial convention in 1774, Moulder joined the Continental Army in 1776 as the captain in command of his artillery company. He recruited a slew of young soldiers from the city's waterfront to his unit—"seamen, longshoremen, block-makers, riggers, and ships' carpenters" by trade.[30] These nautical types assisted the Marbleheaders in rowing the Continentals across the Delaware River on Christmas night, although their role in that endeavor would receive less attention from chroniclers of the Revolution than the efforts of Colonel Glover's regiment. From its position on Queen Street on December 26, Moulder's battery engaged at close range the troops that Colonel Rall was attempting to rally against the American attack.

*****

The redcoats put on a good show as they advanced toward the Assunpink Creek in the fading daylight. This was a proud and arrogant army that had ample reason to feel that way. The experience of the British army during the period leading up to the American Revolution was one of "victory without equal in the world," and its "senior officers and sergeants were seasoned veterans of a great world conflict" in which they had triumphed over France and Spain. During a strife-ridden decade from 1755 to 1764, the crown's army had "fought on five continents and defeated every power that stood against it." An impressive legacy of that remarkable record lay in the various regimental honors that spoke to Britain's global record of military success during this period: in Europe (at Minden and Emsdorf), in India (at Plassey and Pondicherry), in North America (at Louisbourg and Quebec), in the West Indies (at Guadeloupe and Martinique), in Cuba (at Moro and Havana), in the Mediterranean (at Minorca), in the Philippines (at Manila), and in Africa (in Senegal).[31]

The movement of British troops as they approached Assunpink Creek—carefully choreographed in preparation for their twilight assault against the rebel forces—reflected a degree of training, experience, and professional rigor that could easily intimidate an opposing army whose ranks were largely filled with amateur soldiers. Moreover, the redcoats' attire was designed to augment the impression that legions such as theirs sought to convey when contesting 18th century European battlefields. They treated combat as "a dress-up occasion that required fastidious attention to appearance." Their brightly colored uniforms, replete with insignia and accessories, "helped to differentiate among regiments and sides in the smoky confusion of battle," but also suggested to the opposing soldiery how formidable an adversary they faced. The forces of Britannia displayed a variety of adornments and decorations to distinguish between officers and regiments. These included linings and facings of various colors, "waistcoats (vests), hat lace, cockades (a ribbon or feather in a hat), epaulets (shoulder straps often made of strips of cloth, sometimes fringed), [and] gorgets (badges hung around the neck)."[32]

Many of the amateur soldiers now facing these smartly uniformed invaders were dressed in rags. Being on the move for so many months had taken its toll on their shoes and stockings, and "sleeping in the open was hard on clothing."[33] These men "were more concerned with acquiring clothes than caring what color or style they were."[34] When the royals pressed forward on this day, more than a few of the Patriot combatants who had tried to stand against them in earlier battles must have wondered to themselves whether another setback was in the offing.

His Majesty's army had turned the bayonet charge into an art form, and it undoubtedly made an impression on the defenders along the Assunpink—as it often did on American soldiers during the war. The latter instinctively and understandably recoiled from the prospect of facing those lethal blades, and their intense fear of the bayonet seemed in part due to their being much less accustomed to this form of combat than European armies of the time.[35] One account almost waxes poetic in its depiction of Britain's elite warriors as they typically appeared when in battle formation, their

122

ranks advancing "as one man, gleaming steel bobbing before them . . . beautifully disciplined troops coming on steadily even in the face of enemy musket fire," and then, as they reached their objective, "lunging and slashing" with their bayonets. Their infantry "was superb at this sort of thing, the artillery was extremely efficient, and the army's tactical skill may be judged from the fact that in eight years of war the British regulars (not the Hessians or loyalists) lost only a handful of battles to American troops."[36]

The steady advance of Cornwallis's lines would bring the opposing armies closer to their impending clash, as the Hessian troops up front were followed by hundreds of British light infantry, who "were followed by thousands more." Then about 500 yards from the Assunpink bridge, the "British put artillery pieces into position, and soon the cannons were booming." With the support of their big field pieces, the imperial troops began to advance in a solid column, their bayonets fixed. The Continentals and militia, "row upon row on the high ground south of the Assunpink, had their weapons primed." One of them, James Johnston, would recall that they "formed into three lines, front, center, and rear." Although these men and boys were supported by a "tremendous concentration of artillery power," the question remained whether they would "be able to stand their ground under bombardment and attack by the world's best-trained army," which was about to hit them.[37]

*****

The redcoats' use of the bayonet had driven rebel soldiers from the field on prior occasions, but this time the latter were entrenched on high ground with a waterway between them and the advancing enemy, and with plenty of artillery to rain fire down on their adversary. If Washington's troops could hold the narrow stone bridge over the creek and if Cornwallis could not find a feasible alternative crossing point, no British or Hessian bayonets could come close enough to intimidate the defenders. For this scenario to prevail, however, the Continentals and militia had to stand their ground rather than break and run. They were keenly aware of how precarious their position was, with a creek in front of them and a river behind them, no boats available for an evacuation, and an elite opposing force of enormous power staring them in the face.

Fischer writes: "The American troops long remembered that moment, when the enemy appeared before them in their full strength. Many recorded their feelings in remarkably similar ways. Most shared a deep sense of foreboding, deeper than they recalled at any other battle."[38] The comments later put on paper by Washington's soldiers reflect an overwhelming sense of urgency about what was at stake in this confrontation.

Major James Wilkinson would write 40 years later: "If there ever was a crisis in the affairs of the Revolution, this was the moment; thirty minutes would have sufficed to bring the two armies into contact, and thirty more would have decided the combat; and, covered with woe, Columbia might have wept the loss of her beloved Chief and most valorous sons."[39]

Ensign Robert Beale of the 5th Virginia Regiment that was led by Charles Scott reported: "This was the most awful crisis, no possible chance of crossing the River; ice as large as houses floating down, and no retreat to the mountains, the British between us and them."[40]

Captain Stephen Olney of Rhode Island, who had endured the Continentals' siege of Boston, the failed New York campaign, and the harrowing retreat to the Delaware River, "always remembered the stand at Assunpink as the critical moment of the war." This officer recalled: "It appeared to me then that our army was in the most desperate situation I had ever known it." He and his comrades needed no reminder that they "had no boats to carry us across the Delaware" and that it would serve no purpose to withdraw "into the south part of Jersey, where there was no support for an army."[41]

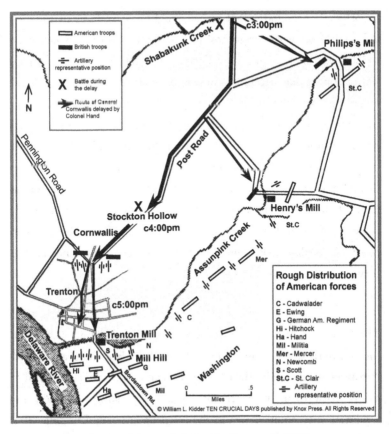

Battle of Assunpink Creek - January 2, 1777

Captain Olney's fellow Rhode Islander, Private Howland, recollected that "on one hour, yes, on forty minutes, commencing at the moment when the British troops first saw the bridge and the creek before them, depended the all-important, the all-absorbing question, whether we should be independent states or conquered rebels!" And he elaborated: "Had the army of Cornwallis within that space have crossed the bridge, or forded the creek, unless a miracle intervened, there would have been an end of the American army."[42]

Captain Thomas Rodney of the Light Infantry Company of Dover, a Delaware militia unit, and younger brother of Caesar Rodney, reported after the battle that he had sought to corral one of the men in his company whose eagerness to join the fray appears to have been lacking, and in so doing he reflected the intensity of the moment. "After sunset this afternoon the enemy came down in a very heavy column to force the bridge," Rodney recalled, while noting: "The fire was very heavy and the light troops were ordered to fly to the support of that important post." As they approached the bridge, he "stepped out of the front to order my men to close up" and observed that "at this time Martinas Sipple was about 10 steps behind the man next in front of him." Directing his wrath at Sipple, the captain immediately drew his sword and "threatened to cut his head off if he did not keep close." According to Rodney, the offending militiaman "then sprang forward and I returned to the front."[43]

*****

The invaders would make three attempts to establish a foothold on the southern side of the Assunpink Creek by launching a series of "probing attacks." The British and Hessian commanders drove their troops forward in the increasing darkness, looking to exploit any weakness they could detect in the rebel defenses and hoping "that one strong blow might send the rebels running as it had so many times before."[44] It was after 5 p.m. "and growing darker moment by moment, when the British line reached the bridge and made its first futile effort to storm the span and gain the other side." Although it was difficult to fire with any accuracy in the fading sunlight, "the Continentals had a great defensive advantage in being able to concentrate on the bridge and keep up withering volleys, throwing out a screen of shot and shell which the redcoats were quite unable to penetrate."[45]

The initial probe was launched by the British light infantry and Hessian jägers at the lower ford near the river. These troops occupied the houses closest to the creek that were directly across from a brigade of New England soldiers deployed between the bridge and the river on the other side of the Assunpink. From there the British and Hessians exchanged fire with the defenders and then pushed down to the edge of the creek. They tried to cross "after sunset but before dark," but "Washington saw them coming and ordered Hitchcock's Rhode Island Continentals to stop them. The attackers were met by a storm of musketry, and the artillery joined in."[46] As New Englanders had fired the first shots of the Revolution on the American side at Lexington and Concord, so now they fired the first shots in the Continental Army's last-ditch stand against the enemy effort to storm across the creek that separated the two armies.

Private Howland, who had joined his fellow Rhode Islanders in retreating across the creek from the advancing enemy, remembered Washington's order and the response by those soldiers. According to Howland, "When I was about halfway across the bridge, the General addressed himself to Col. Hitchcock, the commander of the brigade, directing him to march his men to that field and form them immediately, or instantly, or as quick as possible; which of the terms he used, I am not certain." At the same time, Washington extended his arm and pointed "to a little meadow at a short distance on the south side of the creek [between the Delaware River and the bridge]. . . . This order was promptly obeyed and then we advanced to the edge of the stream, facing the enemy."[47] The latter "soon found it prudent to fall back under cover of the houses" on the north side of the Assunpink.[48]

As Stryker portrays this encounter, Colonel Hitchcock's soldiers "had taken position in a field on the Bloomsbury farm between the bridge and the river, and had thrown up a temporary breastwork," which proved to be a timely maneuver as "a determined party, principally of Hessians, attempted to cross the creek at a good fording-place . . . but the brave New England

Continentals sent a rain of lead on the attacking party, and they quickly abandoned the project."[49]

The second probe was made at the most critical point of defense for Washington's army. A column of Hessian grenadiers from the battalions commanded by Lieutenant Colonel Otto von Linsing and Lieutenant Colonel Heinrich von Block, respectively, charged the bridge.

In this narrow and heavily defended corridor, these veteran troops were tasked with carrying out a mission they were "trained to do, to assault fortified positions with concentrated force."[50] They had come to America from a homeland in which military service was both expected and honored—in which "all able-bodied men were required to undergo military training before either making the military a career or serving part-time in the militia"—and they had anticipated that the effort to defeat the colonial rebellion would be a brief and triumphant venture against an untrained and inexperienced adversary. Furthermore, their officers had been "generally enthusiastic about the war, being eager for active service with its opportunities for recognition and promotion." But now, after several months of fighting in the New World, these combatants from a distant land had been subjected to many of the same hardships as their foe, having to contend with battlefield deaths, wounds, and disease, while in many cases wearing worn uniforms that afforded them inadequate protection against frigid winter temperatures.[51]

The Hessian attackers brought forward four artillery pieces in support of their effort to gain the bridge, while deploying other cannons along the banks of the creek, and they positioned jägers with their trademark short rifles in nearby buildings to target the rebel gun crews. The Hessian cannons launched a barrage that lasted for about 12 minutes, which prompted a reply from the American guns, and then the grenadiers "came forward with bravery and determination."[52] That, and their discipline and training, had availed them against the colonials on earlier battlefields—at Long Island, Kip's Bay, White Plains, and Fort Washington—but any hope they may have had of pushing back the rebels one more time was quite literally blasted within a matter of minutes.

The German assailants encountered a storm of shot and shell that even Europe's most skilled professional warriors could not penetrate, and a bloodbath resulted. The three Virginia regiments under Colonel Scott were waiting for the enemy as they approached the bridge, and those soldiers from the Old Dominion responded with a murderous salvo. Scott's men—with Hand's sharpshooters directly behind them—and their supporting artillery pieces, almost 20 in number, "shredded" the Hessians' advance before they could reach the middle of the bridge.[53] The hail of fire that engulfed the grenadiers killed or wounded 31 of them and compelled 29 others to come forward and surrender "rather than retreat through the heavy fire."[54]

In the final probe, a detachment of redcoats made multiple attempts to cross the bridge, but the American cannons that were concentrated in this area punished them severely. With the Hessians having been repulsed, Cornwallis ordered his British infantry forward to secure a foothold on the other side of the creek; however, the British column stalled at the head of the bridge, "leaving dead and wounded littering the ground." The redcoats "regrouped and surged ahead again, this time forcing their way onto the bridge before they too were forced back," and then Cornwallis launched a final attempt by sending forward "another strong column" to take the bridge. In response, the rebel artillery "pounded the British infantry" and with John Cadwalader's repositioned militia and artillery reinforcing the front line of Continental regulars, the British attackers once more "broke against the bridge and retreated into the darkness."[55]

The narrow bridge became a perfect killing zone in the course of these three attempts by the redcoats to force their way across. In the wake of their final charge, the bloodstained span was littered with the dead and dying of His Majesty's finest soldiery. They had risked their all to achieve the objective assigned to them—to establish a bridgehead on the other side of the creek—because that was what they were trained, and had been ordered, to do.

Cornwallis's army was comprised of men who in various units represented a proud and long-standing tradition of service shared among their regimental peers. Most were of humble origins—farmers, laborers, and tradesmen—while a few were convicts who chose military service over incarceration when given the choice. They had volunteered for the army and many made it their career, as they valued the steady job and pay. However dangerous a soldier's life might be, it represented "an attractive alternative to working class teenagers and young men whose only prospects were long hours of dreary and sometimes hazardous manual labor or an oppressive apprenticeship where they could be overworked or beaten with no recourse."[56]

Many of His Majesty's soldiers "thought, and were encouraged to believe, that their unit was the best in the army. They also felt a deep loyalty to their king that set them in firm opposition to the Americans they were battling."[57] These soldiers were driven by "ideals of loyalty, fidelity, honor, duty, discipline, and service that were as sacred to British Regulars as the cause of liberty was to the American rebels." To those engaged in combat, "the war was not primarily a conflict of power or interest. It was a clash of principles in which they deeply believed."[58]

Sergeant Joseph White of Massachusetts, then about 21 years of age, recalled that the redcoats advanced "in solid columns" in their last probing attack and that the defenders "let them come on some ways. Then, by a signal given, we all fired together. The enemy retreated off the bridge and formed again, and we were ready for them. Our whole artillery was again discharged at them."[59]

An unknown militiaman described how the rebel infantry joined their artillery crews in blasting away at the crown's men:

> . . . our men poured upon them from musketry and artillery a shower of bullets under which, however, they continued to advance, through their speed was diminished. And as the column reached the bridge it moved slower and slower until the head of it was gradually pressed nearly over, when our fire became so destructive that they broke their ranks and fled.
>
> It was then that our army raised a shout, and such a shout I never since heard; by what signal or word of command, I know not. The line [of men] was more than a mile in length and from the nature of the ground the extremes were not in sight of each other, yet they shouted as one man.
>
> The British column halted instantly. The officers restored the ranks and again they rushed the bridge, and again was the shower of bullets poured upon them with redoubled fury. This time the column broke before it reached the centre of the bridge, and their retreat was again followed by the same hearty shout from our line.
>
> They returned a third time to the charge but it was in vain. We shouted after them again but they had had enough of it.[60]

Sergeant White recounted the final British thrust: "They came on a third time. We loaded with canister shot and let them come nearer. We fired all together again, and such destruction it made, you cannot conceive. The bridge looked red as blood, with their killed and wounded and red coats."[61]

Canister and grapeshot—exploding shells of different sizes, in the form of a tin can and canvas bag, respectively—were packed with various objects such as pieces of chain, iron balls, nails, and stones. They were most effective when employed against massed concentrations of enemy infantry. When a cannon fired its canister or grapeshot, the force of the blast ignited the fuse on the shell and it would explode in midair or when it hit the ground and scatter its lethal contents in all directions. This type of ordnance was used to maximum effect against the dense formation of redcoats that funneled its way onto the stone overpass.

The failure of the final British thrust at the bridge ended the close-quarter fighting on January 2. Notwithstanding the exchange of artillery fire that continued for some time—and with the benefit of knowing in retrospect what would happen before daylight reappeared—the Battle of Assunpink Creek was over. With its back to the wall, or more precisely the Delaware River, Washington's army had survived one more fight, and so had the Revolutionary enterprise it symbolized.

Once the redcoats had retreated a safe distance from the bridge, the defenders moved up to the now battle-scarred structure. One of them, militiaman William Hutchinson of Chester County, Pennsylvania, serving with Cadwalader's Philadelphia Associators, recalled the engagement "in which this declarant partook with all the patriotic glow and ardor of a freeman fighting for the liberties of his country," as one in which the attackers "were driven back with great slaughter occasioned by the well-directed fire of our artillery." He described the grisly scene where the enemy combatants had fallen: "Their dead bodies lay thicker and closer together for a space than I ever beheld sheaves of wheat lying in a field over which the reapers had just passed."[62]

Captain Rodney of Delaware summed up the outcome of the fierce struggle at the deadliest crossing point: "We kept possession of the bridge altho' the enemy attempted several times to carry it but were repulsed each time with great slaughter."[63] In echoing this assessment, an unidentified Connecticut officer observed that the crown's men sought "to force the bridge . . . with great vigor . . . several times and were as often broken by our artillery," while noting that some enemy officers drove their men forward by hitting them with the flat of their swords.[64] Lieutenant Charles Willson Peale of the Philadelphia Associators confirmed the intense exchange of fire when he wrote that "some of our artillery stood their ground till the enemy advanced within 40 yards, and they were very near losing the field piece. . . . some unlucky shot from a cannon killed one or two of the 3rd Battalion of Philadelphia troops," as well as some militiamen from Cumberland County, New Jersey.[65]

*****

By 6 p.m., when darkness reigned over the battlefield, the British and Hessian troops had abandoned their efforts to push across the Assunpink Creek, pending the arrival of the rest of Cornwallis's army. The exchange of cannon fire had so dominated this engagement "that participants often later referred to the encounter as a cannonade rather than a battle."[66] Indeed, writers of that era frequently referred to it as "the cannonade at Trent Town."[67] Even after the last enemy charge failed, the rebel artillery "still kept up a determined fire, throwing shot into the town from the high ground on the south side of the creek, which commanded the village," while the British light batteries returned fire "although without effect."[68]

Henry Knox reported that "a few shells we now and then chucked into the town to prevent them enjoying their new quarters securely."[69] Most of the enemy fell back to the high ground at the upper end of town beyond the range of the American field pieces, although "during the evening the streets were thronged with crowds of redcoats."[70]

Lieutenant James McMichael of the 1st Pennsylvania Regiment, a native of Scotland who had emigrated to Pennsylvania and resided in Lancaster County when the war began, kept a diary during his entire service with the Continental Army. In his entry for January 2, he recorded that the British and Hessian forces "reached town at 5 P.M., but our artillery fire was so severe, that the enemy retreated out of town and encamped on an adjacent hill. We continued firing bombs up to seven o'clock P.M., when we were ordered to rest, which we very commodiously did upon a number of rails for a bed."[71]

Stryker's analysis highlights the perilous nature of the American position during the fight along the Assunpink: "It will always appear singular that the invaders did not attempt to cross the creek at some of the many fording places on the east of the town, such as at Henry's Mill or Phillips Ford, the one a mile, the other two miles above the mill-dam at the bridge." As he points out, there was no way for Washington "to protect the whole stream, and had the British forced the American right and driven them toward Trenton Ferry and the river, nothing could have saved the entire army." In Stryker's judgment, a "determined advance" by the imperial forces "along the line and a half hour's fight would have decided the battle. The American army would have been well-nigh annihilated, and with it the fate of America and the hopes of freemen."[72]

In the letter he wrote on January 7 to his wife, Lucy, from Morristown, Henry Knox echoed this recognition of the potential trap awaiting Washington's troops as he described their position at the moment of battle. "The creek was in our front, our left on the Delaware, our right in a wood, parallel to the creek," according to Knox, and the army's "situation was strong, to be sure: but hazardous on this account, that had our right wing been defeated, the defeat of the left would almost have been an inevitable consequence and the whole thrown into confusion or pushed into the Delaware, as it was impassable by boats."[73]

Under the circumstances, it is fair to argue that the dark of night, at least as much as the Americans' determined stand against the enemy sorties along the creek, saved their entire force from disaster on January 2 by curtailing Cornwallis's assault—even if it only postponed until the next morning the likely move by His Majesty's forces to take advantage of the rebels' vulnerable position. As nightfall enveloped both armies, the American soldiers could briefly savor the success of their defensive action against the attackers while Washington and his senior officers contemplated how best to cope with the situation in which they found themselves.

The record of the Assunpink battle was, Fischer writes, "largely missed until the accounts of many individual soldiers and junior officers on both sides emerged to document it in detail. It was not a general engagement . . . but a series of probing attacks, driven home with high courage" by the British and Hessian forces.[74] This was not an all-out assault by Cornwallis because the night set in before he could bring his army's full weight to bear against the rebels, as much of his column was strung out for miles and took some time to arrive on the scene.

Definitive information is unavailable concerning the casualties sustained by both sides during the fighting that day, either on the Princeton Road or in the battle at Assunpink; however, it is estimated that some 365 British and Hessian soldiers were killed, wounded, or captured as compared with about 100 Americans. This included about 140 Hessians and 225 redcoats, with at least 75 of the British casualties occurring on the way to Trenton and 150 in the fighting at the creek. These numbers are probably conservative, as losses on either side may well have been higher.[75] The imperial vanguard of about 1,500 troops bore the brunt of the fighting, because Cornwallis's main body was delayed so long by "the wretched condition of the roads" and the American skirmishers led by Colonel Hand.[76]

*****

In a history of Trenton that was published by the Trenton Historical Society in 1929 to commemorate the city's 250th anniversary,

Frederick Ferris sought to give the Battle of Assunpink Creek its due by comparing the significance of the two encounters at Trenton. In weighing the foray against the Hessian garrison after the Christmas night river crossing against the Assunpink fight a week later, this local historian observed: "[It] is unquestionably true that this later engagement . . . was of even greater moment than the surprise attack on the Hessians the week before." He noted that if Cornwallis's forces had "been successful in their attempts to storm the bridge, Washington might have found his army split asunder and the struggle for national independence brought to a sudden, unfavorable end."[77]

Ferris took into consideration the accounts of American soldiers who were present on January 2 in comparing the two battles at Trenton: "When these descriptive and interpretative statements are considered in the aggregate, it becomes plain that the second Battle of Trenton was, for the Continental army, a defensive operation of vast import." In the raid on the Hessian garrison on December 26, "Washington was the aggressor engaged in attacking what was at best a mere outpost," as contrasted with "the clash at the Assunpink" where "he was defending against a formidable British army under the most competent leadership." In Ferris's estimation, Washington's Assunpink victory "may be said, without any exaggeration, to have been a saving factor for the patriot cause."[78]

In the chapter he contributed to the above work, Ferris referenced an article by John J. Cleary in the November 11, 1923 edition of the *Trenton Sunday Times-Advertiser* about C. C. Haven, a "Trenton historian who was a faithful and earnest student of local Revolutionary lore." In that article, there appeared several verses of a poem probably written by Edward S. Ellis, a former superintendent of the Trenton public schools, who portrayed the fight at the creek in an impassioned tone. His lyrics included the following:

Now tier on tier our patriots ranged themselves upon the ridge,
And now again the redcoats charged upon Assunpink bridge;
Three times Cornwallis' hosts, with ringing shout and shell,
Came rushing down upon us like the very hosts of hell!
But artillery and musketry we poured in deadly rain,
And often as they yelled and charged, we beat them back again,
Until the victory was ours! All hail our Washington!
Assunpink's battle has been fought, Assunpink's battle won![79]

*****

The events of January 2, 1777 provided the essential pivot point from the first American victory of the "Ten Crucial Days" to the last by ensuring that the initial Trenton engagement one week earlier was not a "one-day wonder" but the beginning of a chain of events that altered the whole character of the Revolutionary contest. Had Washington been defeated at Assunpink Creek, his victory at Trenton on December 26, 1776 would have been a historical footnote similar to the Battle of Harlem Heights—a minor American success in September 1776 that did nothing to alter the course of the nearly disastrous New York campaign—and there would have been no victory at Princeton on January 3.

The Assunpink engagement was arguably the most critical moment of the "Ten Crucial Days" and perhaps the most unappreciated American victory in the Revolutionary War. In terms of the number of soldiers involved, it was the largest battle fought during these 10 remarkable days. It was the only one in which the enemy had a numerical advantage, the only one in which Washington's army had to fight both British and Hessian troops, the only one in which the crown's forces were led by a British general—who also happened to be the most competent and energetic field commander in His Majesty's Army, and the only one in which the geographic position of the Patriot forces put them at mortal peril of being trapped between two natural barriers—a creek on one side and a river on the other—with no means of evacuation if they were outflanked and driven back against the riverbank. January 2, 1777 also featured the longest battle of the "Ten Crucial Days" if one counts as a single encounter the resistance by Colonel Hand's men during their fighting withdrawal from Maidenhead to Trenton and the shoot-out at the creek immediately following their delaying action.

Perhaps most importantly, this occasion marked the first time that the Continental Army beat back an attack by British troops during a significant battle. As Fischer observes, "For the American troops it was a great victory. For their general it was a model of a brilliantly managed defensive battle in the same town where Colonel Rall had fought, but with very different results."[80]

Had the rebel army failed to stop the advance of the elite British and Hessian units at Assunpink Creek, the result would in all probability have been the destruction of that army and possibly with it the cause of American independence. And that scenario would almost certainly have entailed fatal consequences for Washington, either on the battlefield or at the end of a British rope—the latter being "a dark specter that hung over many of the rebel leaders" as it was the penalty prescribed for treason against the King of England.[81]

Nathaniel Philbrick opines that if Cornwallis's effort to cross the Assunpink bridge and overrun the rebel army had succeeded, "the war was as good as finished" for the capital city of Philadelphia "would surely [have fallen] that winter, and the Continental Congress in Baltimore might very well [have decided] that a negotiated settlement was in the country's best interests." By choosing to fight on this ground on January 2, "Washington had managed to conflate the standoff at the Old North Bridge in Concord with the Battle of Bunker Hill in Charlestown to create what was, even if it is largely unappreciated today, the make-or-break moment of the War of Independence."[82]

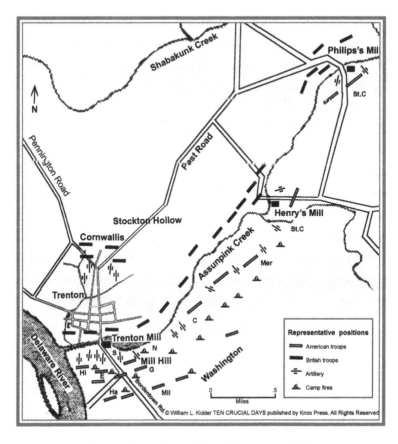

Troop Dispositions, night of January 2, 1777

Mark Maloy shares this assessment of how precarious the American position was: "If the British were able to penetrate Washington's lines or roll up on his flanks, there would be no place to retreat, and his army would be completely crushed. It was important that they prevent the British Regulars from crossing the Assunpink at all." In sum, "the outnumbered Americans appeared to be in a dangerous predicament that could have ended the entire rebellion."[83]

Historians of the Revolution never mention Assunpink Creek in the same breath as Saratoga or Yorktown—the most recognized and significant battles in that struggle, with the former in 1777 leading to France's crucial intervention in the contest and the latter in 1781 breaking the back of England's will to fight against the colonials— but those later engagements might very well have never occurred if January 2, 1777 had turned out differently for Washington's army. The events of that day, including the delaying action by Colonel Hand's men and the fighting at the creek, plausibly created a deciding moment of as great consequence for the cause of American independence as the far better-known confrontations that occurred later in the war. Perhaps no military action in our country's history is more paradoxical than the one on the road to Assunpink Creek, and at the bridge that crossed it, in the sense that its obscurity in the public mind and neglect by many historians is so disproportionate to its impact on the course of a conflict with global implications.

Continental campfires along the mill pond at Assunpink Creek,
January 2, 1777 – 19th century woodcut

All warfare is based on deception. Hence, when we are able to attack, we must seem unable; when using our forces, we must appear inactive; when we are near, we must make the enemy believe we are far away; when far away, we must make him believe we are near.

— Sun Tzu, from *The Art of War*, 5th century B.C.

6

THE GREAT ESCAPE

Once darkness set in and the artillery and small arms fire subsided, the British and Hessians tended to their wounded on the grounds north of the Assunpink Creek and within the town while the Americans did the same for their smaller number of casualties.

The outcome for those soldiers who fell on this and other Revolutionary War battlefields was usually fatal and often gruesome. Richard Ketchum writes: "For many a brave soul, death in battle was merciful compared to the suffering he would have to endure if he were wounded. There were never enough surgeons to go round, and the ones they had were crude, incompetent butchers without adequate supplies or knowledge." Many of the wounded were left to die where they had fallen, "especially if the army had to move quickly, and the unfortunates who made it to the hospital lay there on the ground or on wooden benches, suffering horribly while awaiting their turn with the surgeon, who relied on the saw or some medieval remedy." The hospital environment was ghastly, "filled with the hideous stench of festering wounds and the anguished cries of the dying, who were crowded together with men suffering from all forms of disease."[1] Patriot soldiers commonly "viewed the hospital as a place to be avoided at all costs, and many, if they had actually been in one, had nothing good to say about the experience."[2]

After the battle, Dr. Benjamin Rush helped care for wounded American soldiers at one of the houses near the Delaware River that were turned into makeshift hospitals. He reported that the doctors there slept on the floor with their patients after completing their work, or at least attempted to, and that "for the first time war appeared to me in its awful plenitude of horrors. I want words to describe the anguish of my soul, excited by the cries and groans and convulsions of the men who lay by my side."[3]

The agonies suffered by the injured, who had nothing to ease their pain or heal their infections, reflected the crude state of medicine at the time. For many, there was scant hope of recovery. David Hackett Fischer depicts the appalling reality that awaited these unfortunates in grim terms: "Mortality from amputations of the upper leg were between 60 and 80 percent in that era. Deaths from hip wounds were above 90 percent. Abdominal wounds were almost always fatal." The Hessian grenadiers had "suffered more casualties than the entire American army" on this day, and the agony of their wounded "was beyond description, as they lay on filthy straw three thousand miles from home."[4]

*****

While the wounded were tended to, at least to the extent possible, the commanders of the opposing armies pondered the condition of their respective forces and considered their next move. General

Cornwallis was known as an officer who exhibited concern for his soldiers' welfare and during a forced march would endure "the same deprivation as his men, eating the same food and sleeping in the same conditions."[5] Cornwallis is represented as having been an "honest, kindly, concerned and sympathetic officer," from which ensued the fact that "he was far better liked" in the British army than a number of other generals "could ever hope to be."[6]

His Lordship's regard for the welfare of his troops was one of the considerations that inclined him not to renew his attack on the Americans entrenched behind the Assunpink Creek until the next morning. He was well aware that his men were in need of rest after their long and difficult march to Trenton and extended skirmishing along the way. Mindful not only of his exhausted soldiers but also "the strength of the American artillery," which had startled him, Cornwallis thought it prudent to wait until more troops and cannons arrived from Princeton before commencing the next round of battle.[7]

In spite of these considerations, it appears that the British commander was supremely confident he had the Americans trapped between the Assunpink and the Delaware and could finish them off the next day. After all, no boats were available for the rebels to pull off another miraculous withdrawal during the night as they had done across the East River from Brooklyn Heights to Manhattan after the Battle of Long Island four months before. According to tradition, when Cornwallis convened a council of war at his headquarters on the evening of January 2, he told his senior officers: "We've got the Old Fox safe now. We'll go over and bag him in the morning."[8] One account has the general declaring, "The damned rebels are cornered at last."[9]

Not all his officers shared this optimism. William Erskine, Cornwallis's quartermaster general, warned: "If Washington is the general I take him to be, his army will not be found there in the morning."[10] Erskine urged an immediate attack, but General Grant agreed with the commanding general that the rebels were trapped, with no boats to escape across the river. After their wearying march from Princeton, he argued, the imperial troops needed a night's rest before renewing their assault. In the end, "this chummy British council of fox-hunting men" reached the decision that Cornwallis intended it should. The attendees, including the reluctant Erskine, would defer to their commander's strong desire to postpone the attack until morning.[11]

The reasoning behind Cornwallis's decision rested not only upon a recognition of his soldiers' exhaustion but also unease over the risks inherent in a nighttime operation. Although delaying an action would have run counter to his instincts, "neither did he relish the thought of sending troops into battle blindfolded," as Ketchum explains, "and that was just what it would be like if he tried to turn Washington's flank out there in the blackness along the Assunpink, where his men would have to travel over completely unfamiliar ground, locate the right wing of the rebel army, cross the stream, and attack an entrenched position." The only alternative for the crown's forces would have been to launch a direct frontal assault across a swollen waterway against concentrated artillery fire and "a foe that had plenty of time to dig in."[12]

Cornwallis's determination to delay his move will be forever second-guessed by historians and military analysts. Even so, the British commander's decision has been defended on the grounds that waiting until the next morning made sense in view of how fatigued his troops were and because the Americans, "wherever protected by good terrain, had always been able to give a good account of themselves."[13]

Cornwallis had arranged for reinforcements to support the next day's attack, with orders issued to Colonel Mawhood in Princeton and General Leslie in Maidenhead to join him in the morning. His Lordship also took steps to deploy troops for an early morning strike across the creek at one of the fords upstream. This was the maneuver that he expected would settle matters by outflanking the rebels and sealing the trap shut, and the result was a series of moves and countermoves by the opposing forces in the darkness.

Cornwallis ordered most of his Hessians to withdraw north of the town, out of range of Knox's guns, "probably with the intention of bringing them forward the next day in a demonstration against the American front." He sent British soldiers east of the town, into wooded ground along the upper reaches of the Assunpink. By 10 p.m., Cornwallis had up to 2,000 men in the woods near Philips's Ford positioned to make an early morning splash across the creek and fall upon the right flank of Washington's army, for the British commander, "in his professional way, had been quick to find the fatal weakness in the American position." His patrols having detected the enemy movement, Washington ordered that field fortifications be constructed at Philips's Ford, and St. Clair's New England brigade was "hard at work with axe and shovel, preparing to defend the crossing and the flank of the American army," although they were outnumbered five to one by the enemy regiments across the creek.[14]

Unfortunately for Cornwallis, he neglected to send out cavalry to explore the ground where the rebels' right flank was thought to be in order to ascertain how far their lines extended and to monitor that area for enemy movements. He was not familiar with the terrain and in hindsight would have benefited greatly from the information that such a reconnaissance could have yielded.

*****

Meanwhile, Washington had summoned his senior officers to another council of war to review their strategic options in the wake of the stalled enemy assault across the Assunpink. They assembled at the Alexander Douglass House on Queen Street that was serving as General St. Clair's headquarters. Washington had relocated his own headquarters earlier

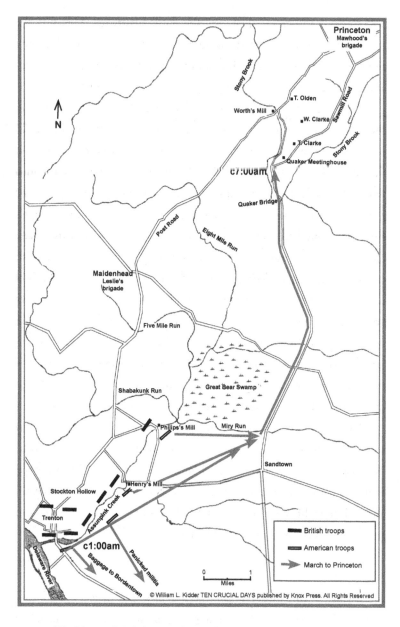

Washington's Night March to Princeton, January 2-3, 1777

that day from the John Barnes house above the creek to Jonathan Richmond's tavern below it, but then was forced to vacate the latter site because it was within reach of British cannon fire.[15]

The most obvious courses of action did not appear promising to the attendees, as William Stryker notes in explaining just how perilous their position was: "It was now almost impossible to retreat across the river with so large and disciplined an army close upon them." But to retreat southward toward Philadelphia "would be certain annihilation" as Cornwallis's larger force would be in hot pursuit and likely to catch the Americans out in the open with neither a strong defensive position to facilitate resistance or any means of evacuating the army across the Delaware to the Pennsylvania side. On the other hand, "to attack the enemy on the morrow and to risk the fortune of a battle was but to court defeat from troops superior in numbers and better skilled in the art of war." Finally, for the defenders "to remain in their earthworks until morning was to invite destruction or an early surrender."[16]

A "freewheeling" discussion in council began immediately after dark. The commanding general wanted a full and frank consideration of options by those present, and that is what occurred.[17] None of the officers who were there doubted who was in charge, but the exchange among them "was not constrained by deference."[18] Those attending included the full panoply of Continental Army leadership: the two division commanders, Generals Nathanael Greene and John Sullivan; the brigade commanders, who included Generals James Ewing, Hugh Mercer, Thomas Mifflin, Arthur St. Clair, and Adam Stephen, along with Colonels John Cadwalader and Daniel Hitchcock; the artillery chief, General Henry Knox; the adjutant general, Colonel Joseph Reed; and others. In addition, local residents were invited to participate and did so.[19]

The commander-in-chief began the meeting with a statement of the army's situation and then asked for advice from those present.

According to General St. Clair, Washington acknowledged that "a battle was certain, if he kept his ground until the morning, and in case of an action a defeat was to be apprehended; a retreat by the only route thought of, down the river, would be difficult and precarious."[20] He concluded by noting that "the loss of the corps he commanded might be fatal to the country."[21] That statement prompted a variety of responses from the officers there, including arguments for a retreat from some and suggestions from others "to hazard all on a general engagement."[22]

Then a third alternative emerged. Some have attributed the notion to General St. Clair, whose brigade was stationed at the army's extreme right, and this additional option garnered widespread support as the discussion continued.[23] The idea was to move the troops around to the right and, under the cover of darkness, proceed along the country lanes that St. Clair's men had patrolled beyond their flank until the Americans reached a point where they could march almost due north to Princeton. There they could proceed along the back roads approaching the town from the southeast— unguarded according to the intelligence Washington had previously received from Reed and Cadwalader—then surprise the British troops in Princeton and race up to Brunswick to capture the coin and supplies in the British magazine that Washington so coveted.

Those present who knew the local terrain confirmed the feasibility of this plan, including Reed and "two men from the country, near the route proposed [who were] called to the council for their opinions of its practicability" and who offered to serve as guides.[24] Washington took this strategy to heart. He wrote that "it would avoid the appearance of a retreat, which was of consequence" both for reasons of "popular opinion" and purely military considerations, as he sought to "give reputation to our arms."[25]

Actually, Washington may very well have had this scheme in mind when he allowed the army "to appear to be trapped in Trenton."[26]

It is likely that this was the plan he had conceived when he rode out from town to personally encourage his skirmishers' resistance against Cornwallis's advance earlier that day and emphasized to them the importance of delaying the enemy until nightfall. Why would the commander-in-chief have done that if he had not already formulated the idea for an operation that was designed to deceive his adversary and achieve a strategic objective under the protective cloak of nighttime? In any case, the decision to make an overnight march to Princeton ultimately won unanimous support from the council participants.[27]

While the rebel officers deliberated about what to do next, the ground was beginning to freeze, and the temperature would drop about 20 degrees overnight—just in time to assist the Patriot cause. The cold front that moved through the Delaware Valley froze the ground solid, thereby saving the Americans from having to contend with the muddy roads that had plagued Cornwallis's troops earlier in the day, and at the same time turning the sky "very black with little starlight."[28]

Washington ordered his supply wagons removed to Burlington in order to enhance the mobility of his advancing columns, and his men wrapped the wheels of their cannons and ammunition wagons in rags to muffle the sound of their movements. Then the various units became part of an elaborate and prolonged maneuver as they extricated themselves from the army's area of encampment below the Assunpink and began advancing in an easterly direction. It took several hours to organize the evacuation, and to get the various regiments "moving on a single road in the dark" proved a "slow and difficult task."[29] Charles Willson Peale reported that his Pennsylvania Associators moved out at midnight, while other troops began their march about an hour later, and Thomas Rodney's company of Delaware militia did not get under way until 2 a.m.

This undertaking was not without its mishaps, as individual soldiers and units did not necessarily act in unison. Some officers who were unaware of the army's movement "had retired to farmhouses somewhat to the rear, to enjoy a much needed rest," and the next day they would have some difficulty in reuniting with their troops after the battle at Princeton.[30] In another instance, Thomas Rodney recalled that in the extreme darkness a Pennsylvania militia regiment mistook another American unit for the enemy near Trenton, and some of those men panicked and fled toward Bordentown; however, "the rest of the column remained firm and pursued their march without disorder."[31]

For the exhausted soldiers who made this journey, it was a challenge to maintain a steady pace. "We moved so slow, on account of the artillery, frequently coming to a halt, or stand still," one participant recalled, "and when ordered forward again, one, two, or three men in each platoon would stand, with their arms supported, fast asleep; a platoon next in the rear advancing on them, they, in walking or attempting to move, would strike a stub and fall." [32]

Rodney's fellow Delawarean, John Haslet, was along for the 12-mile march to Princeton even though his limbs were still badly swollen from his spill in the Delaware River. The undaunted colonel, who had been left without a regiment when the enlistments of his remaining Delaware men expired on December 31, trudged along beside the horse ridden by General Mercer, who was leading a brigade in General Greene's division with Haslet as his second-in-command.[33] This would be the last march that the two leaders of this brigade ever made.

By first light on January 3, at about 6:50 a.m., the army reached Quaker Bridge over the Stony Brook, just six miles from Princeton. There the marchers were slowed by the need to build a wider bridge that could accommodate their artillery and ammunition wagons. The sun rose as they crossed the stream and pushed on toward their objective. That the rebel troops had come so far overnight, given the circumstances, was quite remarkable. It was no small accomplishment for these poorly clad, worn-out men to make "a night march in bitter cold weather and extreme darkness . . . with a train of artillery, and on hard-frozen roads full of ruts and stumps." Even then, as Fischer reminds us, this exercise "astounded professional soldiers of many nations by its audacity and its celerity. It was a triumph of mind and will over material conditions by George Washington himself, his lieutenants, and most of all the sleep-deprived private soldiers who found the stamina to put one frozen foot in front of another."[34]

In order for his end run around Cornwallis's left flank to succeed, Washington had found it necessary to disguise the army's movement toward Princeton. To that end, he left behind a rearguard of about 400 men for part of the night and instructed them to stoke their campfires until "there were several dozen veritable conflagrations blazing on the heights south of Assunpink Creek, convincing the British that the Americans were still there." In addition, this contingent was told to employ such deceptive means of keeping warm on a very wintry night as "clanging picks and shovels on the frozen earth," and the resulting noise convinced the redcoat sentries that the enemy was "building earthworks against tomorrow's assault."[35]

The British sentinels were only about 150 yards from the American lines behind the creek. From there they could easily see the fires that the defenders had created, using "huge piles of cedar rails all along their lines." They could also hear the sound made by the colonials' use of their picks and shovels, which suggested that the rebels were literally digging in for a renewed battle in the morning.[36]

This activity did not fail to engender a British response, but the reaction was based on a misunderstanding of what was happening. British pickets reported "this theatrical performance that was elaborately staged for their benefit," and Cornwallis did indeed take action to address the situation as he perceived it. His Lordship inferred that the rebels were about to attack him in the dark in a reprise of their Christmas night strike against the Rall brigade. Exhibiting the due diligence expected of a proven military professional, he moved to stop this anticipated blow by ordering some of his best troops to take up defensive positions at the upper fords of the Assunpink. But in doing so, "this highly intelligent commander committed one of the most common fallacies of military reasoning" by preparing to fight the last battle.[37]

*****

When Cornwallis turned in for the night, he was undoubtedly convinced that his adversary was trapped in "a cul-de-sac from which there was no breaking out."[38] His Lordship probably entertained visions of a crushing victory that would ensue from a crucial flanking movement such as the one the British army had executed at the Battle of Long Island in August, which was decisive in the outcome of that engagement. There some 10,000 imperial soldiers—almost half of General Howe's force—had marched around the Americans' extreme left overnight in a broad, sweeping maneuver and attacked the Continentals from the rear.[39] But this time, Cornwallis could well have reasoned that the result would be even more conclusive. Now Washington's entire army would be at risk on the battlefield, rather than at Long Island when half his troops were posted on the other side of the East River in Manhattan. And without any appreciable number of boats at hand for an evacuation and lacking well-established fortifications to delay the enemy advance, both of which the Americans had at Brooklyn Heights after the Long Island debacle, there would be no way for the colonials to escape across the Delaware as they had been able to do on the New York river.

Only dawn's arrival on January 3 would dissuade the British general from the ill-fated conviction that his opponent's fate was sealed. Describing the scene that presented itself to Cornwallis and his staff as they emerged from their quarters to scrutinize the rebel defenses, Ketchum infers that these officers "looked through the wisps of morning fog lifting from the creek and saw not a single cannon or soldier on the ridge beyond," because the only indications that an opposing army had been entrenched on that ground would have been "mounds of freshly dug earth and the smoldering coals of countless campfires." The fox that Cornwallis thought was trapped had eluded him, and not until shortly after 8 a.m., "when the distant rumble of artillery was heard off to the north, did the British general have the vaguest idea where he had gone."[40] It was quite literally a rude awakening for a commander bent on winning a decisive victory over a cunning opponent on this day, and for the army he had expected to produce that final triumph over Washington's upstart colonial force.

This is an important period to America, big with great events. God only knows what will be the issue of this Campaign, but everything wears a much better prospect than they have for some weeks past.

— Nathanael Greene, from a letter to his wife, Catharine, December 30, 1776

7

FURY ON FROZEN GROUND

As his forces approached Princeton on the wintry morning of January 3, 1777, Washington divided them into separate columns to carry out their impending attack, much as he had done prior to the raid at Trenton on December 26. Frozen snow lay on the ground, and the temperature hovered in the low 20's.[1]

When the army arrived at the edge of Princeton, its left wing, comprising General Mifflin's brigade of 1,500 Pennsylvania Continentals and militia, advanced along the Quaker Road in a northwesterly direction towards the Princeton Road, intending to cut off any possible British movement southward from Princeton and to ensure that no enemy reinforcements from Trenton could reach the town. Colonel Haussegger was ordered to seal off any possible escape route to the north with his German Regiment, which would prove to be an unsuccessful effort. The rest of the army veered off to the right, from the Quaker Road onto the Saw Mill Road (which does not exist today), and headed north in the direction of Princeton.

A column of more than 700 redcoats, comprising the elite 17th Regiment of Foot and elements of other units under Colonel Mawhood, had exited the town and was marching south on the Princeton Road to reinforce Cornwallis's army in Trenton when Mawhood observed the American troops who were approaching Princeton from the Saw Mill Road on his left flank. Mawhood was "an excellent regimental commander" with 24 years of military service, who was "highly respected by the men who served under him" and esteemed by both Generals Howe and Cornwallis.[2] As soon as he discerned the movement of rebel forces in the distance, Mawhood dispatched soldiers from his column to warn the rest of the garrison inside the town and then ordered the bulk of his column to attack the intruders.

The two sides spotted each other at about 7:45 a.m. and closed rapidly. General Mercer was leading a small brigade of only 350 Continental soldiers in Mawhood's direction, not realizing that he was about to collide with a much larger enemy force. Mercer's contingent was part of General Greene's division, which also included about 1,100 of Cadwalader's Philadelphia Associators. Colonel Haslet proceeded on foot by Mercer's side with the handful of his remaining men from the Delaware Regiment in tow. At the same time, General Sullivan's division, with more than 2,000 men, advanced on Mercer's right flank in order to deliver the primary assault against the main body of redcoats who were expected to be in the town.

The battle began when Mercer's brigade traded fire with the British in the apple orchard on William Clarke's farm two miles from Princeton. The brigade, outnumbered at least two-to-one by Mawhood's contingent, was forced to fall back in the face of a fierce bayonet charge that the Americans were ill-equipped to withstand. As the redcoats pressed forward, they repeatedly stabbed and clubbed the few wounded soldiers who were left behind in the rebel retreat.[3]

Mercer's horse was shot from under him, and the encircling enemy soldiers knocked him to the ground. Because the general "was handsomely uniformed, even to a cravat," the British regulars thought they had captured Washington.[4] Mercer refused their demand to surrender and lunged at them with his sword, only to be bayoneted seven times and left to die—which he did nine days later in the nearby Thomas Clarke house.

Colonel Haslet joined the others in Mercer's brigade as they retreated toward the barn on Thomas Clarke's farm, about half a mile from the orchard. As he was either attempting to rally those soldiers or go to the aid of the wounded Mercer, Haslet took a musket ball to the head and died at once. With both Mercer and Haslet out of action, their brigade fled to the rear and appeared to be on the verge of crumbling as Continental officers made a desperate effort to organize resistance against Mawhood's advance. Cadwalader's brigade attempted to stem the British, but these raw militia reversed direction when they saw Mercer's Continentals being driven back by the redcoats' bayonet charge.

The experience and professionalism of the crown's men had paid dividends to this point—a tribute to Mawhood's leadership and the discipline of his regulars.[5] They were on the verge of routing the demoralized troops of Greene's division before the latter could be reinforced by other American units. However, Captain Moulder and the score of youthful artillerists from the Philadelphia waterfront who comprised his battery crew had other ideas. Moulder commanded two long-barreled four-pounder cannons, stationed to the right of the Thomas Clarke house, which he brought quickly into action. They sent "deadly rounds of grape and canister" into the enemy ranks and halted their advance.[6] According to William Stryker,

Moulder's gunners "made every shot tell as they mowed down the ranks of the redcoats."[7] Despite their youth, the captain's battery crew proved unflappable at this critical juncture; their "artillery fire was accurate and their courage unwavering during the battle."[8]

Captain Rodney of Delaware, whose militia were supporting Moulder's battery, remembered that these "two pieces of artillery stood their ground and were served with great skill and bravery," and that his unit was situated in such a manner that the enemy was uncertain as to the size of this opposing force. The Delaware militia "kept up a continuous fire on the enemy" from behind nearby haystacks and farm buildings that concealed their numbers; and, according to Rodney, "in all probability it was this circumstance that prevented the enemy from advancing, for they could not tell the number we had posted behind these covers and were afraid to attempt passing them; but if they had known how few they were, they might easily have advanced . . . and routed the whole body."[9]

The significance of this stand by Moulder's crew and the accompanying militia was paramount in the outcome of the Princeton battle: "Had Mawhood realized that all that faced him . . . were two guns and perhaps a score of determined men he certainly would have ordered his troops to charge the position. . . . [but] Moulder and his gunners bought the rebel army just enough time." In addition, Mawhood perceived what appeared to be a large American force in the nearby woods and had no idea how many there might be "waiting to sweep down on him."[10] While the Continental officers urgently tried to rally their men, Moulder's pair of cannons "continued to pour grape upon the enemy."[11] Given the pivotal nature of this moment, it has been rightly said of Moulder's effort "that without his services on January 3, 1777, the story of the American Revolution might have turned out rather differently."[12]

Moulder's artillery was quickly joined by other field guns as more American infantry arrived on the scene, with Washington urging them on: "Parade with us, my brave fellows! There is but a handful of the enemy, and we will have them directly."[13] The rebel counterattack was fashioned from elements of General Mifflin's brigade who assaulted Mawhood's right flank and soldiers from Colonel Hitchcock's brigade and Colonel Hand's regiment who stormed the British left, together with Colonel Cadwalader's brigade in the center of this alignment. The commander-in-chief led the rallying Continentals and militia into the center of the action, waving them forward with his hat as he rode to within 30 paces of the enemy lines. There ensued what has been described as "one of the most extraordinary moments of the American Revolution."[14]

At this moment in the battle, Washington—six feet, two-and-a-half-inches in height, riding a white horse, and clearly identified as a general by his uniform—had made himself an easy and obvious target for any redcoat who wanted to dispatch the rebel leader.[15] Yet not a bullet touched him. One can speculate that this was due more to the sensibilities of the British regulars about shooting an opposing general during this early stage of the war than to poor marksmanship, but their treatment of General Mercer in the same battle suggests they would have had no such reservations. Whatever the reason, Washington escaped without a scratch, much to the amazement of a very anxious subordinate. The commanding general has been depicted as being "apparently oblivious to the danger of his position which seemed to one of his officers, Colonel John Fitzgerald, so perilous that, as the British guns opened fire again, the Colonel pulled his hat over his eyes so that he would not be a witness to the General's death." However, when Fitzgerald uncovered his eyes, Washington was still astride his horse and uninjured. Unable to restrain his tears of joy, the colonel exclaimed: "Thank God. Your excellency is safe!" The fortunate Washington replied: "Bring up your troops, my dear Colonel. The day is our own."[16]

Mawhood's outnumbered force was outflanked and compelled to bolt from the field. Some fled toward Princeton and others into the surrounding countryside, as Washington jubilantly exhorted the rebel soldiers to pursue an adversary who for so many months had been pursuing them: "It is a fine fox chase, my boys!"[17]

Meanwhile, the army's other division under General Sullivan forced its way into town over the weak resistance offered by the few remaining defenders. When a number of British soldiers took refuge in Nassau Hall, then the largest stone building in the colonies, the New York artillery unit that was commanded by Captain Hamilton fired on the building—at least according to legend. Various accounts suggest that one of Hamilton's guns sent a cannonball through a window, perforating a portrait of King George II and decapitating him in the process, which the beleaguered occupants "must have viewed . . . as an ominous sign."[18] In any case, they capitulated in short order. Hamilton later referred to "the enterprises of Trenton and Princeton . . . as the dawnings of that bright day which afterwards broke forth with such resplendent luster."[19]

As Washington's victorious but weary army withdrew from Princeton northward, Captain Moulder's battery made a further contribution to the Americans' success by assisting in a "small but important rearguard action" that helped to retard the advance guard of Cornwallis's light troops and mounted dragoons who were in hot pursuit of the elusive rebels. Moulder's gun crew, joined by some 20 or more Philadelphia cavalry, "discouraged the pursuers, who let the Americans go on their way."[20]

Thomas Paine, among many others supporting the Patriot cause, marveled at the audacity of Washington's escape from the clutches of Cornwallis's superior force at Trenton and his coup at Princeton. Paine later wrote in *The American Crisis*, Number V (March 21, 1778) that the victory on January 3, 1777 "by a harrassed and wearied party, who had been engaged the day before and marched all night without refreshment, is attended with such a scene of circumstances and superiority of Generalship, as will ever give it a place on the first line in the history of great actions."[21]

The brief but fierce clash at Princeton proved to be one of the few major battles of the Revolution in which Washington's army gained "a clear-cut victory over British troops," although the sizable numerical advantage it enjoyed over the enemy in this contest "was hardly incidental to the outcome."[22] Washington deployed nearly 5,000 combatants against Mawhood's brigade, which has been estimated at between 1,200 and 1,500 men. To be sure, a substantial portion of the rebel force comprised inexperienced militia, but on the other hand, only one of the three infantry regiments serving under Mawhood—the 17th Foot—was considered an elite unit. Much of his brigade was cobbled together with convalescents and transfers from other regiments.[23]

The engagement lasted little more than an hour but was among the most savage of the whole conflict.[24] The Americans sustained some 60 to 75 casualties—that is, killed, wounded, captured, or missing in action—as compared with about 450 redcoats. The frozen ground ensured that the blood shed on the field of combat remained to discolor the surface, which amplified one's sense of horror at the scene of carnage. The battlefield "was strewn with the bodies of British and American soldiers," and some of them were buried together in a mass grave the next day.[25] The loss of General Mercer and Colonel Haslet was a bitter pill for Washington to swallow, Mercer being a friend as well as peer and Haslet having emerged as one of the commander-in-chief's most reliable officers. Legend even has it that he wept over the colonel's lifeless body on the Princeton battlefield.[26]

Some analysts have suggested that the Princeton battle was really an extension of the fighting at Assunpink Creek the day before, so that the two events should be considered as one engagement. Obviously the encounter at the creek segued into the overnight American march that led directly to the victory at Princeton. However, some stark differences between the two encounters present themselves. Washington was outnumbered at Assunpink with a river at his back, whereas he had a significant numerical advantage at Princeton and no waterway with which to contend. While his army was potentially in mortal peril at the creek, it had a clear means of escape at Princeton. In the latter battle, the British contingent fighting the Americans was too small to annihilate Washington's army, so that the best outcome it could realistically have achieved would have been to repulse the rebels' attack and drive them out of Princeton. If that had happened, Washington in all probability would have been forced to do what he did anyway. He would have proceeded with his troops to Morristown in order to elude Cornwallis's army that was pursuing him from Trenton on the morning of January 3 and to seek a safe haven for the winter nestled in the Watchung Mountains. In short, Washington's army faced an existential threat at Assunpink Creek; at Princeton, it did not.

As it was, the small redcoat garrison at Princeton won a moral victory of sorts. It "had attacked the entire American army and stopped its advance for a critical moment," which enabled the larger part of Colonel Mawhood's brigade to escape from Princeton in the direction of Brunswick, along with most of its supplies and artillery.[27] Even more important, "Mawhood's gallant resistance succeeded in stopping the Americans long enough to disrupt a major part of Washington's operation," for the Princeton engagement "drained the energy from the American army." As a result, Washington would be forced to abandon what he described in a January 5, 1777 letter to Congressional President John Hancock as his "original plan when I set out from Trenton . . . to have pushed on to Brunswick."[28]

Unfailingly aggressive by instinct, the commander-in-chief considered following up the Princeton victory with a raid on the British supply depot at Brunswick; however, Generals Greene and Knox, among others, dissuaded him from such a precarious venture at this juncture. They knew that Cornwallis's main force was coming up from Trenton and would be joined by General Leslie's troops in Maidenhead as they pursued Washington's army. The Continental officers were well aware that they were outnumbered by the pursuing enemy and that their men were exhausted from the whirlwind campaign of the last 10 days and in no condition to continue their winter offensive. These soldiers "had now been under arms for 40 continuous hours . . . with no interval for rest or to cook a meal," and they "were actually falling asleep on the frozen ground."[29]

Still, the rebel troops had driven the British out of Princeton and gained a significant psychological lift from having defeated His Majesty's finest, outnumbered though the latter may have been. The real value of this victory to the Revolutionary enterprise lay in the morale boost that it provided to a weary army and the confidence that "Washington's undoubted personal courage on the battlefield instilled in his soldiers."[30]

Not wanting to risk everything the army had achieved by its herculean effort during the past several days, Washington elected to forgo a strike at Brunswick and instead marched his troops to Somerset Court House (Millstone today) and then to the village of Morristown. There, out of harm's way, the men could settle into winter quarters. By January 6, the rebel soldiers had arrived at their destination, which offered a number of important advantages as a hibernal base of operations. Morristown "sat on a fertile plateau surrounded by the rugged Newark Mountains," known today as the Watchung Mountains. Few roads entered the village, each of which "was easily defended, especially in the winter, when deep snow made the area difficult to penetrate." Another important consideration was that the local farmers were generally supportive of the Patriot cause.[31] Furthermore, the Continentals, while entrenched in these hills, "could be supplied easily from broad valleys further north, which ran from the Hudson nearly to Philadelphia."[32]

Here the army found a safe haven that the enemy could approach "only though narrow, rugged gorges . . . [with] wood in abundance for log huts and fires, and food in the surrounding countryside." The village was only 30 miles from New York, which enabled Washington to monitor any possible British movement from that direction. While at Morristown, he was preoccupied with keeping together the remainder of his army once the six-week period for which he had provided bonuses to avoid a mass departure of soldiers on December 31 came to an end. New recruits were slow to arrive, "but when they did, it would be on Washington's own terms—a three-year enlistment."[33]

*****

The "Ten Crucial Days" of the Revolution ended with the victory at Princeton on January 3, having yielded a degree of success by the Patriot forces that was nothing short of spectacular. During this brief span of time, more than 1,700 British and Hessian soldiers were killed, wounded, captured, or missing in action, while the American forces suffered fewer than 200 casualties. Moreover, Washington's troops seized a significant quantity of arms and supplies and expelled their adversary from most of New Jersey.

Their triumphant campaign would ultimately be judged by professional analysts to be "one of the most brilliant in military history."[34] The Patriot army overcame an enemy who was better trained and more experienced, notwithstanding an array of hardships that stood in the Americans' way: "shortages of supplies; brutal weather; desertions; expiring enlistments; and the effects of malnutrition, disease, and exhaustion."[35]

It has been asserted that if Washington achieved nothing before or after the "Ten Crucial Days" campaign, his actions during that period "would alone assure him high mention in the annals of military history."[36] Indeed, Frederick II, the Prussian ruler who during his long reign (1740-1786) made his kingdom the leading military power in Europe and became known as Frederick the Great, rated the feats of "Washington and his little band of compatriots" during this period as "the most brilliant of any recorded in the annals of military achievements."[37] Among the less-renowned observers of these developments, a representative view of the import of these events was expressed by Samuel DeForest, a Connecticut militiaman: "The events of two weeks appears to have rolled on a pivot which has sealed and gave a stamp to the destiny of America."[38]

Victory proved a tonic for Washington's reputation as well as the fortunes of his army. He was no longer the general who had lost every major battle he had fought and who a growing number of people, including some of his officers and members of the Continental Congress, had come to view as an indecisive and inept leader. Now he was seen by many as a military mastermind and a national hero.

Writing to John Adams, a member of Congress who had pushed for Washington's appointment as commander of the army and would later serve as his Vice President and then second President of the United States, his wife, Abigail, with her customary acumen, recognized "that our late misfortunes have called out the hidden excellencies of our commander-in-chief."[39] When, almost seven years later, the new nation's foremost warrior passed through Trenton at war's end en route to resigning his military commission and returning to Mount Vernon, he would be greeted by Governor William Livingston of New Jersey and other dignitaries with a tribute evoking memories of a legendary winter campaign that had "rendered [Trenton] famous to the latest posterity, by the most unexampled effort of military genius; and [by] your signal victory over an enemy till then, through the great superiority of their numbers, the triumphant possessors of this part of the country."[40]

The newfound appreciation of Washington's talents was accompanied by a more optimistic outlook among those in the general public who supported the Revolution. According to one account, "Superstitious folk had feared the coming of 1777, for the numerals resembled a gallows: Rebels would hang that year. But suddenly the gallows seemed remote."[41] And this spirit of confidence and hope expressed by supporters of the rebellion—"a renewed faith of the nation in the army and its general"—was matched by an enhanced self-assurance among Washington's men. More of the American officers and soldiers now believed in themselves, and there was broad agreement among them that their recent victories "had transformed the Revolution, which once again was a cause that could be won."[42]

Another element contributed to young America's success at this time and is perhaps unappreciated for its role then and what it presaged for Great Britain's soon-to-be global struggle against not only the colonists but other rival nations who sought to chip away at England's empire. The arms and munitions being quietly provided by French, Spanish, and Dutch merchants, which were finding their way into the hands of rebel soldiers, were beginning to impact the contest in North America.

By the end of 1776, this military assistance totaled at least 10,000 muskets and nearly 1,000,000 pounds of gunpowder. At the beginning of the conflict, some militia units were sharing one musket between four men with only 15 rounds for each of them, but at Trenton on December 26, 1776, each soldier carried his own musket and 60 rounds into battle. A "modern archeological survey of shot recovered at the Princeton battlefield" indicates that nearly half was fired by muskets made in France, Spain, and

Liège (a principality in what is now the eastern part of Belgium) and used only by the Americans, while the other half corresponded to British- and American-manufactured muskets and American-made rifles. With respect to the battles fought during the "Ten Crucial Days," it can be said that "Dutch gunpowder and Spanish, French, and Liège muskets were not winning the war, but they were certainly preventing it from being lost."[43]

On the British side, the events of this period amply demonstrated to General Howe the degree of vulnerability that was attached to the string of outposts his troops had established across New Jersey, and he reacted by withdrawing them from all but Brunswick and Perth Amboy. The British command's "comfortable plan for winning the war [was] utterly shattered," as it had been proven "not only impractical but dangerous to try, against an army as mobile and unconventional as Washington's, to hold down a large area with a network of posts." The danger was amplified by the fact that the crown's hopes for His Majesty's colonial subjects to rally to the support of the mother country had been largely disappointed.[44]

In his letter of January 20, 1777 to Lord George Germain, the British Secretary of State for North America and principal architect of his government's strategy for defeating the rebellion, Howe conveyed his concern that the American victories had "thrown us further back than was at first apprehended, from the great encouragement it has given the rebels." He confessed: "I do not now see a prospect of terminating the war, but by a general action, and I am aware of the difficulties in our way to obtain it, as the enemy moves with so much [more] celerity than we possibly can."[45]

The men of Howe's army now confronted a new reality that carried with it different expectations about the future of the conflict and the nature of their opponent. Colonel William Harcourt confessed his concern about the newly recognized fighting capacity of the Patriot forces in a March letter to his father: "Though it was once the fashion of this army to treat them in the most contemptible light, they are now become a formidable enemy."[46] Moreover, these events reinforced the doubts among those in Britain who questioned the government's colonial policy and for many of the public there made it clear that the effort to conquer America was doomed to fail.[47]

The forces of the British crown never had a better chance to destroy Washington's army than they had prior to the "Ten Crucial Days" or than they did at Assunpink Creek on January 2, 1777, although it is arguable that they came perilously close at Brandywine Creek the following September during a notable British victory that stemmed from what was "probably Washington's worst battlefield performance of the war."[48] At least there, however, the Americans had more room to maneuver as they were not fighting with a river at their back and so were able to escape from the battlefield with the army intact.

To be sure, Washington and the troops under his command encountered any number of reversals and challenges that imperiled their cause before and after the "Ten Crucial Days." Most notably, these included: the whipping they suffered on Long Island in August 1776 when half the army was in danger of being trapped on Brooklyn Heights by General Howe; the devastating loss of Fort Washington overlooking the Hudson River that November; the bitter defeats at Brandywine and Germantown in late 1777; the difficult winter encampment at Valley Forge in 1777-1778 followed by the even more brutal experience at Morristown during the ferocious winter of 1779-1780; and the grueling slugfest in the blistering heat of the June 1778 battle at Monmouth Court House (now Freehold, New Jersey)—the last major engagement of the Revolution fought in the northern states—when the commander-in-chief personally rallied his retreating soldiers to avert what could have been a costly setback.

Even so, Washington's army would not have survived long enough to confront the difficulties it faced well after the "Ten Crucial Days" ended had the events of January 2, 1777 turned out differently. It is difficult to argue that this army was ever in greater peril than it was on the banks of the Assunpink Creek, when the rebels were on the verge of being trapped between two waterways and crushed under the weight of a larger, better trained, more experienced, elite enemy force commanded by the best fighting general in the British army. But just when Cornwallis's moment of triumph over the army of rebellion seemed so near, everything faded away for him: daylight vanished too soon, the rebels disappeared overnight, and the opportunity for a decisive victory receded into the realm of what-might-have-been. And as darkness descended on the Assunpink Creek that day, the sun also set on what may have been Great Britain's best chance to retain her North American colonies.

Celestial choir! enthroned in realms of light,
Columbia's scenes of glorious toils I write.
While freedom's cause her anxious breast alarms,
She flashes dreadful in refulgent arms. . . .
Muse! how propitious while my pen relates
How pour her armies through a thousand gates. . . .
Fix'd are the eyes of nations on the scales,
For in their hopes Columbia's arm prevails.
Anon Britannia droops the pensive head,
While round increase the rising hills of dead.
Ah! cruel blindness to Columbia's state!
Lament thy thirst of boundless power too late.

— Phillis Wheatley, African American poet, from a poem sent to
George Washington as a tribute, October 26, 1775

8

THE ROAD FROM ASSUNPINK CREEK

From an embattled stream along Trenton's southern boundary, the road to eventual victory in the Revolutionary War was long, convoluted, and challenging, as were the subsequent efforts to place a newly independent confederation of states on the path to achieving an enduring republic and building an expansive democracy that would gradually diffuse its attendant rights among an ever-widening swath of the population. The "Ten Crucial Days" were only the end of the beginning of a conflict that would run for almost five more years before the climactic battle at Yorktown, Virginia, and more than six-and-a-half years before a formal cessation of hostilities and the long-sought recognition of America's independence by the British crown under the Treaty of Paris in September 1783.

Much to his frustration, Washington, after the Battle of Monmouth in June 1778, was forced to sit on the sidelines while the struggle continued in other theaters of the war. He longed for an opportunity to indulge his aggressive military instincts and strike a game-changing blow with the assistance eagerly awaited from the forces of King Louis XVI of France, who had formally allied with the New World revolutionaries in early 1778. This interlude must have seemed interminable to a general so disposed to action and intensely committed to the "glorious cause," his term for America's quest for liberty.[1] Edward Lengel notes that "Washington was never very good at waiting, but that is how he spent the years between 1778 and 1781." The commander-in-chief sought a deciding battle with the enemy, but while "the main British army in America camped in New York, he felt constrained to hover nearby. And so, for three years, he had to do without leading troops in the field."[2]

That was until General Cornwallis unwittingly dug a trap for his army at Yorktown that eventuated in a victorious siege of His Lordship's outnumbered and outgunned garrison by a combined American-French force under Washington and the Comte de Rochambeau. That signal triumph in October 1781 fatally undermined Britain's willingness to carry on the war, although sporadic fighting continued for some time thereafter.

The factors that contributed to young America's eventual triumph in its quest for independence have been exhaustively analyzed by various scholars.[3] To reduce their interpretive work to its essence, the outcome of the Revolutionary struggle was determined by three key considerations.

The first was that the crown "lacked the military capacity to conquer and control the vast expanse of territory encompassed by the colonies" without receiving more support from the Loyalist population than they were able or willing to provide. Secondly, the rebels did not necessarily have to win battles in order to succeed, "but only needed to persevere until Britain's willingness to expend its blood and treasure was exhausted, which is what occurred." And finally, foreign assistance, primarily French but also Spanish and Dutch, which ranged from covert aid in the beginning of the war to more conspicuous intervention later in the struggle, "sustained the American war effort and eventually drew Britain into a global conflict that diverted military and naval resources from its effort to subdue the American rebellion."[4]

With regard to the geographic circumstances that factored into the war's outcome, it cannot be overemphasized that His Majesty's forces never demonstrated an ability to conquer and control the "sheer immensity and wilderness" of the territory comprising the upstart nation that they sought to strangle in its cradle. Their base "remained the Atlantic Ocean and the navigable rivers leading upcountry from it." British naval assets could not penetrate the American interior where the crown's military ambitions were ultimately thwarted, not only by rebel opposition but also by "the difficult terrain and the hardships of moving an army about," to which General Howe's letters to Lord Germain and others in London often alluded.[5]

Any effort to subjugate a population that was spread over so large an area would have been severely hampered by the deficiencies in command and control that plagued Britain's war effort. These included a degree of persistent "administrative gridlock" that was "fueled by incompetence, infighting, and overlapping spheres of authority" among the various government departments, as well as an "unwieldy and inefficient" military command structure that for most of the war suffered from not having a single commander-in-chief responsible for directing all land operations in North America— including the 13 colonies and Canada—against the rebel opposition.[6]

Finally, an ancillary factor of no small weight in Britain's failure to quash the colonial uprising was an immense ocean. Each "weapon, musket ball, and grain of powder, every boot and uniform button" utilized by the British expeditionary force "had to be transported 3,000 miles across the Atlantic in slow, cranky transports."[7] And the distances involved posed an obvious and significant impediment to communications. Even a swift vessel "carrying urgent dispatches seldom took much less than two months to cross over from an English port," while some messages took three or four, and on occasion even six or seven, months to make that voyage.[8]

In the end, Great Britain's failure to subdue the rebellion among her North American colonies may very well have been the worst disaster her storied empire ever suffered, and in 1783 that defeat constituted a stunning and humiliating setback for what was at the time the closest thing to a global superpower. This calamity occurred even while the crown was "putting one in every seven or eight eligible men under arms, and recruiting large auxiliary forces in Germany to fight alongside white Loyalists as well as Native Americans and former slaves."[9]

Aside from its geopolitical ramifications, the war imposed an enormous cost on the mother country—40,000 casualties and 50 million pounds—for which it gained nothing.[10] For Britannia, it was a monumental tragedy in which at least 20,000 of her soldiers and seamen perished in America, the West Indies, or at sea, either killed "in battle or dying in their own filth from wounds or disease, with rarely a stone to mark the grave of anyone below commissioned [officer] rank."[11] And thousands of Loyalists, Native Americans, and Hessian soldiers also died in the support of Britain's effort to suppress the colonial rebellion. Moreover, the struggle imposed an enormous sacrifice on the Loyalist community at its conclusion when about one in 40 of these Americans chose, or were driven into, permanent exile—the equivalent of approximately 7.5 million people today.[12]

The lengthy period of hostilities exacted a "ghastly toll" on the Patriot side as well, with the mortality rate among American soldiers exceeded only by the Civil War among all conflicts in the history of the United States. An estimate of about 25,000 to 30,000 fatalities would be regarded as very conservative.[13] To put those numbers in perspective, the total of Continental soldiers and militiamen killed during the war would easily exceed three million in terms of today's population and a considerably larger figure if we consider these deaths as a percentage of only the Patriot population during the Revolution.[14]

The figures on combatant mortality exclude the unknown number of civilian deaths—perhaps "well into the thousands"—from diseases unintentionally spread by soldiers on both sides and violent deaths resulting from naval attacks on coastal communities, Native American raids, the use of tactics that would be described as "guerrilla warfare" today, and siege operations that affected civilian populations.[15] Often the violence that extended to civilians was perpetrated with alacrity and cruelty on both sides. In addition to injury and loss of life, it included widespread loss of property at the hands of soldiers as well as physical assault. Such large-scale "plundering brought the war right to people's farms and into their homes," deprived "them of their belongings and destroyed their sense of safety."[16]

Disciples of the Patriot cause engaged in "campaigns of terror" against the Loyalist community, but they generally sought to distinguish "acceptable from illegitimate forms of violence" and thereby align their tactics with their political values. The rebels called attention to what they claimed was "the enemy's brutishness while striving to stay within the limits permitted by the prevailing codes of war," and in that way they sought "to win the moral war that accompanied the war on the ground."[17]

*****

Out of this carnage, there emerged a new legal national entity. To be sure, it resulted from the efforts of a people who sought to secure their political and economic rights within the context of the British empire until they felt compelled to seek independent status and who, throughout the rebellion and even afterward, generally identified themselves more by regional or local affiliations than by any concept of nationhood. It can be argued that the colonists were "reluctant nationalists," and that the Revolution "began, rather than culminated, a long, slow, and incomplete process of creating an American identity and nation."[18]

To this day, historians differ over how far-reaching the Revolution was in its consequences. Some have found little in the way of substantive change and highlight trends that continued from the colonial era while others emphasize the expansion of economic opportunities and spreading political participation among "common white men." It has been argued that the Revolution augmented trends already underway, including enhanced political engagement by common men, territorial expansion at the expense of Native Americans, and the westward expansion of slavery.[19] A counterargument to this thesis acknowledges that the colonial insurrection did not impact slavery or social arrangements such as those between men and women, but contends that it went hand-in-hand with a broad, radical social transformation that converted a society of "monarchical, hierarchy-ridden subjects on the margin of civilization" into one whose inhabitants became "almost overnight, the most liberal, the most democratic, the most commercially minded, and the most modern people in the world"—all without the benefit of those forces that are usually associated with modernization such as industrialization or urbanization.[20]

Clearly the struggle for freedom that the Revolutionary enterprise claimed to embody rang hollow when it came to acknowledging the interests of the 20 percent of the colonial population who were enslaved. The Patriot leaders, "in the wake of their historic revolution, which they had boldly declared to be in the service of human liberty itself," allowed economic and political considerations to supersede their moral qualms about human bondage and so "extravagantly failed their own challenge."[21] It would take another eight decades and an even bloodier war to end America's most infamous institution.

The Revolutionary era from 1765 to 1787 served as the original laboratory of American democracy in which the founding fathers spearheaded a popular uprising that evolved into an armed insurgency against British colonial policy, engineered a political divorce from the mother country, crafted the documents that became the touchstones of our republic in the Declaration of Independence and the federal Constitution, and created a representative government designed to control itself as well as those it governed. The uprising of the 1770s may be viewed as an upheaval that not only launched America on its quest for independence but also in perpetual search of a republican ideal it is still seeking today.

From the republic's turbulent beginning emerged an unceasing process and tradition in which succeeding generations have debated, defined, and defended American democracy. "Indeed, the lesson of our history," it has been observed, "is that the task of merely maintaining strong and sturdy the structures of a constitutional order is unending, the continuing and ceaseless work of every generation."[22] This unrelenting obligation to protect and preserve the sinews of our democracy, as well as to defend it from foreign foes, was articulated at the time of America's inception by Thomas Paine in *The American Crisis,* Number IV (September 12, 1777): "Those who expect to reap the blessings of Freedom must . . . undergo the fatigue of supporting it."[23]

A plausible argument can be made that the Revolutionary War merely accelerated an attainment of American independence from England that in all probability was inevitable. Although it is possible the Revolution could have been avoided if a spirit of accommodation had prevailed in both Parliament and the colonies, it is likely that at some point Britain and her North American subjects would have gone their separate ways, either by conflict or a decision by Britain to grant the United States independence in the same way it did with Canada in 1867.[24] One can reasonably assume that the American colonies would have gradually progressed toward independence in the 19th century as their political and economic strength developed "within the protective constraints of the British Empire," but instead the creation of the new nation occurred in a revolutionary, rather than evolutionary, manner.[25]

Even so, the ramifications of North America's Revolutionary turmoil spread far beyond its shores in the late 18th century and well into the next one. The colonists' struggle for independence would inspire insurgent movements in France, Mexico, South America, and Europe that sought to emulate the republican form of government taking root in the United States, and in that sense it provided a template for advocates of representative democracy across the globe. These developments buttressed the claim made by Paine in Common Sense that the "cause of America is in a great measure the cause of all mankind."[26]

*****

At a more personal level, the story of the American Revolution is also the story of George Washington's evolution as an individual and a leader. No doubt, he was an enigma, "an elusive quarry" of whom it has been said that the "closer he seems, the more easily he slips away." "Washington fostered this with his own demeanor" because he was acutely aware of his role as a public figure and so "crafted an outward persona that obscured his private being."[27] Lengel sums up the man's admixture of qualities this way: "As a soldier, he was erratic but competent. As a man he was impulsive, vindictive, brave, hardworking, intelligent, and virtuous. And as a leader, he was great."[28]

The paradoxical qualities to be found in the father of our country are many and varied. The Washington who in his formative years was a self-interested, sometimes brash youth and a provincial Virginian became in his wartime role a selfless leader who exhibited prudent judgment and a steady hand in the cause of his country's independence while adopting the perspective of an ardent nationalist.

In terms of his character, Washington might be described as an individual of driving ambition but modest public persona and as someone who experienced powerful emotions but publicly maintained an aloof and dignified demeanor. As a planter, he proved to be a shrewd businessman but struggled in his quest for financial security. A demanding slaveholder, he nevertheless became the only "founding father" to free those he held in servitude. And while generally demonstrating sound judgment, he needed ample time to make decisions.

As a public figure, Washington exhibited keen political skills but is not generally regarded as an accomplished politician. Although not an intellectual, he committed himself wholeheartedly to the pursuit of certain ideas. He was a warrior who resolutely adhered to the principal of civilian control over the military, a general who lost more battles than he won but ultimately emerged victorious in America's fight for independence, and an army commander who refused to accept a salary for his services yet kept a meticulous record of his expenses—for which he expected to be, and was, reimbursed by the Continental Congress at the end of the war. Finally, this was a leader who was used to exercising enormous power but appears to have eagerly relinquished it and in doing so demonstrated the full measure of his greatness, both when he resigned his commission as commander-in-chief of the Continental Army in 1783 and when he left office after serving two terms as the first president of the United States in 1797.

Washington was not a brilliant general in a purely military sense and certainly made his share of battlefield blunders early in the war. But the Continental Congress, which had conferred upon him the honor and burden of heading its fledgling army in 1775, came to recognize that Washington combined those traits best suited to managing the various political and military aspects of the army's operations in a very challenging environment. Many, if not most, members of that body appreciated "the difficulties with which he coped—poorly supplied armies, callow soldiers, unworthy officers, and a formidable adversary," as well as the qualities of "character, judgment, circumspection, industry, meticulousness, example, and diplomatic and political skills" that uniquely qualified Washington to command the Continental Army.[29]

Washington's conduct of military operations was continually undermined by the absence of two key means of support for his troops. First, he had to contend with a national government that had insufficient authority to compel the states to back the army with more than rhetorical gestures, as Congress had no power to require that state governments contribute manpower, supplies, or tax revenue to the Patriot cause. Second, Washington was plagued by the poor infrastructure in colonial America—a lack of roads, wagons, and wagoners—that made it difficult to regularly supply the army with the items it sometimes desperately needed: food, warm clothing, tents, blankets, and clean straw. Still, the perseverance and resourcefulness of "America's first leader" paid off in the end, for despite the persistent circumstances of a weak central authority and inadequate supply system, Washington "fought his way through using what was available to hold off superior forces in almost every battle" and only at Yorktown in 1781 went into combat "with a favorable hand."[30]

In the process of directing the war effort, the American commander-in-chief came to personify the quest for independence in a way that transcended his purely military role. He, more than anyone else, "by his actions and example, held together the political structure that constituted the United States." Robert Middlekauff asserts that if Washington had not persevered in the service of his "glorious cause," the Revolution would have slowly collapsed, for no one else "in the army, the Congress, or the states commanded the moral force he embodied."[31]

Washington's attributes—"composure, dignity, presence, a deep determination, and an absolute unwillingness to accept defeat"—inspired enough of his soldiery to fight on until success was achieved.[32] His leadership brought an army back from the brink of total defeat during the "Ten Crucial Days," held it together under the most adverse conditions for eight long years, and ultimately prevailed in a grueling war of attrition against the mightiest empire on earth. For those who believe that America would have lost its bid for independence were it not for Washington's leadership, he will forever be regarded "for all his flaws, as the savior of his country."[33] And he left nothing to chance when it came to documenting his wartime conduct for future generations. The rebel leader was scrupulous about maintaining extensive records to ensure "his side of the story was safely preserved for posterity," for he "had a profound sense of history and his role in it."[34]

Washington's persistence throughout the conflict was remarkable, as he outlasted four British commanders-in-chief. He "stayed the course" while a succession of His Majesty's generals who faced him in battle—William Howe, Henry Clinton, and Charles Cornwallis—"headed back home to their firesides and their extenuating speeches and memoirs."[35] Washington's moment of climactic triumph over Lord Cornwallis's army in 1781 must have produced in this man who so earnestly sought to hide his emotions in public the greatest intensity of feeling he ever experienced. After "years of privations and disappointments and bloodstained footprints in the snow of the men for whom he could not obtain decent footwear," one can easily infer that this occasion would have moved him deeply even though these emotions were never "confided to any person or age."[36]

The memory of that monumental achievement and the feelings that arose from it undoubtedly accompanied the leader of America's first army when he became America's first national chief executive in April 1789. He began that chapter in his life by journeying from his beloved Mount Vernon to the new nation's capital in New York City to assume the presidency, in the process returning to the banks of the stream where he had led his men in battle a dozen years before.

As Washington neared the bridge over Assunpink Creek, he saw that an elaborate floral arch had been erected in his honor with the date, "December 26, 1776," sewn from leaves and flowers. He rode closer and encountered "thirteen young girls, robed in spotless white . . . with flower-filled baskets, scattering petals at his feet." Sitting astride his horse with tears in his eyes, "he returned a deep bow and noted the 'astonishing contrast between his former and actual situation at the same spot.'"[37] A hand-colored lithograph published by Currier & Ives in 1845 depicts the scene with the floral arch bearing the words that proclaimed Washington's heroic status in the eyes of his admirers: "The defender of the mothers will be the protector of the daughters."[38]

*****

Notwithstanding Washington's central, and perhaps indispensable, role in the outcome of the war for independence, any realistic appraisal of the factors behind the young nation's ultimate success must obviously acknowledge the contributions of the enlisted soldier as well. They were the men who volunteered for duty or could not afford to pay a fine or hire a substitute to serve in their place when drafted into the Continental Army. The common soldiers became part of "a small regular army of poor men [who] sustained the

Patriot cause by enduring years of hard duty and public neglect," and although often initially conscripted, they "developed a commitment to the cause greater than their more fortunate neighbors who stayed home."[39]

Those who chose to join the army did so for a wide variety of reasons. In some cases it was a commitment to fight for liberty and independence, in others the opportunity for financial gain derived from a bounty (a cash payment received for enlisting) or being hired as a substitute, while some enlistees were motivated by a desire to break away from a parent or master, or simply by an adventurous impulse or eagerness to serve with a friend. Whatever their reasons, many "came to feel part of something larger than themselves" by virtue of sharing and enduring "the experiences of war, its occasional excitement and terror and its prolonged drudgery." In the process, they became professional soldiers, overcoming the severity of military life and its attendant hardships as well as neglect by those in the larger community who were indifferent to the army's needs. Ultimately, with the help of foreign intervention, they "succeeded in driving out a larger and more experienced enemy."[40]

Washington's growing capacity as a wartime leader would have had far less significance than it did "if his generals, junior officers, and enlisted men had not grown commensurately in competence and assurance."[41] His ability to preserve the Continental Army over the long haul—regardless of the "defeats, desertions, expired enlistments, threatened and actual mutinies, disease, and chronic shortages of equipment, food, and supplies" that bedeviled him— was predicated upon the fact that "enough Continental soldiers and militiamen stood by the cause to deny the British outright victory and overcome the opposition of American loyalists," while prolonging the war long enough for American and French forces to score the all-important victory over the crown's troops at Yorktown.[42]

Among the unsung Patriot heroes, none had a greater impact at a more crucial moment in the Revolution than the rifle commander from Lancaster whose leadership orchestrated a valiant defense against overwhelming odds on the second day of 1777 and foiled Cornwallis's plan to knock out Washington's army once and for all. Edward Hand continued to distinguish himself as the Revolution unfolded. He earned a promotion to brigadier general in April 1777, when he was assigned to command the American troops at Fort Pitt in western Pennsylvania, followed by command of a brigade of light infantry in the division led by the Marquis de Lafayette, and then in January 1781 he become adjutant general of the Continental Army—the last man to occupy the position during the war. In that capacity, Hand was at Washington's side, with responsibility for the transmission of most general orders to the army, personnel administration, supervision of outposts, and security matters.

The fighting general "would be there at the end—storming the British works at Yorktown."[43] When the besieged Cornwallis capitulated, Hand accompanied Generals Washington and Rochambeau as they rode out to one of the captured British redoubts to receive the official document of surrender.[44] At the war's close in September 1783, he was made a brevet major general in recognition of his service.[45] Perhaps the crowning recognition of his contribution to the Patriot cause came four months later when Washington wrote his faithful comrade in arms to convey "my entire approbation for your public conduct."[46]

When peace came, Hand resigned from the army and returned home to Lancaster where he later built a Georgian-style brick mansion on several hundred acres of land that he had purchased. It became known as Rock Ford Plantation, and he lived there from 1794 until his death. Hand practiced medicine, served as a member of the Congress of Confederation in 1784-85 and the Pennsylvania Assembly in 1785-86, and was chosen as a delegate to the Pennsylvania Constitutional Convention in 1790. Tradition has it that he played host to his former commander-in-chief, President Washington, during the latter's visit to Lancaster in 1791. Hand's death on September 3, 1802 at age 57 was attributed to "Cholera Morbus," then used to describe a variety of cholera-like symptoms.[47] He was interred in the St. James Episcopal Church Cemetery in Lancaster, leaving a legacy of service to cause and country that defined him as "the stuff of which the hard core" of America's first army was made.[48]

*****

The democratic impulse behind the efforts of Edward Hand and his men reflected a desire to be free of arbitrary governmental authority and to enjoy the prerogatives of political and economic self-determination that have since the Republic's founding been gradually extended to more and more Americans. That motivation has been frequently and notably expressed in many ways and by many individuals since the Revolution but was perhaps never more succinctly articulated than it was by a more recent military hero who rose from the nation's heartland, Dwight Eisenhower, when he was asked to comment on the events of D-Day—the invasion of German-occupied France on June 6, 1944 that he commanded under the code name, Operation Overlord.

During an interview on Omaha Beach for a special CBS television program marking the 20th anniversary of that engagement, the old soldier spoke against the backdrop of the English Channel, which the American, British, and Canadian troops of the Allied Expeditionary Force[49] had traversed on that June day—the most celebrated nautical undertaking by American infantry since Christmas night 1776. From there they stormed the French beaches during the most decisive battle of the Second World War and went on to liberate western Europe from the tyranny of Nazi rule. Looking out at the history-laden waterway, America's 34th president reflected with a compelling simplicity on the force of an aroused democracy: "It just shows what free men will do rather than be slaves."[50]

The Road from Assunpink Creek

General George Washington at Trenton (John Trumbull), 1792
Yale University Art Museum

It doesn't take a hero to order men into battle. It takes a hero to be one of those men who goes into battle.

— General H. Norman Schwarzkopf, from his autobiography, *It Doesn't Take a Hero*, 1992

9

GATHERING LAURELS

Unlike today, when generals who command forces in combat do so at distances far afield from the actual fighting, their 18th century counterparts needed to be on the battlefield in order to provide direction, encouragement, and even inspiration to their troops. Generals such as George Washington and Charles Cornwallis were known for being in the thick of the fight and braving whatever dangers their men faced. Each commander gave ample evidence on multiple occasions of a willingness to risk his life in the service of his country alongside the soldiers he led, and the level of personal courage and determination they displayed is inextricably intertwined with the fame attached to their names.

For his part, Washington exhibited "great personal bravery and coolness under fire, and his composure in times of crisis helped him earn the respect of the soldiers he commanded in the Revolutionary War."[1] On the other hand, it is argued that he repeatedly took "the most foolhardy risks" in combat.[2] Indeed, it has been said of the commander-in-chief that the "sound of gunfire drew him like a magnet."[3] It had done so ever since he was a young colonel during the French and Indian War, and no more dramatic exhibition of those instincts occurred than at the Battle of Princeton on January 3, 1777.

Not to be outdone in this regard, Cornwallis "personally led assaults at the front of his army" and "was almost reckless in exposing himself to the enemy," like Washington having horses shot from under him.[4] Two such incidents serve to reinforce this point. One was at the Battle of Long Island in August 1776 when he "personally led his troops in a spirited charge along the Gowanus Road" and exposed himself "to enemy fire with almost reckless abandon."[5] And at the Battle of Guilford Courthouse in March 1781, the earl "was foolhardy in his personal bravery" when two horses were killed beneath him and he was slightly wounded but would not allow himself to be listed as a casualty.[6]

At the same time, the gentlemanly code of conduct among military officers during the 18th century provided for a degree of civility in the interaction of these two commanders that we might regard as quaintly charming today. After his surrender at Yorktown near the mouth of the Chesapeake Bay in October 1781, Lord Cornwallis is said to have toasted the victorious Washington as follows: "When the illustrious part that your Excellency has borne in this long and arduous contest becomes a matter of history, fame will gather your brightest laurels rather from the banks of the Delaware than from those of the Chesapeake."[7] In so doing, Cornwallis accorded the American commander-in-chief a tribute that recognized the significance of the "Ten Crucial Days" in regard to the ultimate outcome of the protracted conflict.

Because Cornwallis was present for only one of the engagements at Trenton, the Battle of Assunpink Creek, it is reasonable to assume that the latter encounter was foremost in his mind when he offered his gracious toast to the squire of Mount Vernon. In that revealing instant, the British commander acknowledged how key the outcome of the Assunpink shoot-out was to the future course of events.

It would appear that the famed American painter of the Revolutionary War era, John Trumbull, concurred with General Cornwallis about the importance of the events at the creek. In his 1792 work, *General George Washington at Trenton*, Trumbull depicted the commander of the Continental Army on that January night after the battle at Assunpink and before the army's overnight march to Princeton. The painting has been pronounced one of Trumbull's "most interesting works," and Washington is represented here in what both the artist and the general "believed to be the critical moment of the Revolution."[8]

Paul Staiti describes the portrait, which its creator claimed was the best he ever produced:

> In the painting, Trumbull showed Washington calm and focused as chaos encircles him. His skittish charger pulls against the reins held by its groom. Piles of broken cannons and carriages litter the foreground, and in the distance, beneath a fluttering American flag, soldiers move around haphazardly under a winter sky, building fires meant to fool Cornwallis into thinking the Americans had settled into camp. To the right a gnarled tree stands to the side of Washington, one broken stub of a branch ominously pointing at his head. The thoughtful, classically thinking Trumbull used a print of Apollo for Washington's pose, and he included precise details, such as Washington's gilt-trimmed field glasses and the leopard-skin saddlecloth he liked to put on his horse.[9]

Given the perception of the Assunpink fray's significance reflected in Cornwallis's toast to Washington at Yorktown and Trumbull's magisterial effort at memorializing this event, one might infer that Lord Cornwallis would have thought January 2, 1777 to be the most desperate moment of the war for Washington and his army. In hindsight, the fighting earl surely knew that he could have demolished the rebel force facing him across a narrow creek that day had his troops reached their objective with sufficient daylight remaining to accomplish their task.

Of all the crown's military principals, Cornwallis was best equipped by talent and temperament to secure that final victory over Washington. It has been argued that His Lordship should have been "the outstanding British general in the American Revolution" based on his combat experience, his military academy training, and a knowledge of strategy and tactics far surpassing that of the average British officer.[10] But whatever his record and abilities, Cornwallis ran out of time when his men were detained by the muddy road conditions that impeded their advance from Princeton to Trenton and by the fierce resistance that was mounted by an outnumbered but battle-tested and obstinate band of Continental skirmishers along that route. It might be said that the weather was guided by the hand of fate and the defenders by the Hand of Pennsylvania.

The man who led the Pennsylvania riflemen and others in their running battle with Cornwallis's juggernaut on January 2, 1777 has been ranked among those American officers who "had that special aptitude for leading men in battle... [and] were, when the chips were down, capable of delivering the best any general could demand."[11] When the fate of the Continental Army that embodied the Patriot cause hung in the balance, the colonel's hardy few urgently needed to fulfill George Washington's demand for exemplary soldiering against a formidable invader. One might judge their readiness to meet that challenge by employing a time-honored means of interpreting human affairs—that is, by borrowing a line from Shakespeare. The way his character Mercutio memorably describes his fatal wound in *Romeo and Juliet* is how the Bard of Avon might have regarded Edward Hand's small but steadfast contingent: ". . . 'tis not so deep as a well, nor so wide as a church door, but 'tis enough. 'Twill serve."[12]

EPILOGUE

Today the road to Assunpink Creek is a study in historical understatement, both metaphorically and literally. Its significance for America's Revolutionary struggle has been downplayed by historians and the wider community, and the evidence for that contention is twofold. It lies first in the lack of scholarly attention devoted to the critical military encounter that occurred along what is now Route 206 in Lawrence Township and Trenton, New Jersey (variously known in 1777 as the Princeton Road, the Princeton-Trenton Road, or the Post Road running from Princeton through Maidenhead to Trenton). It is also to be found in the obvious dearth of conspicuous historical markers that would otherwise indicate the importance of what occurred here on January 2, 1777.

This work has attempted to enhance the salience of the engagement fought on that day along a road that should be regarded as hallowed ground, one which may very well have saved George Washington's army and perhaps with it the American Revolution. However, a book by itself cannot alter the physical location or display of markers that arguably fail to do justice to the legacy of the brave men who risked their lives beside this embattled thoroughfare in the cause of American liberty and independence. The locations that were part of this historic event—little Shabakunk Creek, Big Shabakunk Creek, and Stockton Hollow—deserve greater

197

recognition and a corresponding display of signage that befits their status as noteworthy sites on the road to a history-laden creek and America's emergence as a new nation.

Upgrading the appearance and visibility of the markers that delineate the route along which Edward Hand's men fought a desperate and determined battle against the forces of the British crown would be a fitting way to celebrate the approach of the 250th anniversary of the Declaration of Independence. The case for doing so honors their memory and reminds us of how ordinary people have done extraordinary things in the course of our national journey: to gain our independence, create a new republic, cultivate an enduring set of democratic traditions and values, and build a nation that, however gradually and tentatively, expanded freedom and opportunity at home while attaining an unparalleled degree of influence and respect abroad. In the process our land became a beacon of liberty and hope to people from across the globe, and if we lose the sense of purpose and pride connected with that American heritage and the moral imagination that is its animating spirit, we and the world will be the poorer for it. For America's greatness inheres in that legacy and the idealism of its people.

Epilogue

APPENDIX A.

THE "TEN CRUCIAL DAYS": A CHRONOLOGY OF EVENTS

Prelude - December 14 - 25, 1776: The Continental Army troops led by General George Washington are encamped on the Pennsylvania side of the Delaware River, where they are regrouping from a nearly disastrous New York campaign against the British and Hessian forces and a long retreat across New Jersey. In New Jersey, Continental soldiers and militiamen engage Hessian troops in the area of Mount Holly while other militia units continually harass the Hessian brigade occupying Trenton. Thomas Paine's pamphlet, *The American Crisis*, inspires the weary Continentals to fight on, and it is read to and by many of Washington's troops.

Day 1 - Wednesday, December 25, 1776: A Continental Army force of 2,400 soldiers, organized into seven brigades, crosses an ice-choked Delaware River to New Jersey over a period of 9-10 hours that stretches into the early morning of December 26— without losing a single soldier, cannon, horse, wagon, or boat in the process—and marches almost 10 miles to Trenton in a raging blizzard to assault the 1,500 Hessian troops occupying the town.

Day 2 - Thursday, December 26, 1776: First Battle of Trenton - The Continental Army defeats the Hessians at Trenton in the midst of a snowstorm to win its first significant victory of the war and suffers minimal casualties, then returns to Pennsylvania with its prisoners and captured arms, ammunition, horses, and wagons. The commander of the Hessian brigade at Trenton, Colonel Johann Rall, is mortally wounded during the American raid, and about 1,000 enemy soldiers are killed, wounded, or captured.

Days 3 and 4 - Friday and Saturday, December 27 - 28, 1776: After returning to Pennsylvania, Washington and his generals decide to cross the Delaware back to New Jersey in like manner as Colonel John Cadwalader's Philadelphia Associators, who have already crossed over from Pennsylvania and discovered that the Hessian forces have withdrawn from their posts at Bordentown and Burlington south of Trenton.

Days 5 and 6 - Sunday and Monday, December 29 - 30, 1776: The Continental Army crosses the river for the fourth time that month and returns to Trenton. There Washington's troops combine with militia to form a consolidated force of about 7,000 men that entrenches itself below the Assunpink Creek on the southern edge of the town. Washington and his other officers persuade a bare majority of the soldiers whose enlistments are to expire on December 31 to remain with the army for another six weeks, based on a promise to pay each of them a $10 bonus in hard coin.

Days 7 and 8 - Tuesday and Wednesday, December 31, 1776 - January 1, 1777: Several Continental Army regiments advance from Trenton toward enemy-occupied Princeton and take up positions along the Princeton Road in Maidenhead (today Lawrence Township). There they skirmish with British and Hessian troops on New Year's Day.

Day 9 - Thursday, January 2, 1777: Battle of Assunpink Creek (or the Second Battle of Trenton) - Continental Army units led by Colonel Edward Hand, totaling about 1,000 men, fight a delaying action against 8,000 British and Hessian troops under General Charles Cornwallis in Maidenhead and the outskirts of Trenton for several hours. Aided by muddy roads resulting from overnight rain and unusually warm temperatures, the rebel skirmishers slow Cornwallis's march from Princeton to Trenton long enough to prevent a full-scale, coordinated assault in daylight against Washington's army arrayed behind the Assunpink Creek. The opposing armies at the creek engage in a fierce artillery duel, and the Continental soldiers and militia beat back a series of probing attacks by British and Hessian forces in the area of the stone bridge over the creek as darkness descends on the battlefield. This is the only engagement of the "Ten Crucial Days" in which Washington's army fights British and Hessian troops in the same action, is outnumbered by the enemy, and faces soldiers commanded by a British general. It is also the one involving the largest number of soldiers, as well as the longest battle of that period if one counts Colonel Hand's delaying action and the fighting at the creek that immediately followed as a single encounter. In the course of this extended confrontation, casualties among the crown's forces outnumber American losses by more than three to one.

Day 10 - Friday, January 3, 1777: Battle of Princeton - Overnight, the Continental Army marches some 12 miles around Cornwallis's left flank, from behind the Assunpink Creek to Princeton, and in a brief but ferocious encounter defeats a small British force under the command of Lieutenant Colonel Charles Mawhood for the capstone American victory of the "Ten Crucial Days." Washington personally rallies his troops on the battlefield at great personal risk and turns the tide of battle during one of the few occasions in the war when his army scored a victory over British troops. Casualties among the latter exceed American losses by at least six to one in this bloody affair.

Postscript - January 3 - 6, 1777: The Continental Army makes its way from Princeton to Morristown, New Jersey, where it establishes its winter quarters behind the safety of the Watchung Mountains and thereby ends the military campaign associated with the "Ten Crucial Days."

APPENDIX B.

THE DISPOSITION OF FORCES AT THE BATTLE OF ASSUNPINK CREEK, JANUARY 2, 1777

Note: Army, division, and brigade commanders for both armies are indicated in parentheses. At the time of the battle, Continental Army regiments were often referred to by the name of a regimental colonel rather than their numerical designation, even when that officer had been captured or promoted. The numbers of soldiers indicated for the various units are estimates.

AMERICAN TROOPS: 7,000 soldiers - Continental Army
(Commander-in-Chief, General George Washington)

Sullivan's Division (Major General John Sullivan) - 1,200
    St. Clair's Brigade (Brigadier General Arthur St. Clair)
        - Poor's, Reed's, and Stark's New Hampshire
        Continental Regiments
        - Paterson's 1st Massachusetts Continental Regiment
    Glover's Brigade - remnants combined with St. Clair's Brigade
        - 4th, 14th, and 19th Massachusetts Continental Regiments
        - Bailey's Massachusetts Continental Regiment
    Sargent's Brigade (Colonel Paul Dudley Sargent) - remnants
        combined with St. Clair's Brigade
        - 13th and 16th Massachusetts Continental Regiments

- Ward's Connecticut Regiment
- Connecticut State Troops

Greene's Division (Major General Nathanael Greene) - 1,400
    Mercer's Brigade (Brigadier General Hugh Mercer)
      - Smallwood's Maryland Continental Regiment
      - Miles's Pennsylvania Rifle Regiment
      - Rawlings's Maryland and Virginia Rifle Regiment
      New Jersey State Artillery
    Stirling's Brigade - remnants combined with Mercer's Brigade
      - Haslet's Delaware Continental Regiment
      - Read's 1st Virginia Continental Regiment
      - Weedon's 3rd Virginia Regiment
      - Williams's 6th Maryland Regiment
    Stephen's Brigade (Colonel Charles Scott)
      - Elliott's 4th Virginia Continental Regiment
      - Scott's 5th Virginia Continental Regiment
      - Buckner's 6th Virginia Continental Regiment
    Fermoy's Brigade (Brigadier General Matthias-Alexis
      de Roche Fermoy)
      - Pennsylvania and Maryland German Regiment
      - Hand's 1st Pennsylvania Rifle Regiment

Ewing's Brigade, Pennsylvania Militia (Brigadier General James Ewing)
    - 600
    - Bucks, Cumberland, Lancaster, and York County Militias

Cadwalader's Brigade, Philadelphia Associators (Colonel John
    Cadwalader) - 1,150
    - Bayard's, Morgan's, and Nixon's Philadelphia Militia Regiments
    - Matlack's Philadelphia Rifle Battalion
    - Henry's Philadelphia Light Infantry
    - Chester County Militia
    - Kent County Delaware Militia
    - Marines
    - Pennsylvania Artillery

Hitchcock's Brigade (Major Israel Angell) - 350
- Hitchcock's, Lippitt's, and Varnum's Rhode Island Continental Regiments
- 4th and 12th Massachusetts Continental Regiments

Mifflin's Brigade (Brigadier General Thomas Mifflin) - 1,800
- 2nd, 4th, 10th, and 11th Pennsylvania Continental Regiments
- 12th Pennsylvania Continental Rifle Regiment

Griffin's Brigade, New Jersey Militia (Colonel Silas Newcomb) - 500
- Cumberland, Gloucester, and Salem County Militias

Total Artillery - 40 guns

BRITISH AND HESSIAN TROOPS: 10,700 - Cornwallis's Division
(Major General Charles Cornwallis)
Vanguard (Colonel Carl von Donop) - 1,500
- Hessian Jäger Corps, Foot - 1 company
- Hessian Jäger Corps, Mounted - 1 company
- Hessian Grenadiers - 100 picked men
- 16th Light Dragoons - 2 troops

Main Force - 6,500

Light Infantry Brigade (Major General James Grant)
- 1st and 2nd Light Infantry Battalions
- Hessian Grenadier Battalion Köhler
- 42nd and 71st Regiments of Foot

British Grenadiers and Guards Brigade (Lieutenant Colonel Henry Monckton)
- 1st and 2nd British Grenadier Battalions
- 2nd British Guards Battalion

Hessian Brigade Grenadiers and Fusiliers
- Grenadier Battalions Block, Linsing, and Minnigerode
- Fusilier Battalion Loos
- Remnants of the Rall Brigade

Total Artillery - 28 guns

Reserve at Maidenhead - 1,500

Second British Brigade (Brigadier General Alexander Leslie)
- 5th, 28th, 35th, and 49th Regiments of Foot

Reserve at Princeton - 1,200

Fourth British Brigade (Lieutenant Colonel Charles Mawhood)
- 17th, 40th, and 55th Regiments of Foot
- Royal Artillery (6 guns)

SOURCES:

David Hackett Fischer, *Washington's Crossing* (New York: Oxford University Press, 2004);

David Bonk, *Trenton and Princeton 1776-77: Washington crosses the Delaware* (New York: Osprey Publishing, 2009);

William S. Stryker, *The Battles of Trenton and Princeton* (Boston: Houghton, Mifflin and Company, 1898).

APPENDIX C.

THE FATE OF CERTAIN INDIVDUALS WHOSE END IS NOT REVEALED IN THE NARRATIVE

William Alexander (Lord Stirling): The brigadier general who commanded a Continental Army brigade during the "Ten Crucial Days" was considered one of Washington's most loyal officers. He was too ill to participate in the battles at Assunpink Creek and Princeton but was promoted to major general early in 1777 and saw action at the battles of Brandywine, Germantown, and Monmouth. Known for eating and drinking to excess, he died from gout in Albany, New York, at age 56 in 1783.

John Cadwalader: The colonel of the Philadelphia Associators was appointed brigadier general of the Pennsylvania militia in 1777 but declined Continental Army appointments to brigadier general and to brigadier and commander of the cavalry. In 1778, he left military service and returned to his family's estate in Shrewsbury, Maryland.

That year, he fought a duel with Washington's nemesis, Thomas Conway, over the latter's alleged "cabal" among certain army officers against Washington's leadership, inflicting a nonfatal wound on Conway. After the war, Cadwalader moved from Pennsylvania to Maryland and served in its House of Delegates. He died in Shrewsbury at age 44 in 1786.

Charles Cornwallis: The most aristocratic and aggressive of Great Britain's generals during her war against the American Rebellion (as the colonies' quest for independence was known in England) was unsuccessful in his efforts to destroy Washington's army at Assunpink Creek in 1777 and to do the same to Nathanael Greene's southern army in 1781. He recovered from his signal defeat against the combined American and French forces at Yorktown, Virginia, in 1781 to become governor-general of India in 1786. Cornwallis was created a marquess (a rank of nobility above an earl and below a duke) for his services and later served as viceroy of Ireland. He was reappointed governor-general of India in 1805 and died in Ghazipur, India, at age 66 in 1805.

Carl von Donop: The Hessian colonel had overall command of the German troops stationed in the Trenton-Bordentown-Burlington area of New Jersey in December 1776. He was mortally wounded during an attack on Fort Mercer on the Delaware River below Philadelphia, known as the Battle of Red Bank, in October 1777. At the time of his death, he was age 45.

William Erskine: The British quartermaster general to General Cornwallis, who unsuccessfully urged the latter to attack Washington's army at Assunpink Creek without delay on the night of January 2, 1777, had been knighted for his military exploits prior to the American Rebellion. Known as "Woolly" by his fellow officers, he was promoted to brigadier general and then major general during the course of the war and saw action in the Philadelphia campaign in 1777 and at the Battle of Monmouth the following year. Erskine returned to England in 1779 and later commanded troops in Britain's war against revolutionary France. He died at age 67 in 1795.

Johann Ewald: The Hessian captain, who came to America in 1776 and served under Colonel Carl von Donop during the "Ten Crucial Days," participated in many of the war's significant battles and was with Cornwallis's army when it surrendered at Yorktown in 1781. He kept a diary that contained a comprehensive account of his experiences throughout the war and created numerous maps of the areas in which he fought, which included the placement of troops and fortifications. Ewald later served in the Danish army, rising to the rank of lieutenant general. He died in Kiel, in the northern German state of Schleswig-Holstein, at age 69 in 1813.

Matthias-Alexis de Roche Fermoy: The brigadier general from the West Indies who abandoned his post on January 2, 1777 in the face of Cornwallis's march to Trenton, leaving Colonel Edward Hand to assume command of Fermoy's troops, would end his military career in disgrace. In July 1777, he endangered his troops at Fort Ticonderoga when he set fire to his quarters during an attempt at a secret nighttime evacuation of the fort and thereby prematurely revealed the American withdrawal to the British forces nearby. After he was rejected for a promotion to major general, he resigned from the army in January 1778 and returned to the West Indies where he died sometime afterwards.

Thomas Forrest: The artillery captain whose battery fought in all three battles of the "Ten Crucial Days" played a prominent role in the delaying action waged by American skirmishers under Colonel Hand between Princeton and Trenton on January 2, 1777. He was promoted to major shortly afterward and then to lieutenant-colonel in 1778. Resigning from the army in 1781, Forrest entered politics after the war and served in the U.S. House of Representatives. He died in Philadelphia at about age 78 in 1825.

John Glover: The colonel commanded the seafaring men of the 14th Massachusetts Continental Regiment from Marblehead, who played an indispensable role in the Delaware River crossing of December 25, 1776. He was left without a regiment after December 31, 1776 because of expired enlistments. Glover went home to attend to family and business matters after his regiment disbanded but returned to the army in 1777 and served for the remainder of the war. He was promoted to brigadier general in 1777 and made a brevet major general in 1783. He died in Marblehead at age 64 in 1797.

James Grant: The Scottish-born major general served as the British commander in New Jersey during the "Ten Crucial Days" until General Cornwallis assumed command in the wake of the American victory at Trenton on December 26, 1776. Grant was probably the most contemptuous of all British generals in his attitude toward the rebels. He saw action in the Philadelphia campaign in 1777 and later commanded a small British force in the West Indies. A member of the British House of Commons before the war, Grant re-entered politics in England afterward but remained in the army until 1805. He died a year later at age 86.

Nathanael Greene: The major general who led one of Washington's two divisions during the "Ten Crucial Days" subsequently became quartermaster general of the Continental Army. He later earned fame as the successful commander of the southern army against General Cornwallis, in which role he was credited with waging a brilliant military campaign against a superior foe. After the Revolution, Greene was awarded liberal grants of money by South Carolina and Georgia and settled on an estate near Savannah in 1785. He died there at age 43 in 1786.

Samuel Griffin: The colonel led the militia raid that diverted Colonel von Donop's Hessian troops away from Bordentown to Mount Holly, New Jersey, and rendered them incapable of assisting their fellow German soldiers in Trenton during the battle there on

December 26, 1776. He returned to his native Virginia after the war. An attorney, Griffin went on to a successful political career as a member of the Virginia Board of War, mayor of Williamsburg, county sheriff, and member of the state House of Delegates and the U.S. House of Representatives. He died at age 64 in 1810.

Alexander Hamilton: The young artillery captain became an aide-de-camp to Washington with the rank of lieutenant-colonel in 1777 and proved to be of inestimable value in his services to the commander-in-chief. He attained battlefield glory by leading the assault on British redoubt number 10 at Yorktown in 1781, then returned to New York City where he practiced law and entered politics. Hamilton supervised and co-authored *The Federalist Papers* with James Madison and John Jay in 1787 in support of the proposed federal constitution. As Washington's secretary of the treasury from 1789 to 1795, he played an essential role in shaping young America's national government and facilitating the development of its capitalist economy, while emerging as the leading spokesperson for the political faction known as the Federalists. He died in New York City in 1804 from a mortal wound sustained in a duel with his bitter political rival, Aaron Burr. At the time of his death, Hamilton was age 49.

Daniel Hitchcock: The colonel led a brigade of Massachusetts and Rhode Island soldiers that turned back a probing attack by the enemy at the Battle of Assunpink Creek. He was a Yale University graduate and had practiced law in Massachusetts and Rhode Island before the war. Hitchcock died in Morristown, New Jersey, only 11 days after the Assunpink battle from a combination of wounds, pneumonia, and possibly tuberculosis. At the time of his death, he was age 37.

William Howe: The British army's commander in North America from 1775 to 1777 returned to England in 1778. In response to criticism of his military leadership, he demanded a parliamentary committee of inquiry in order to vindicate his conduct in America, but the committee of inquiry adjourned without reaching a conclusion. Howe assumed a significant role in supervising the defenses of England against Napoleon Bonaparte's France and served in various governmental positions, including as a member of the Privy Council and as governor of Berwick-upon-Tweed and then Plymouth. He died in Plymouth, England, at age 85 in 1814.

Henry Knox: The Continental Army's artillery commander was promoted to major general in 1782 and succeeded George Washington as the army's commander-in-chief in 1783, serving briefly in that position. Having been at General Washington's side during every battle of the war, Knox became the nation's first secretary of war under President Washington and then retired to his estate in Maine in 1795. He died there at age 56 in 1806 as the result of an infection from a chicken bone that lodged in his throat.

Charles Lee: The major general who was Washington's second in command when captured by the British in December 1776 was returned in a prisoner exchange in the spring of 1778. He led the Continental Army's vanguard against the enemy at the Battle of Monmouth in June 1778, when he was humiliated in a battlefield confrontation with Washington. A court-martial that Lee requested to clear his name found him guilty of insubordination, and he was dismissed from the army in 1780. He lived as a recluse in retirement, first on his Virginia estate and then in Philadelphia, where he died alone in a tavern at age 51 in 1782.

Alexander Leslie: The brigadier general who commanded the British brigade that occupied Princeton when the "Ten Crucial Days" campaign began was stationed in Maidenhead with a reserve force on January 2, 1777, while the main body of Cornwallis's army advanced on Trenton. His nephew, Captain William Leslie, was mortally wounded at the Battle of Princeton the next day. Leslie was promoted to major general in 1782 and continued to serve in the military after the war. He died in Edinburgh, Scotland, at age 63 in 1794.

Charles Mawhood: The colonel led a spirited resistance by outnumbered British troops against Washington's army at the Battle of Princeton on January 3, 1777 and was highly regarded in England afterwards. He served in the Philadelphia campaign of 1777 and subsequently raised a new regiment that fought against the Spanish siege of British-held Gibraltar, where he died at age 50 in 1780 after suffering from a gallstone.

Thomas Mifflin: The general persuaded the soldiers of a New England regiment to remain with the Continental Army when their enlistments expired on December 31, 1776, by offering each a financial bonus for agreeing to serve another six weeks, and thereby inspired Washington to do the same when appealing to other units. Mifflin had been a Philadelphia merchant and politician who served as a delegate to the Continental Congress before joining the army. He rose through the ranks to become a major general but experienced tensions with Washington over Mifflin's handling of his duties as the army's first quartermaster general. After his military service ended, he again served as a delegate to the Continental Congress and subsequently as a delegate to the 1787 Constitutional Convention. He became the first governor of Pennsylvania in 1790 and served for nine years. Mifflin died in Lancaster at age 56 in 1800.

James Monroe: The lieutenant who was wounded at the Battle of Trenton on December 26, 1776 saw further military service and after the war returned to his native Virginia. He went on to enjoy an illustrious political career, becoming a United States senator, governor of Virginia, ambassador to France, secretary of state and war, and finally the fifth president of the United States (1817-1825). He is best known for asserting, in his annual message to Congress in 1823, the "Monroe Doctrine" that declared opposition to European intervention in the Western Hemisphere, which became a cornerstone of American foreign policy. He died in New York City at age 73 in 1831.

Joseph Moulder: The artillery captain whose battery played a critical role in winning the Battle of Princeton died in Philadelphia at age 65 in 1779. A marker was created in 1998 by Chris Wang of Boy Scout Troop 88 of Princeton and erected by the Division of Parks and Forestry in the New Jersey Department of Environmental Protection to identify the spot on the Princeton battlefield where the captain's guns were positioned. It informs the reader that Moulder's "defence was a major factor in the American victory being crucial in buying time for Washington to arrive on the field and organize a counterattack."

Stephen Olney: The Rhode Island captain who fought at the Battle of Assunpink Creek saw further action at the Battle of Monmouth in 1778 and the siege of Yorktown in 1781. Resigning from the army in 1782, he returned to his native North Providence, Rhode Island, and served as president of the North Providence town council and as a member of the Rhode Island General Assembly. Olney died in North Providence at about age 76 in 1832.

Thomas Paine: The English-born author of *Common Sense* and *The American Crisis*, the two pamphlets with an outsized impact on the American Revolution, produced other works after the war that contributed to his reputation as a renowned political propagandist. These included *Rights of Man*, a defense of the French Revolution and republican principles, and *The Age of Reason*, an examination of the role of religion in society. After living in Europe from 1787 to 1802, first in England and then France, Paine returned to America, where he was widely condemned for his views on religion. He died in New York City at age 72 in 1809.

Joseph Reed: The lawyer and colonel who served as the Continental Army's adjutant general during the "Ten Crucial Days" was offered both a position as brigadier general and as chief justice of the Pennsylvania Supreme Court in 1777, but he turned both down because he had been elected to the Continental Congress. In 1778, he was elected president of the Supreme Executive Council of Pennsylvania (equivalent to the position of governor) and in that position oversaw the enactment of a 1780 law providing for the abolition of slavery in Pennsylvania. Reed died in Philadelphia at age 43 in 1785.

John Riker: The physician who saved the life of Lieutenant James Monroe at the Battle of Trenton on December 26, 1776 served as an army guide afterwards. Assigned as a surgeon to a New Jersey Continental regiment, he was captured by a Loyalist regiment near Brunswick, New Jersey, in October 1779 but freed as part of a prisoner exchange shortly afterward. After the war, Riker returned to his native Newtown, New York (Queens County), where he practiced medicine. He died there at age 56 in 1794.

Thomas Rodney: The Delaware militia captain and younger brother of Caesar Rodney, a signer of the Declaration of Independence, fought in the battles of Assunpink Creek and Princeton, and pursued an extended political and judicial career after the war. Rodney's positions included: chief justice of the Kent County Court in Delaware; delegate to the Continental Congress; member and then speaker of the Delaware General Assembly; associate justice of the Delaware Supreme Court; and senior federal judge for the Mississippi Territory. He died in Natchez, Mississippi, at age 66 in 1811.

Benjamin Rush: The Philadelphia physician, professor, and political activist in support of the Revolution was appointed surgeon general of the middle department of the Continental Army in 1777. He later authored Philadelphia newspaper essays in support of the Federal constitution and was elected to the Pennsylvania convention that adopted the constitution. Rush served as treasurer of the U.S. Mint from 1797 to 1813 but also taught and practiced medicine until the end of his life. Perhaps the most celebrated American physician of his time, he died in Philadelphia at age 67 in 1813.

Arthur St. Clair: The Continental Army brigadier general may have been the first officer to suggest to Washington the idea of an overnight march from Trenton to Princeton on January 2-3, 1777. He was promoted to major general in 1777 and later fought in the southern theater. St. Clair left the army in 1783 and became a delegate to the Continental Congress. He served as governor of the Northwest Territory from 1787 to 1802 and, during a brief return to military duty, suffered a severe defeat against Native American tribes at the 1791 Battle of the Wabash. He died in Pennsylvania at age 82 in 1818.

Charles Scott: The colonel who led a Virginia brigade as part of Colonel Hand's delaying action and at the Battle of Assunpink Creek was promoted to brigadier general in 1777 and brevetted to major general in 1783. After the war ended, Scott settled in Kentucky, which was then part of Virginia. He led a Kentucky regiment in battle against Native American tribes and served in the Virginia General Assembly. Kentucky became the 15th state when it was admitted to the Union in 1792, and Scott was elected its fourth governor in 1808. He served for four years and then retired from public life in 1812. He died at his Kentucky plantation at age 74 in 1813.

Adam Stephen: The brigadier general who commanded a Continental Army brigade during the "Ten Crucial Days" was promoted to major general shortly afterward and saw action at the battles of Brandywine and Germantown. His heavy drinking precipitated a court-martial and dismissal from the army in late 1777. He returned to his home in Virginia where he resumed his medical practice, farmed, and engaged in local politics. He died in Virginia at about age 73 in 1791.

John Sullivan: The major general who led one of Washington's two divisions during the "Ten Crucial Days" commanded American troops fighting against the Native American tribes of the Iroquois Confederacy and their Loyalist allies later in the war. After the

218

Revolution, the New Hampshire-born attorney served as attorney general and governor of his state and as a federal district judge. He died in Durham, New Hampshire, at age 54 in 1795.

George Washington: The Commander-in-Chief of the Continental Army resigned his commission when the war ended in 1783 and returned to his estate at Mount Vernon in Virginia, but was later recalled to public service. He presided over the 1787 convention in Philadelphia that adopted the federal constitution and became the first President of the United States in 1789. In that role, he forged the federal government's executive branch, established a set of enduring precedents that would guide his successors—perhaps most importantly creating a tradition of presidential term limits by refusing to serve for a third term—and spearheaded the effort to convert the promise of constitutional democracy into a living reality. Washington retired from public life in 1797, returning once again to Mount Vernon. In what is known as his farewell address to the American people upon leaving the presidency, he exhorted his fellow countrymen to assume a greater sense of national identity in their capacity as citizens of the United States. Washington died at Mount Vernon at age 67 in 1799.

William Washington: The captain and distant cousin of George Washington was wounded at the Battle of Trenton on December 26, 1776 and earned a promotion to major and then colonel. He distinguished himself as a cavalry officer in the southern theater and received a silver medal from Congress, one of only 11 awarded during the war, for his role at the Battle of Cowpens in 1781. After the Revolution, Washington settled in South Carolina and served in the state legislature. He died at age 58 in 1810.

James Wilkinson: The major who fought in all three battles of the "Ten Crucial Days" served as adjutant general to General Horatio Gates in 1777-78. After the war, he settled in Kentucky, was given a lieutenant-colonel's commission in the U.S. Army, and became governor of a portion of the Louisiana Territory in 1805. He engaged in various intrigues, including a furtive attempt to conquer the Mexican provinces of Spain and establish an independent government, but survived a series of courts-martial and congressional investigations. Wilkinson was promoted to major general, but his poor performance as a commander during the War of 1812 brought his military career to an ignoble end. He died in Mexico City at age 68 in 1825.

SOURCE NOTES

1. A CREEK AT THE CROSSROADS

1. This statue of Washington crossing the Delaware River, which is
    north of the South Montgomery Street Bridge over the Assunpink
    Creek, was sculpted in Italy by Mahlon Dickerson Eyre and first
    displayed in 1876 at the Centennial Exposition in Philadelphia,
    the first World's Fair held in the United States. Purchased by the
    City of Trenton in 1889, it was placed in the city's Cadwalader
    Park in 1892 and then moved to its current location in the Mill
    Hill Historic District in connection with the 1976 bicentennial
    celebration. The author is grateful to Richard Hunter, President/
    Principal Archaeologist of Hunter Research, Inc., Trenton, New
    Jersey, and Laura Poll, Archivist in the Trentoniana Room at the
    Trenton Free Public Library, for their assistance in obtaining
    information about the statue. See Al Frazza, *Revolutionary War New
    Jersey: The Ultimate Field Guide to New Jersey's Revolutionary War Historic
    Sites! – Revolutionary War Sites in Trenton, New Jersey.* http://www.
    revolutionarywarnewjersey.com/new_jersey_
    revolutionary_war_sites/towns/trenton_nj_revolutionary_war_
    sites.htm.

2. William M. Dwyer, *The Day Is Ours!: November 1776 - January
    1777: An Inside View of the Battles of Trenton and Princeton.*
    (New York: The Viking Press, 1983), 320.

3. William L. Kidder, *Crossroads of the Revolution: Trenton, 1774-1783.*
    (Lawrence Township, NJ: Knox Press, 2017), 4.

4. In addition to being the capital of New Jersey since 1790, Trenton is
    today the county seat of Mercer County, which was established by
    the New Jersey State Legislature in 1838 by combining parts of
    Burlington, Hunterdon, Middlesex, and Somerset counties. The new
    county was named for General Hugh Mercer of the Continental
    Army, who died from wounds sustained at the Battle of Princeton
    on January 3, 1777.

5. For a comprehensive study of Trenton during the Revolutionary War
    era, see Kidder, *Crossroads of the Revolution: Trenton, 1774-1783.*

6. Arthur S. Lefkowitz, *The Long Retreat: The Calamitous American
    Defense of New Jersey, 1776.* (New Brunswick, NJ: Rutgers University
    Press, 1999), 121-122.

7. Hal Taylor, *The Illustrated Delaware River: The History of a Great
    American River.* (Atglen, PA: Schiffer Publishing Ltd., 2015), 12-13.

8. Ibid., 14.

9. The Province of New Jersey comprised two political divisions, West Jersey and East Jersey, from 1674 to 1702, when they became a single Royal Colony.

10. Richard M. Ketchum, *The Winter Soldiers.* (Garden City, NY: Doubleday & Company, Inc., 1973), 281.

11. J. Roscoe Howell, *The Assunpink Creek, in Pictorial History of Lawrence Township, 1697-1997: A Tricentennial Publication.* (Lawrenceville, NJ: Township of Lawrence, 1997), 15.

12. The name of the mill near the Assunpink Creek bridge in the 1770s was confirmed by Richard Hunter, President/Principal Archaeologist of Hunter Research, Inc., in a personal communication with the author.

13. Rev. Manasseh Cutler, *New Jersey, Pennsylvania and Ohio, in 1787-8: Passages from the Journals of Rev. Manasseh Cutler, Proceedings of the New Jersey Historical Society,* Second Series, 3 (1874), 94.

14. Nadine Sergejeff, Damon Tvaryanas, Ian Burrow, and Richard Hunter, *Chapter 2: Land Use History, in The Assunpink Creek in Mill Hill: A History and Consideration of Historic Interpretive Opportunities.* Trenton Historical Society, December 2002. www.trentonhistory.org/documents/millhillreport.html.

15. Frederick L. Ferris, *Chapter III, The Two Battles of Trenton, in A History of Trenton, 1679-1929: Two Hundred and Fifty Years of a Notable Town with Links in Four Centuries.* Trenton Historical Society, 1929. www.trentonhistory.org/his/battles.html.

16. Ferris (per note number 15 above) writes that the stone bridge built on the Assunpink Creek in 1766 was a single-arched crossing. For concurrence with that description of the bridge, see William S. Stryker, *The Battles of Trenton and Princeton.* (Boston: Houghton, Mifflin and Company, 1898), 263. However, various sources suggest otherwise. A description of the bridge by Rev. Manasseh Cutler from about 1787 (per note number 13 above) refers to a bridge with "arches." Richard Hunter, President/Principal Archaeologist of Hunter Research, Inc., as well as author Larry Kidder (per note number 5 above), in personal communications with the author, opined that the 1766 bridge had two arches. And the former provided visual evidence to suggest this was the case, in particular a detail from a map showing a bridge with two arches (c. 1804, prior to known substantial reconstructive work on the bridge following flood damage in the 1820s and 1840s). See also Graham Turner's visual rendition of the bridge that depicts two arches in David Bonk, *Trenton and Princeton 1776-77: Washington crosses the Delaware.* (New York: Osprey Publishing, 2009), 74-75. That artwork is on the cover of this book.

17. Ketchum, 397.

2. DURHAMS AND ENDURANCE

1. Eric Nelson, *The Royalist Revolution: Monarchy and the American Founding.* (Cambridge, MA: The Belknap Press of Harvard University Press, 2014), 4.

2. Christopher Hibbert, *Redcoats and Rebels: The American Revolution Through British Eyes.* (New York: W. W. Norton & Company, 1990), xviii.

3. Ibid., xviii.

4. Alan Taylor, *American Revolutions: A Continental History, 1750-1804.* (New York: W. W. Norton & Company, 2016), 52.

5. Hibbert, 5-6.

6. Jon Meacham, *Thomas Jefferson: The Art of Power.* (New York: Random House, 2012), 113.

7. Holger Hoock, *Scars of Independence: America's Violent Birth.* (New York: Crown Publishers, 2017), 106.

8. Alan Taylor, 161.

9. Derek W. Beck, *Igniting the American Revolution, 1773-1775.* (Naperville, IL: Sourcebooks, 2015), 77.

10. Hoock, 18.

11. Alan Taylor, 138.

12. Beck, *Igniting the American Revolution, 1773-1775,* 77-78.

13. William Cobbett, *Cobbett's Parliamentary history of England from the Norman Conquest in 1066 to the year 1803, Volume XVIII, AD 1774 to 1777,* in Henry Steele Commager and Richard B. Morris, eds. *The Spirit of 'Seventy-Six: The Story of the American Revolution as Told by Participants.* (New York: Harper & Row, Publishers, 1967), 238.

14. David Price, *Rescuing the Revolution: Unsung Patriot Heroes and the Ten Crucial Days of America's War for Independence.* (Lawrenceville, NJ: Knox Press, 2016), 4-5.

15. Joseph J. Ellis, *Revolutionary Summer: The Birth of American Independence.* (New York: Alfred A. Knopf, 2013), 35.

16. Christopher L. Ward, *The Delaware Continentals, 1776-1783.* (Wilmington, DE: The Historical Society of Delaware, 1941), 19.

17. Ibid., 46.

18. Samuel Stelle Smith, *The Battle of Trenton.* (Monmouth Beach, NJ: Philip Freneau Press, 1965), 5.

19. Ketchum, 209.

20. Nathaniel Philbrick, *Valiant Ambition: George Washington, Benedict Arnold, and the Fate of the American Revolution.* (New York: Viking, 2016), 61.

21. Ketchum, 170.

22. David McCullough, *1776.* (New York: Simon & Schuster, 2005), 251.

23. Christopher L. Ward, 104.

24. Edward G. Lengel, *General George Washington: A Military Life.* (New York: Random House, 2005), 9.

25. David Hackett Fischer, *Washington's Crossing* (New York: Oxford University Press, 2004), 151.

26. Mark Edward Lender, "Introduction," in Lefkowitz, *The Long Retreat,* xxiv.

27. Hibbert, 64-65.

28. Lengel, *General George Washington,* 62.

29. Ibid., 66.

30. Ibid., 78-79.

31. Douglas Southall Freeman, *George Washington: A Biography, Volume Two.* (New York: Charles Scribner's Sons, 1948), 390.

32. Ibid., 392.

33. Willard Sterne Randall, *George Washington: A Life.* (New York: Henry Holt and Company, 1997), 189.

34. Russell Shorto, *Revolution Song: A Story of American Freedom.* (New York: W. W. Norton & Company, 2017), 5.

35. Randall, 190.

36. Don Higginbotham, *George Washington and the American Military Tradition.* (Athens, GA: University of Georgia Press, 1985), 40-41.

37. Lengel, *General George Washington,* 81.

38. Ron Chernow, *Washington: A Life.* (New York: The Penguin Press, 2010), 181.

39. Hoock, 89.

40. Shorto, 5.

41. Fischer, 19-21.

42. Higginbotham, 72.

43. Ibid., 72.

44. Christopher L. Ward, 4.

45. Higginbotham, 51-52.

46. Hoock, 69.

47. Lengel, *General George Washington*, 98.

48. Ketchum, 218.

49. Lengel, 139.

50. Alan Taylor, 169.

51. Maldwyn A. Jones, *Sir William Howe: Conventional Strategist*, in George Athan Billias, ed., *George Washington's Opponents: British Generals and Admirals in the American Revolution*. (New York: William Morrow and Company, Inc., 1969), 64.

52. Ketchum, 224.

53. Christopher L. Ward, 100.

54. Andrew Jackson O'Shaughnessy, *The Men Who Lost America: British Leadership, the American Revolution, and the Fate of the Empire*. (New Haven, CT: Yale University Press, 2013), 252.

55. Enoch Anderson, *Personal Recollections of Captain Enoch Anderson*. (Wilmington, DE: The Historical Society of Delaware, 1896 Reprint: Arno Press, Inc., 1971), 28.

56. Jones, in Billias, ed., *George Washington's Opponents*, 49.

57. William S. Stryker, *The Battles of Trenton and Princeton*. (Boston: Houghton, Mifflin and Company, 1898), 48n2.

58. O'Shaughnessy, 13.

59. James L. Kochan and Don Troiani. *Don Troiani's Soldiers of the American Revolution*. (Guilford, CT: Stackpole Books, 2007), 61.

60. Phillip Papas, *Renegade Revolutionary: The Life of General Charles Lee*. (New York: New York University Press, 2014), 202.

61. Ibid., 203.

62. Christopher L. Ward, 108.

63. Ibid., 109.

64. Ketchum, 243.

65. Christopher L. Ward, 118.

66. Eric Foner, *Tom Paine and Revolutionary America*. (New York: Oxford University Press, 2005), 78.

67. Hibbert, 114.

68. Alan Taylor, 158.

69. Thomas Paine, *Collected Writings*. (New York: The Library of America, 1955), 91.

70. Ibid., 92.

71. Ibid., 96.

72. Fischer, 142.

73. Jones, in Billias, ed., *George Washington's Opponents*, 57.

74. Price, 6-7.

75. Lefkowitz, *The Long Retreat*, 142.

76. Ibid., 143.

77. Fischer, 220.

78. Stryker, 134.

79. William P. Upham, *Memoir of General John Glover, of Marblehead.* (Salem, MA: Charles W. Swasey, 1863), 21.

80. Fischer, 21.

81. John Ferling, *Almost a Miracle: The American Victory in the War of Independence.* (New York: Oxford University Press, 2007), 344.

82. Henry Wiencek, *An Imperfect God: George Washington, His Slaves, and the Creation of America.* (New York: Farrar, Straus and Giroux, 2003), 215.

83. Caroline Cox, *A Proper Sense of Honor: Service and Sacrifice in George Washington's Army.* (Chapel Hill, NC: The University of North Carolina Press, 2004), 17.

84. Fischer, 22.

85. Gordon S. Wood, *Revolutionary Characters: What Made the Founders Different.* (New York: The Penguin Press, 2006), 38.

86. Hibbert, 117.

87. Hoock, 95.

88. Ibid., 397-398.

89. Alan Taylor, 22.

90. Peter Osborne, *No Spot In This Far Land Is More Immortalized: A History of Pennsylvania's Washington Crossing Historic Park.* (Yardley, PA: Yardley Press, 2014), 53.

91. Chernow, *Washington: A Life*, 272.

92. Price, 24.

93. Ibid., 25.

94. William M. Welsch, *Christmas Night 1776: How Did They Cross?*, in *Journal of the American Revolution.* October 16, 2013, Vol. 1, 108: 100-109. www.allthingsliberty.com.

95. Fischer, 228.

96. General Hugh Mercer's Brigade Orders to Colonel John Durkee, December 25, 1776, in Smith, *The Battle of Trenton*, 32.

97. Price, 26-27.

98. Christopher L. Ward, 121.

99. Price, 26.

100. Jacob Francis, *Military Pension Application Narrative, in John C. Dann, ed., The Revolution Remembered: Eyewitness Accounts of the War for Independence.* (Chicago: University of Chicago Press, 1980), 394-395. It is questionable whether Francis actually saw Washington as he described and his narrative was written some 60 years after the event he sought to recall, so a somewhat imprecise memory is to be expected. In any case, his description conveys the sense of entrapment that the Hessian defenders must have felt as they were caught between the Greene and Sullivan divisions attacking them from opposite sides of the town. In addition, because Washington was with the troops in Greene's division as the assault unfolded and Francis was with Sullivan's division, one might interpret Francis's statement as a figurative rather than a literal reference to the commander-in-chief. In other words, he saw the troops in Greene's division advancing under Washington's direction with the enemy positioned between them and Sullivan's men. This interpretation would be consistent with Francis's depiction of the Hessians as being caught "between us and them," with the latter referring to the soldiers in Greene's brigades, in the context of the applicable sentence: "General Washington was at the head of that street coming down towards us and some of the Hessians between us and *them*." (italics added)

101. Ketchum, 310.

102. Hoock, 154.

103. Price, 107-108.

104. Stephen E. Haller, *William Washington: Cavalryman of the Revolution.* (Bowie, MD: Heritage Books, Inc., 2001), 4.

105. Fischer, 406.

106. Ibid., 405.

107. Ferling, *Almost a Miracle*, 178.

108. Marcus Cunliffe, *George Washington: George Washington's Generalship*, in Billias, ed., *George Washington's Generals*, 10.

109. Fischer, 256-257, and Dwyer, 270-271.

110. Fischer, 199.

111. Ibid., 200.

112. Ibid., 200.

113. Dennis Rizzo and Alicia McShulkis. *The Widow Who Saved a Revolution.* December 2012. www.gardenstatelegacy.com.

114. Dwyer, 217.

115. Hoock, 43.

116. Alan Taylor, 200.

117. Lengel, *General George Washington*, 369.

118. Ketchum, 206.

119. Fischer, 253.

120. Shorto, 285.

3. Coming Together

1. Lengel, *General George Washington*, 190.

2. Ibid., 366.

3. Ibid., 176.

4. Ibid., 189.

5. Ketchum, 334.

6. Higginbotham, 76-77.

7. Fischer, 316.

8. Committees of Safety were established throughout the colonies in 1774 to support the Patriot cause in connection with the Continental Association. The latter was created by the first Continental Congress as a vehicle for encouraging the common interests and values endorsed by the congressional delegates. It represented an agreement passed by the Congress under which the colonies undertook to boycott British goods. This non-importation, non-consumption, non-exportation policy was to be enforced by local committees in each colony.

9. Kemble Widmer, *The Christmas Campaign: The Ten Days of Trenton and Princeton* (New Jersey's Revolutionary Experience, No. 22). (Trenton, NJ: New Jersey Historical Commission, 1975), 19.

10. Christopher L. Ward, 133.

11. Fischer, 266.

12. Lefkowitz, *The Long Retreat*, 8.

13. Thomas Fleming, *Liberty! The American Revolution.* (New York: Viking, 1997), 316.

14. Fischer, 153.

15. Jack Kelly, *Band of Giants: The Amateur Soldiers Who Won America's Independence* (New York: Palgrave Macmillan, 2014), 57.

16. North Callahan, *Henry Knox: American Artillerist*, in George Athan Billias, ed., *George Washington's Generals*. (New York: William Morrow and Company, Inc., 1964), 245.

17. Charles P. Whittemore, *John Sullivan: Luckless Irishman*, in Billias, ed., *George Washington's Generals*, 137.

18. Hoock, 275.

19. James Johnston, *Military Pension Application Narrative*, in Dann, 401.

20. Bonk, 64.

21. Kelly, 107.

22. Ketchum, 330.

23. William Burnett, *Military Pension Application Narrative*, in Dann, 372. Washington's life guard was a special unit of soldiers assigned to protect the commander-in-chief and the official papers and money traveling with the Continental Army. The unit was officially designated as "His Excellency's Guard" or the "General's Guard," and its motto was "Conquer or Die."

24. Cox, 38.

25. Ketchum, 332.

26. Ibid., 332.

27. Fischer, 274.

28. Ketchum, 333.

29. Fischer, 274.

30. Ibid., 410.

31. Ketchum, 335.

32. Ibid., 335.

33. Ibid., 337.

34. Fischer, 277-278.

35. Ibid., 278.

36. Ibid., 278.

37. Ibid., 278.

38. Phillip Thomas Tucker, *George Washington's Surprise Attack: A New Look at the Battle That Decided the Fate of America.* (New York: Skyhorse Publishing, 2014), 262.

39. Fred B. Walters, *John Haslet: A Useful One.* (News Horizons Ipub, 2005), vi.

40. Christopher L. Ward, 86.

41. Tucker, 333.

42. Christopher L. Ward, 496.

43. Dwyer, 120.

44. Ketchum, 233.

45. McCullough, 1776, 171.

46. Patrick K. O'Donnell, *Washington's Immortals: The Untold Story of an Elite Regiment Who Changed the Course of the Revolution.* (New York: Atlantic Monthly Press, 2016), 61.

47. Fischer, 95.

48. Tucker, 56.

49. Fischer, 219.

50. John Haslet to Caesar Rodney, January 1, 1777, in Rodney, Caesar, *Letters to and from Caesar Rodney, 1756-1784.* Edited by George Herbert Ryden,(Philadelphia: Historical Society of Delaware, 1933), 152-153.

51. Fischer, 280.

52. The Sons of Liberty were organized groups of colonial protesters that formed in various communities during the agitation over the Stamp Act in 1765 and continued their activities in the period leading up to the war. The term, "Sons of Liberty," was first applied to these political activists by Colonel Isaac Barré during a speech in Parliament against the stamp tax.

53. Fischer, 287.

54. Philbrick, 80.

55. Ibid., 80.

56. O'Shaughnessy, 251.

57. Cox, 42.

58. Ketchum, 216.

59. Hibbert, 149.

60. Hoock, 64-65.

61. O'Shaughnessy, 250-251.

62. Christopher L. Ward, 144.

63. Bonk, 66.

64. Fischer, 292.

65. Ibid., 292.

66. Ibid., 292.

67. Ibid., 291.

68. Ibid., 291.

69. Hugh F. Rankin, *Charles Lord Cornwallis: Study in Frustration,* in George Athan Billias, ed., *George Washington's Opponents,* 222.

70. Ibid., 225.

4. HAND'S HEROICS

1. Bonk, 68.
2. Fischer, 293.
3. Brady J. Crytzer, *Hessians: Mercenaries, Rebels, and the War for British North America.* (Yardley, PA: Westholme Publishing, 2015), 21.
4. Ketchum, 341.
5. Arthur S. Lefkowitz, *Eyewitness Images from the American Revolution.* (Gretna, LA: Pelican Publishing Company, 2017), 135.
6. Christopher L. Ward, 51.
7. Ibid., 52.
8. Kochan, 66.
9. Fischer, 293-294.
10. Samuel Stelle Smith, *The Battle of Princeton.* (Monmouth Beach, NJ: Philip Freneau Press, 1967), 13.
11. Dwyer, 314.
12. Kidder, *Crossroads of the Revolution,* 171.
13. According to most accounts with which the author is familiar, Captain Forrest's battery that fought against the enemy advance to Trenton on January 2, 1777 included two cannons. See Stryker and more recent authors who follow his lead such as Dwyer, Ketchum, and Kidder, although Smith and Fischer write that the battery had six cannons. The circumstances suggest that the smaller number of field pieces is correct since the mobility of Forrest's battery would have been key to its effective operation. The guns were deployed as part of a fighting retreat along a stretch of several miles, requiring the battery crews to maneuver their pieces in an expeditious manner throughout the engagement in order to prevent their capture by the enemy as the American skirmishers withdrew toward Trenton. Moving a half-dozen cannons would have been an unwieldy and perilous undertaking in these circumstances.
14. Fischer, 283.
15. Shorto, 24.
16. Michel Williams Craig, *General Edward Hand: Winter's Doctor* (Lancaster, PA: Rock Ford Plantation, 1984), 1.
17. Richard Reuben Forry, *Edward Hand: His Role in the American Revolution.* (Durham, NC: Duke University Press, 1976), 20.
18. Gordon Wood, *The Radicalism of the American Revolution.* (New York: Alfred A. Knopf), 110.
19. Forry, 53.

20. Ibid., 38.

21. Tucker, 128.

22. Forry, 64.

23. Ketchum, 341.

24. Kochan, 91-92.

25. Forry, 66.

26. Fischer, 23.

27. Lefkowitz, *Eyewitness Images from the American Revolution*, 73.

28. Ferling, *Almost a Miracle*, 89.

29. Derek W. Beck, *The War Before Independence, 1775-1776*. (Naperville, IL: Sourcebooks, 2016), 196.

30. Ibid., 197.

31. Price, 71.

32. Ketchum, 219-221.

33. Richard Brookhiser, *Founding Father: Rediscovering George Washington*. (New York: The Free Press, 1996), 31.

34. Christopher L. Ward, 206.

35. Hoock, 251.

36. Lengel, *General George Washington*, 100.

37. Ketchum, 341.

38. Fischer, 109.

39. Christopher L. Ward, 76.

40. Fischer, 295.

41. Ibid., 295.

42. Forry, 106.

43. Fischer, 296.

44. Ketchum, 341-342.

45. Forry, 112.

46. Fischer, 296.

47. Tucker, 119.

48. Ibid., 93.

49. Edward Hand to Katherine Ewing Hand, December 17, 1777, in *Edward Hand papers* (Collection 261), Historical Society of Pennsylvania.

50. Craig, 12.

51. Ketchum, 219.

52. Denis Hambucken, *Soldier of the American Revolution: A Visual Reference.* (Woodstock, VT: The Countryman Press, 2011), 14.

53. Ketchum, 342.

54. Fischer, 296,

55. Ketchum, 343.

56. Hoock, 252.

57. Lefkowitz, *Eyewitness Images from the American Revolution*, 111.

58. Ketchum, 342.

59. George Athan Billias, *John Burgoyne: Ambitious General*, in Billias, ed., *George Washington's Opponents*, 162-163.

60. Theodore P. Savas and David J. Dameron. *A Guide to the Battles of the American Revolution.* (El Dorado Hills, CA: Savas Beatie, 2013), 88.

61. Forry, 106.

62. Stryker, 259.

63. Ferling, *Almost a Miracle*, 182.

64. Forry, 107.

65. Stryker, 260.

66. Fischer, 297.

67. Ibid., 297.

68. Ibid., 297.

69. Dwyer, 316.

70. Fischer, 298.

71. Ibid., 298.

72. Stryker, 261.

73. Ibid., 260-261.

74. Bonk, 69.

75. Smith, *The Battle of Princeton*, 15.

76. Stryker, 261.

77. Dwyer, 317.

78. Bonk, 69.

79. Fischer, 300.

80. Kidder, *Crossroads of the Revolution*, 175.

81. Hoock, 159.

82. *Reverend John Rosbrugh (1714-1777)*. PCCMP: Presbyterians Caring for Chaplains and Military Personnel.http://pccmp.org/who-we-are/history/reverend-john-rosbrugh-presbyterian-chaplain-1714-1777.

83. Fischer, 300.

84. Stryker, 263.

85. Robert Selig, Matthew Harris, and Wade P. Catts, *Battle of Princeton Mapping Project: Report of Military Terrain Analysis and Battle Narrative. Prepared for the Princeton Battlefield Society.* (West Chester, PA: John Milner Associates, Inc., September 2010), 45.

86. Colonel Nicholas Haussegger to George Washington, 16 January 1777, in *Founders Online*, National Archives, last modified June 13, 2018, http://founders.archives.gov/documents Washington/03-08-02-0087.

87. Fischer, 528n32.

88. Colonel Nicholas Haussegger to George Washington, n3.

89. Kidder, *Crossroads of the Revolution*, 179-180.

90. Ibid., 178.

5. THE DESPERATE HOUR

1. Fischer, 301.

2. Ibid., 301.

3. Dwyer, 319-320.

4. Ibid., 317-318.

5. Smith, *The Battle of Princeton*, 15 and 17.

6. Fischer, 301.

7. Ibid., 153.

8. Tucker, 119.

9. Harry M. Ward, *Charles Scott and the Spirit of '76.* (Charlottesville, VA: University of Virginia Press, 1988), 1.

10. Dwyer, 320.

11. Fischer, 305.

12. Kidder, *Crossroads of the Revolution*, 178.

13. Price, 88.

14. Fischer, 303.

15. Hambucken, 14.

16. Higginbotham, 59.

17. William L. Kidder, *A People Harassed and Exhausted: The Story of a New Jersey Militia Regiment in the American Revolution.* (CreateSpace, 2013), 12.

18. Kidder, *Crossroads of the Revolution*, 176.

19. Fischer, 303.

20. Dwyer, 321.

21. Fischer, 303.

22. Ibid., 301.

23. Dwyer, 324.

24. Henry Knox to Lucy Flucker Knox, January 7, 1777, in Stryker, 450.

25. Callahan, in Billias, ed., *George Washington's Generals*, 247.

26. Ibid., 242.

27. Kelly, 57.

28. Lefkowitz, *The Long Retreat*, 95.

29. Shorto, 330.

30. Fischer, 217.

31. Ibid., 33.

32. Cox, 55.

33. Ibid., 57.

34. Ibid., 58.

35. Hoock, 252.

36. Ketchum, 221.

37. Dwyer, 319.

38. Fischer, 303.

39. Ibid., 303.

40. Ibid., 303.

41. Ibid., 304.

42. Kidder, *Crossroads of the Revolution*, 190.

43. Thomas Rodney and Caesar A. Rodney. *Diary of Captain Thomas Rodney, 1776-1777.* (Wilmington, DE: The Historical Society of Delaware, 1888. Reprint: Kessinger Publishing, LLC), 31.

44. Fischer, 304.

45. Ferris.

46. Fischer, 305.

47. Ibid., 301

48. Ibid., 305.

49. Stryker, 266.

50. Fischer, 305.

51. Kidder, *Crossroads of the Revolution*, 120-121.

52. Fischer, 305.

53. Bonk, 73.

54. Fischer, 305.

55. Bonk, 73.

56. Lefkowitz, *Eyewitness Images from the American Revolution*, 25.

57. O'Donnell, 42.

58. Fischer, 50.

59. Ibid., 306.

60. Dwyer, 323-324.

61. Fischer, 306-307.

62. William Hutchinson, *Military Pension Application Narrative*, in Dann, 146.

63. *Diary of Captain Thomas Rodney*, 31.

64. Dwyer, 324.

65. Ibid., 324-325.

66. Kidder, *Crossroads of the Revolution*, 181-182.

67. Introduction by Caesar A. Rodney, in *Diary of Captain Thomas Rodney*, 5.

68. Stryker, 268.

69. Ibid., 268.

70. Ibid., 268.

71. William P. McMichael, *Diary of Lieutenant James McMichael, of the Pennsylvania Line, 1776-1778*, in *The Pennsylvania Magazine of History and Biography. XVI:2* (1892), 140.

72. Stryker, 268.

73. Henry Knox to Lucy Flucker Knox, January 7, 1777, in Stryker, 450.

74. Fischer, 307.

75. Ibid., 412.

76. Ketchum, 343.

77. Ferris.

78. Ibid.

79. Ibid.

80. Fischer, 307.

81. Ketchum, 177.

82. Philbrick, 82.

83. Mark Maloy, *Victory or Death: The Battles of Trenton and Princeton: December 25, 1776-January 3, 1777.* (El Dorado Hills, CA: Savas Beatie LLC, 2018), 97.

6. The Great Escape

1. Ketchum, 221-222.
2. Cox, 156.
3. Fischer, 309.
4. Ibid., 309.
5. O'Shaughnessy, 251.
6. Hibbert, 149.
7. Fischer, 313.
8. Ibid., 313.
9. Hibbert, 150.
10. Ketchum, 344.
11. Fischer, 313.
12. Ketchum, 344.
13. Rankin, in Billias, ed., *George Washington's Opponents*, 196-197.
14. Fischer, 310.
15. Kidder, *Crossroads of the Revolution*, 184.
16. Stryker, 269.
17. Fischer, 313.
18. Ibid., 313.
19. Ibid., 313.
20. Ibid., 313.
21. Ibid., 314.
22. Ibid., 314.
23. Ibid., 314.
24. Ibid., 315.
25. Ibid., 315.
26. Kidder, *Crossroads of the Revolution*, 185.
27. Fischer, 315.
28. Ibid., 316.
29. Ibid., 318.

30. Stryker, 275.

31. *Diary of Captain Thomas Rodney*, 32.

32. George F. Scheer and Hugh F. Rankin, *Rebels and Redcoats: The American Revolution Though the Eyes of Those Who Fought and Lived It.* (New York: Da Capo Press, 1957), 217.

33. *Diary of Captain Thomas Rodney*, 33.

34. Fischer, 322-323.

35. Fleming, 223.

36. Ketchum, 344-345.

37. Fischer, 317.

38. Ketchum, 345.

39. Fischer, 95.

40. Ketchum, 345.

7. FURY ON FROZEN GROUND

1. Fischer, 401.

2. Ibid., 326-327.

3. Hoock, 160.

4. Fischer, 332.

5. Ibid., 329.

6. Ibid., 334.

7. Stryker, 284.

8. Lefkowitz, *Eyewitness Images from the American Revolution*, 149.

9. *Diary of Captain Thomas Rodney*, 35-36.

10. Ketchum, 361.

11. Christopher L. Ward, 150.

12. Ketchum, 360.

13. Ibid., 361.

14. Lefkowitz, *Eyewitness Images from the American Revolution*, 150.

15. Fischer, 334. For a contrary perspective, see Maloy, 55. He contends that while most accounts of the battles at Trenton and Princeton describe Washington as riding a white horse, he probably rode his dark gray horse, Blueskin, during those engagements. His other primary mount, Nelson, was a white horse.

16. Hibbert, 150.

17. Fischer, 336.

18. Mark Puls, *Henry Knox: Visionary General of the American Revolution*. (New York: St. Martin's Press, 2008), 83.

19. Ron Chernow, *Alexander Hamilton: A Life*. (New York: The Penguin Press, 2004), 85.

20. Ketchum, 376.

21. Paine, 157-158.

22. Price, 112.

23. Fischer, 327.

24. Scheer, 218.

25. Hoock, 155.

26. Walters, 7.

27. Fischer, 336-339.

28. Ibid., 340.

29. Christopher L. Ward, 153.

30. Selig, 7.

31. Lefkowitz, *The Long Retreat*, 70.

32. Dave Richard Palmer, *The Way of the Fox: American Strategy in the War for America, 1775-1783*. (Westport, CT: Greenwood Press, 1975), 134.

33. Ketchum, 379.

34. Fischer, 367.

35. Price, 10.

36. Palmer, 134.

37. Chernow, *Washington: A Life*, 283.

38. Samuel DeForest, *Military Pension Application Narrative*, in Dann, 47.

39. David McCullough, *John Adams*. (New York: Simon & Schuster, 2001), 168.

40. Kidder, *Crossroads of the Revolution*, 329.

41. Bart McDowell, *The Revolutionary War*. (Washington, DC: National Geographic Society, 1967), 109.

42. Robert Middlekauff, *Washington's Revolution: The Making of America's First Leader*. (New York: Alfred A. Knopf, 2015), 139.

43. Larrie D. Ferreiro, *Brothers at Arms: American Independence and the Men of France and Spain Who Saved It*. (New York: Vintage Books, 2017), 69.

44. James Thomas Flexner, *Washington: The Indispensable Man*. (Boston:

Little, Brown and Company, 1974), 98.

45. Ketchum, 382-383.

46. William Harcourt to Simon Harcourt (the 1st Earl Harcourt), March 17, 1777, in Commager, 524.

47. Ketchum, 385.

48. Lengel, *General George Washington*, 242.

8. THE ROAD FROM ASSUNPINK CREEK

1. Robert Middlekauff, *The Glorious Cause: The American Revolution, 1763-1789*. (New York: Oxford University Press, 2005), 302.

2. Lengel, *General George Washington*, 307.

3. See chapter 25 in Ferling, *Almost a Miracle*, pp. 562-575, and the Conclusion in O'Shaughnessy, pp. 353-361.

4. Price, 119.

5. Ketchum, 224-225.

6. Lengel, *General George Washington*, 97.

7. Ketchum, 223.

8. Hibbert, 335.

9. Hoock, 15.

10. Ellis, *Revolutionary Summer*, 178.

11. Nick Bunker, *An Empire on the Edge: How Britain Came to Fight America*. (New York: Alfred A. Knopf, 2014), 12.

12. Hoock, 17.

13. Ferling, *Almost a Miracle*, 558.

14. Hoock, 17.

15. Ferling, *Almost a Miracle*, 559.

16. Hoock, 134.

17. Ibid., 12.

18. Alan Taylor, 4.

19. Ibid., 479.

20. Wood, *The Radicalism of the American Revolution*, 6-7.

21. Shorto, 438.

22. Charles Krauthammer, *Things That Matter: Three Decades of Passions, Pastimes and Politics*. (New York, Crown Forum, 2013), 4.

23. Paine, 147.

24. Richard M. Strum, *Causes of the American Revolution*. (Stockton, NJ: Ottn Publishing, 2005), 54-55.

25. Ellis, *Founding Brothers: The Revolutionary Generation*. (New York: Alfred A. Knopf, 2003), 5.

26. Paine, 5.

27. Edward G. Lengel, *Inventing George Washington: America's Founder, in Myth and Memory*. (New York: Harper, 2011), 211.

28. Lengel, *General George Washington*, 371.

29. John Ferling, *The Ascent of George Washington: The Hidden Political Genius of an American Icon*. (New York: Bloomsbury Press, 2009), 369.

30. Middlekauff, *Washington's Revolution*, 305-306.

31. Ibid., 304.

32. Ketchum, 395.

33. Lengel, *General George Washington*, 371.

34. William M. Fowler, Jr., *American Crisis: George Washington and the Dangerous Two Years After Yorktown, 1781-1783*. (New York: Walker & Company, 2011), 225.

35. Cunliffe, 17.

36. Barbara W. Tuchman, *The First Salute*. (New York: Alfred A. Knopf, 1988), 284.

37. Chernow, 561-562.

38. The Currier & Ives lithograph is entitled: *Washington's reception by the ladies, on passing the bridge at Trenton, N.J. April 1789, on his way to New York to be inaugurated first president of the United States.* The wording displayed on the arch—*The defender of the mothers will be the protector of the daughters*—also appears in a c.1929 illustration of this scene by Trenton artist George Bradshaw for the Trenton Historical Society. Another image of this event, a 1930 N.C. Wyeth mural entitled *Reception To Washington on April 21, 1789, at Trenton on his way to New York to Assume the Duties of the Presidency of the United States*, depicts the floral arch bearing two dates—"Dec. 26, 1777" and "Jan. 2, 1777"—instead of the one date, "Battle of Trenton Dec. 26th, 1776," shown in the lithograph, and with a modest difference in the wording displayed on the arch: *The defender of the mothers will also protect the daughters.*

39. Alan Taylor, 199.

40. Cox, 240-241.

41. Cunliffe, 15.

42. Price, 120.

43. Ketchum, 341.

44. Craig, 95.

45. This was a type of military commission used at the time of the Revolution as a way to reward an officer for meritorious service by promoting him to a higher rank without providing the corresponding pay or full authority associated with that rank. It was often granted as an honor immediately before an officer's retirement from the army.

46. Craig, 105

47. Sean Heuvel, *Washington's Adjutant: General Hand and His Contributions to the American Revolution.* Unpublished booklet. (Lancaster, PA: Rock Ford Plantation, n.d.), 14.

48. Ketchum, 341.

49. The Allied Expeditionary Force included a smattering of Free French, Poles, Norwegians, and other nationalities in addition to the American, British, and Canadian troops. See Stephen E. Ambrose, *D-Day, June 6, 1944: The Climactic Battle of World War II.* (New York: Simon & Schuster, 1994), 20.

50. Ibid., 583.

9. GATHERING LAURELS

1. Lengel, *General George Washington*, 78.

2. Flexner, 36.

3. Lengel, *General George Washington*, 370.

4. O'Shaughnessy, 251.

5. Rankin, in Billias, ed., *George Washington's Opponents*, 195.

6. Ibid., 212.

7. Fischer, 362.

8. Ibid., 429-430.

9. Paul Staiti, *Of Arms and Artists: The American Revolution through Painters' Eyes.* (New York: Bloomsbury Press, 2016), 224.

10. Rankin, in Billias, ed., *George Washington's Opponents*, 193.

11. Ketchum, 297.

12. William Shakespeare, *The Tragedy of Romeo and Juliet.* Barbara Mowat and Paul Werstine, eds., (Washington: Folger Shakespeare Library, n.d.), III. 1. 100-101.www.folgerdigitaltexts.org/html/Rom.html.

BIBLIOGRAPHY

PRIMARY SOURCE DOCUMENTS

Anderson, Enoch. *Personal Recollections of Captain Enoch Anderson.* Wilmington, DE: The Historical Society of Delaware, 1896. Reprint: Arno Press, Inc., 1971.

Cadwalader Family Papers. The Historical Society of Pennsylvania, 2007. http://hsp.org/sites/default/files/legacy_files/migrated/findingaid1454cadwaladerpart1.pdf.

Commager, Henry Steele, and Richard B. Morris, eds. *The Spirit of 'Seventy-Six: The Story of the American Revolution as Told by Participants.* New York: Harper & Row, Publishers, 1967.

Cutler, Rev. Manasseh. *New Jersey, Pennsylvania and Ohio, in 1787-8: Passages from the Journals of Rev. Manasseh Cutler.* Proceedings of the New Jersey Historical Society, Second Series, 3 (1874).

Dann, John C., ed. *The Revolution Remembered: Eyewitness Accounts of the War for Independence.* Chicago: University of Chicago Press, 1980.

Edward Hand papers. Historical Society of Pennsylvania. www.hsp.org.

McMichael, William P. *Diary of Lieutenant James McMichael, of the Pennsylvania Line, 1776-1778,* in *The Pennsylvania Magazine of History and Biography,* XVI:2, 1892.

Paine, Thomas. *Collected Writings.* New York: The Library of America, 1955.

Rodney, Caesar, and George Herbert Ryden, ed. *Letters to and from Caesar Rodney, 1756-1784.* Philadelphia: Historical Society of Delaware, 1933.

Rodney, Thomas, and Caesar A. Rodney. *Diary of Captain Thomas Rodney, 1776-1777.* Wilmington, DE: The Historical Society of Delaware, 1888. Reprint: Kessinger Publishing, LLC.

Scheer, George F., and Hugh F. Rankin. *Rebels and Redcoats: The American Revolution Though the Eyes of Those Who Fought and Lived It.* New York: Da Capo Press, 1957.

The Captain Johann von Ewald Diaries: Maps of the Revolutionary War. https://library.bloomu.edu/Archives/Maps/mapindex.htm.

BOOKS

Ambrose, Stephen E. *D-Day, June 6, 1944: The Climactic Battle of World War II*. New York: Simon & Schuster, 1994.

Beck, Derek W. *Igniting the American Revolution, 1773-1775*. Naperville, IL: Sourcebooks, 2015.

————, *The War Before Independence, 1775-1776*. Naperville, IL: Sourcebooks, 2016.

Billias, George Athan, ed. *George Washington's Generals*. New York: William Morrow and Company, Inc., 1964.

————. *George Washington's Opponents: British Generals and Admirals in the American Revolution*. New York: William Morrow and Company, Inc., 1969.

Bonk, David. *Trenton and Princeton 1776-77: Washington crosses the Delaware*. New York: Osprey Publishing, 2009.

Brookhiser, Richard. *Founding Father: Rediscovering George Washington*. New York: The Free Press, 1996.

Bunker, Nick. *An Empire on the Edge: How Britain Came to Fight America*. New York: Alfred A. Knopf, 2014.

Chernow, Ron. *Alexander Hamilton*. New York: The Penguin Press, 2004.

————. *Washington: A Life*. New York: The Penguin Press, 2010.

Cox, Caroline. *A Proper Sense of Honor: Service and Sacrifice in George Washington's Army*. Chapel Hill, NC: The University of North Carolina Press, 2004.

Craig, Michel Williams. *General Edward Hand: Winter's Doctor*. Lancaster, PA: Rock Ford Plantation, 1984.

Crytzer, Brady J. *Hessians: Mercenaries, Rebels, and the War for British North America*. Yardley, PA: Westholme Publishing, 2015.

Dwyer, William M. *The Day Is Ours!: November 1776 - January 1777: An Inside View of the Battles of Trenton and Princeton*. New York: The Viking Press, 1983.

Ellis, Joseph J. *Founding Brothers: The Revolutionary Generation*. New York: Alfred A. Knopf, 2003.

————. *Revolutionary Summer: The Birth of American Independence*. New York: Alfred A. Knopf, 2013.

Bibliography

Ferling, John. *Almost a Miracle: The American Victory in the War of Independence*. New York: Oxford University Press, 2007.

———. *The Ascent of George Washington: The Hidden Political Genius of an American Icon* New York: Bloomsbury Press, 2009.

———. *Whirlwind: The American Revolution and the War That Won It*. New York: Bloomsbury Press, 2015

Ferreiro, Larrie D. *Brothers at Arms: American Independence and the Men of France and Spain Who Saved It*. New York: Vintage Books, 2017.

Fischer, David Hackett. *Washington's Crossing*. New York: Oxford University Press, 2004.

Fleming, Thomas. *Liberty! The American Revolution*. New York: Viking, 1997.

Flexner, James Thomas. *Washington: The Indispensable Man*. Boston: Little, Brown and Company, 1974.

Foner, Eric. *Tom Paine and Revolutionary America*. New York: Oxford University Press, 2005.

Forry, Richard Reuben. *Edward Hand: His Role in the American Revolution*. Durham, NC: Duke University Press, 1976.

Fowler, William M., Jr. *American Crisis: George Washington and the Dangerous Two Years After Yorktown, 1781-1783*. New York: Walker & Company, 2011.

Freeman, Douglas Southall. *George Washington: A Biography, Volume Two*. New York: Charles Scribner's Sons, 1948.

Haller, Stephen E. *William Washington: Cavalryman of the Revolution*. Bowie, MD: Heritage Books, Inc., 2001.

Hambucken, Denis. *Soldier of the American Revolution: A Visual Reference*. Woodstock, VT: The Countryman Press, 2011.

Hibbert, Christopher. *Redcoats and Rebels: The American Revolution Through British Eyes*. New York: W. W. Norton & Company, 1990.

Higginbotham, Don. *George Washington and the American Military Tradition*. Athens, GA: University of Georgia Press, 1985.

Hoock, Holger. *Scars of Independence: America's Violent Birth*. New York: Crown Publishers, 2017.

Howell, J. Roscoe. *The Assunpink Creek, in Pictorial History of Lawrence Township, 1697-1997: A Tricentennial Publication*. Lawrenceville, NJ: Township of Lawrence, 1997.

Kelly, Jack. *Band of Giants: The Amateur Soldiers Who Won America's Independence.* New York: Palgrave Macmillan, 2014.

Ketchum, Richard M. *The Winter Soldiers.* Garden City, NY: Doubleday & Company, Inc., 1973.

Kidder, William L. *A People Harassed and Exhausted: The Story of a New Jersey Militia Regiment in the American Revolution.* CreateSpace, 2013.

————. *Crossroads of the Revolution: Trenton, 1774-1783.* Lawrence Township, NJ: Knox Press, 2017.

Kochan, James L., and Don Troiani. *Don Troiani's Soldiers of the American Revolution.* Guilford, CT: Stackpole Books, 2007.

Krauthammer, Charles. *Things That Matter: Three Decades of Passions, Pastimes and Politics.* New York: Crown Forum, 2013.

Lefkowitz, Arthur S. *Eyewitness Images from the American Revolution.* Gretna, LA: Pelican Publishing Company, 2017.

————. *The Long Retreat: The Calamitous Defense of New Jersey, 1776.* New Brunswick, NJ: Rutgers University Press, 1999.

Lengel, Edward G. *General George Washington: A Military Life.* New York: Random House, 2005.

————. *Inventing George Washington: America's Founder, in Myth and Memory.* New York: Harper, 2011.

Maloy, Mark. *Victory or Death: The Battles of Trenton and Princeton: December 25, 1776-January 3, 1777.* El Dorado Hills, CA: Savas Beatie LLC, 2018.

Marshall, Jeffrey L. *Early History of Upper Makefield Township, Bucks Co., PA.* Upper Makefield, PA: Upper Makefield Historical Society, 1990.

McCullough, David. *John Adams.* New York: Simon & Schuster, 2001.

————. *1776.* New York: Simon & Schuster, 2005.

McDowell, Bart. *The Revolutionary War.* Washington, DC: National Geographic Society, 1967.

Meacham, Jon. *Thomas Jefferson: The Art of Power.* New York: Random House, 2012.

Middlekauff, Robert. *The Glorious Cause: The American Revolution, 1763-1789.* New York: Oxford University Press, 2005.

————. *Washington's Revolution: The Making of America's First Leader.* New York: Alfred A. Knopf, 2015.

Bibliography

Nelson, Eric. *The Royalist Revolution: Monarchy and the American Founding*. Cambridge, MA: The Belknap Press of Harvard University Press, 2014.

O'Donnell, Patrick K. *Washington's Immortals: The Untold Story of an Elite Regiment Who Changed the Course of the Revolution*. New York: Atlantic Monthly Press, 2016.

Osborne, Peter. *No Spot In This Far Land Is More Immortalized: A History of Pennsylvania's Washington Crossing Historic Park*. Yardley, PA: Yardley Press, 2014.

O'Shaughnessy, Andrew Jackson. *The Men Who Lost America: British Leadership, the American Revolution, and the Fate of the Empire*. New Haven, CT: Yale University Press, 2013.

Palmer, Dave Richard. *The Way of the Fox: American Strategy in the War for America, 1775-1783*. Westport, CT: Greenwood Press, 1975.

Pappas, Phillip. *Renegade Revolutionary: The Life of General Charles Lee*. New York: New York University Press, 2014.

Philbrick, Nathaniel. *Valiant Ambition: George Washington, Benedict Arnold, and the Fate of the American Revolution*. New York: Viking, 2016.

Price, David. *Rescuing the Revolution: Unsung Patriot Heroes and the Ten Crucial Days of America's War for Independence*. Lawrenceville, NJ: Knox Press, 2016.

Puls, Mark. *Henry Knox: Visionary General of the American Revolution*. New York: St. Martin's Press, 2008.

Randall, Willard Sterne. *George Washington: A Life*. New York: Henry Holt and Company, 1997.

Savas, Theodore P., and J. David Dameron. *A Guide to the Battles of the American Revolution*. El Dorado Hills, CA: Savas Beatie, 2013.

Shorto, Russell. *Revolution Song: A Story of American Freedom*. New York: W. W. Norton & Company, 2017.

Smith, Samuel Stelle. *The Battle of Trenton*. Monmouth Beach, NJ: Philip Freneau Press, 1965.

————. *The Battle of Princeton*. Monmouth Beach, NJ: Philip Freneau Press, 1967.

Staiti, Paul. *Of Arms and Artists: The American Revolution through Painters' Eyes*. New York: Bloomsbury Press, 2016.

Strum, Richard M. *Causes of the American Revolution*. Stockton, NJ: Ottn Publishing, 2005.

Stryker, William S. *The Battles of Trenton and Princeton*. Boston: Houghton, Mifflin and Company, 1898.

Taylor, Alan. *American Revolutions: A Continental History, 1750-1804*. New York: W. W. Norton & Company, 2016.

Taylor, Hal. *The Illustrated Delaware River: The History of a Great American River*. Atglen, PA: Schiffer Publishing Ltd., 2015.

Tuchman, Barbara W. *The First Salute*. New York: Alfred A. Knopf, 1988.

Tucker, Phillip Thomas. *George Washington's Surprise Attack: A New Look at the Battle That Decided the Fate of America*. New York: Skyhorse Publishing, 2014.

Upham, William P. *Memoir of General John Glover, of Marblehead*. Salem, MA: Charles W. Swasey, 1863.

Walters, Fred B. *John Haslet: A Useful One*. News Horizons Ipub, 2005.

Ward, Christopher L. *The Delaware Continentals, 1776-1783*. Wilmington, DE: The Historical Society of Delaware, 1941.

Ward, Harry M. *Charles Scott and the Spirit of '76*. Charlottesville, VA: University of Virginia Press, 1988.

Wiencek, Henry. *An Imperfect God: George Washington, His Slaves, and the Creation of America*. New York: Farrar, Straus and Giroux, 2003.

Wood, Gordon S. *Revolutionary Characters: What Made the Founders Different*. New York: The Penguin Press, 2006.

————. *The Radicalism of the American Revolution*. New York: Alfred A. Knopf, 1992.

PAMPHLETS, PERIODICALS, AND REPORTS

Glickstein, Don. *How General Leslie Really Died*, in *Journal of the American Revolution*, October 11, 2013. https://allthingsliberty.com/2013/10/general-leslie-really-died/.

Schenawolf, Harry. *British General James Grant. Revolutionary War Journal*. October 19, 2013. www.revolutionarywarjournal.com/general-james-grant.

Selig, Robert, and Matthew Harris, and Wade P. Catts. *Battle of Princeton Mapping Project: Report of Military Terrain Analysis and Battle Narrative*. Prepared for the Princeton Battlefield Society. West Chester, PA: John Milner Associates, Inc., September 2010.

Bibliography

Welsch, William M. *Christmas Night 1776: How Did They Cross?*, in *Journal of the American Revolution*, October 16, 2013, Vol.1, 108: 100-109. https://allthingsliberty.com/2013/10/christmas-night-1776-cross/.

Widmer, Kemble. *The Christmas Campaign: The Ten Days of Trenton and Princeton (New Jersey's Revolutionary Experience, No. 22)*. Trenton, NJ: New Jersey Historical Commission, 1975.

OTHER ONLINE SOURCES

Brigadier General Edward Hand. National Park Service: Yorktown Battlefield. www.nps.gov.

Captain Stephen Olney House. www.preservationri.gov/pdfs_zips_downloads/national_pdfs/north_providence/nopr_smithfield-road-138_capt-stephen-olney-house.pdf.

Charles Cornwallis, 1st Marquess and 2nd Earl Cornwallis. Encyclopædia Britannica.https://www.britannica.com/biography/Charles-Cornwallis-1st-Marquess-and-2nd-Earl-Cornwallis.

Charles Lee. United States History. http://www.u-s-history.com/pages/h1117.html.

Charles Mawhood. Civil War Trust. https://www.civilwar.org/learn/biographies/charles-mawhood.

Col Carl Emil Kirk Von Donop. Find A Grave. June 20, 2005. https://www.findagrave.com/cgi-binfg.cgi?page=gr&GRid=11207429.

Col Daniel Hitchcock. Find A Grave. May 8, 2014. https://www.findagrave.com/cgi-bin/fg.cgi?page=gr&GRid=129412272.

Fermoy, Matthias Alexis de Roche. Encyclopedia of the American Revolution: Library of Military History. http://www.encyclopedia.com/history/encyclopedias-almanacs-transcripts-and-maps/fermoy-matthias-alexis-de-roche.

Ferris, Frederick L. *Chapter III, The Two Battles of Trenton*, in *A History of Trenton, 1679-1929: Two Hundred and Fifty Years of a Notable Town with Links in Four Centuries*. Trenton Historical Society, 1929. www.trentonhistory.org/his/battles.html.

5th Virginia Regiment (Revolutionary War). www.familysearch.org.

Foner, Philip S. *Thomas Paine, British-American Author*. Encyclopædia Britannica.https://www.britannica.com/biography/Thomas-Paine.

Fore, Samuel K. *Adam Stephen*. George Washington's Mount Vernon: George Washington Digital Encyclopedia. www.mountvernon.org/ digital-encyclopedia/article/adam-stephen.

—————. *William Washington*. George Washington's Mount Vernon: George Washington Digital Encyclopedia. http://www. mountvernon.org/digital-encyclopedia/article/william-washington.

Founders Online, National Archives, last modified June 13, 2018, http://founders.archives.gov/documents/Washington/ 03-08-02-0087.

Frazza, Al. *Revolutionary War New Jersey: The Ultimate Field Guide to New Jersey's Revolutionary War Historic Sites! – Revolutionary War Sites in Trenton, New Jersey*. http://www.revolutionarywarnewjersey.com/new_ jersey_revolutionary_war_sites/ towns/trenton_nj_revolutionary_ war_sites.htm .

General Charles Scott. www.rootsweb.ancestry.com.

General Sir William Erskine of Torrie, later Bt.1728-95. www.silverwhistle. co.uk/lobsters/erskine.html.

Hanson, Ashley. *John Cadwalader*. George Washington's Mount Vernon: George Washington Digital Encyclopedia. http://www.mountvernon.org/digital-encyclopedia/article/ john-cadwalader.

James Wilkinson, United States Military Officer. Encyclopædia Britannica. https://www.britannica.com/biography/James-Wilkinson.

John Sullivan, American Politician and Officer. Encyclopædia Britannica. https://www.britannica.com/biography/John-Sullivan-American-politician-and-office.

Johnson, Jared D. *Thomas Mifflin*. George Washington's Mount Vernon: George Washington Digital Encyclopedia. www.mountvernon.org/ digital-encyclopedia/article/thomas-mifflin.

Kentucky Governor Charles Scott. Governors/Former Governors' Bios, National Governors Association. www.nga.org.

Major General Arthur St. Clair. National Museum of the United States Army. January 27, 2015. https://armyhistory.org/major-general-arthur-st-clair.

McIntyre, James. *William Alexander, Lord Stirling*. George Washington's Mount Vernon: George Washington Digital Encyclopedia. http:// www.mountvernon.org/digital-encyclopedia/article/william-alexander-lord-stirling.

Bibliography

Nathanael Greene, United States General. Encyclopædia Britannica. https://www.britannica.com/biography/Nathanael-Greene.

Pavao, Esther. *Joseph Reed.* www.revolutionary-war.net/joseph-reed.html.

Reverend John Rosbrugh (1714-1777). PCCMP: Presbyterians Caring for Chaplains and Military Personnel. http://pccmp.org/who-we-are/history/reverend-john-rosbrugh-presbyterian-chaplain-1714-1777.

Rizzo, Dennis, and Alicia McShulkis. *The Widow Who Saved a Revolution.* December 2012. www.gardenstatelegacy.com.

Rodney, Thomas (1744-1811). Biographical Directory of the United States Congress. http://bioguide.congress.gov/scripts/biodisplay. pl?index=R000380.

Sergejeff, Nadine, and Damon Tvaryanas, Ian Burrow, and Richard Hunter. *The Assunpink Creek in Mill Hill: A History and Consideration of Historic Interpretive Opportunities.* Trenton Historical Society, December 2002. www.trentonhistory.org/documents/millhillreport.html.

Shakespeare, William. *The Tragedy of Romeo and Juliet.* ed. Barbara Mowat, and Paul Werstine. Folger Shakespeare Library. www. folgerdigitaltexts.org/html/Rom.html.

Signers of the Declaration of Independence. Benjamin Rush, 1745-1813. http://www.ushistory.org/declaration/signers/rush.html.

Some of Trenton's History. City of Trenton, NJ, 2010. www.trentonnj.org/Cit-e-Access/webpage.cfm?TID=55&TPID=5612.

Note: All websites listed above were accessed during the period from January 2017 through July 2018.

UNPUBLISHED SOURCES

Bereiter, Gregory D., *Campaigning in America: Captain Johann Ewald's Hessians in the American Revolution.* April 24, 2001. Honors Project, Illinois Wesleyan University. Paper 20. http://digitalcommons.iwu.edu/history_honproj/20.

Gallagher, Kim. *Princeton Battlefield Society Notes for Battlefield Park Tour.* April 15, 2017.

Heuvel, Sean M. *Washington's Adjutant: General Hand and His Contributions to the American Revolution.* Unpublished booklet. Lancaster, PA: Rock Ford Plantation (n.d.).

The Princeton Battlefield: Come Home to Your American Revolution. Unpublished brochure. Princeton, NJ: The Princeton Battlefield Society (n.d.).

64th Annual Reenactment of Washington Crossing the Delaware River: December 11 & 25, 2016. 2016 Program Book. Washington Crossing, PA: Washington Crossing Historic Park. Pennsylvania Department of Conservation and Natural Resources and the Friends of Washington Crossing Park.

The 56th Annual Colonel Hand Historic March: Reenactment of the Delaying Tactics of Colonel Edward Hand and his Pennsylvania Riflemen on January 2, 1777. Lawrence Township, NJ. 2017 Program Booklet. January 13, 2018.

ACKNOWLEDGMENTS

Although I am a historical interpreter at Pennsylvania's Washington Crossing Historic Park (WCHP) and conduct guided tours there on behalf of the Friends of Washington Crossing Park (FWCP), I am speaking in these pages for myself only. The views expressed in this work are mine exclusively, except where they are specifically attributed to another author or historical account. While gratefully acknowledging the assistance of others in connection with this work, I must—for better or worse—accept sole responsibility for its content.

During my time at WCHP, I have come to know many volunteers and staff with the FWCP and to appreciate their knowledge, dedication, and eagerness to share information about the "Ten Crucial Days" and other aspects of the American Revolution and life in early America. I am indebted to all these persons and particularly to a fellow historical interpreter, Judi Biederman, for reviewing and commenting on a draft of this work. Judi, who is currently Regent of the Washington Crossing Chapter (Pennsylvania) of the Daughters of the American Revolution, has been a stalwart supporter of my literary efforts, which is especially important to me given her writing and editing acumen and historical knowledge.

Jennifer Martin, the FWCP executive director, and Connie Unangst, the WCHP bookstore manager, have been very supportive of my efforts in connection with writing this book, as well as the earlier one that also relates to my interpretive work at WCHP. WCHP veteran Dianne Breen has talked up my previous book to park visitors, for which I am most appreciative, and I hope she will feel the same about this one. Tom Maddock, a WCHP historical interpreter whom I consider a mentor, was kind enough to contribute to my bibliography by loaning a useful volume from his Revolutionary War library.

This project has benefited considerably from the input provided by Larry Kidder, author of *A People Harassed and Exhausted: The Story of a New Jersey Militia Regiment in the American Revolution* and *Crossroads of the Revolution: Trenton, 1774-1783*. Larry, who has a wealth of demonstrated expertise on colonial Trenton and the Revolution offered a perceptive critique of the manuscript and shared valuable insights on several matters as well as primary source materials. His stylistic suggestions improved the flow of the narrative, and he was particularly helpful in regard to supplying information about the 18th century Assunpink Creek stone bridge. In addition, he generously lent his mapmaking skills to these pages. I also thank Larry for his work on the design and production of this book. I am thankful for all of Larry's assistance and support and I recommend his newest work, *Ten Crucial Days: Washington's Vision for Victory Unfolds*.

Many thanks also to William Welsch, President of the American Revolution Round Table of Richmond and Co-founder of the Congress of ARRTs, for reviewing this work and sharing his insights about various aspects of the narrative. Bill is widely known for his extensive store of Revolutionary knowledge, and his comments and suggestions are most appreciated.

As she did with my first such venture, former newspaper editor Linda Lehans, aka my sister-in-law, contributed her rigorous editing to this project and thereby enhanced the quality of the final product. Thank goodness for those eagle eyes. I owe her again.

Thanks are especially due to publisher Roger Williams for turning a manuscript of mine into a published work for the second time, and his insights on various issues relating to historical literature and the preservation of history for this and future generations are a welcome bonus. .

At the David Library of the American Revolution—the singularly renowned research institution on American history between 1750 and 1800—librarian Kathie Ludwig and volunteer Parker Cohen provided a hand with Hand when I was looking for additional details about the Pennsylvania colonel. And Kaitlyn Pettengill, Digital Services Archivist at the Historical Society of Pennsylvania, retrieved a PDF of a letter from Hand to his wife that I earnestly sought. Richard Hunter, President/Principal Archeologist of Hunter Research, Inc., and an authority on Trenton area history, and Laura Poll, Archivist in the Trentoniana Room at the Trenton Free Public Library, responded in a very timely manner to my inquiries regarding the Revolutionary War era version of the Assunpink Creek bridge and the George Washington statute near the Assunpink Creek in Trenton's Mill Hill Historic District. I am grateful to all these individuals.

I want to give a shout-out to Joe Garrera, Executive Director of the Lehigh Valley Heritage Museum in Allentown, Pennsylvania, for the useful suggestion he provided in regard to the book's title when I visited his very impressive facility in connection with the speaker series that he and his staff organize for the benefit of the historically minded in their community. The title ultimately went in a different direction, but it's the thought that counts.

And a tip of the hat goes to Rob Fraser, the rummage sale book guru at Trinity Episcopal Church in Princeton, New Jersey, for keeping me in mind when he comes across anything that bears on Washington or the Revolution. Rob has unearthed some real treasures that now occupy an honored place on our living room bookshelf.

My first book reminded me—and if anything, this effort has even further heightened my awareness—of how beholden we are to the historians whose work informs our study and discussion of the "Ten Crucial Days." These include, in particular, William Dwyer, David Hackett Fischer, Richard Ketchum, David McCullough, and William Stryker. This volume seeks to build on their scholarship while also incorporating revisions as necessitated by more recent research findings.

The members of the community in which I have lived for more than three decades have provided a source of inspiration to me in writing a book that honors the memory of Edward Hand and the soldiers he led into combat on January 2, 1777. In that regard, I feel connected to the residents of Lawrence Township, New Jersey, which Hand's men would have known as Maidenhead— the people who live where those backwoodsmen fought along the road from Princeton to Trenton—with respect to their long-running endeavor to recognize the crucial role played by Hand's contingent in contributing to the successful outcome of the Battle of Assunpink Creek. The township has been doing that in January of every year since 1962 in an event that highlights its role in the Revolution. And each year since 1981, the role of Colonel Hand has been performed by local resident William Agress, who is joined on this occasion by other re-enactors, Revolutionary War enthusiasts, members of the Boy Scouts, township officials, and local residents. Kudos to these local history buffs. (One might say they deserve "a Hand" for their efforts.)

As I did once before, I would like to thank my wife Alison for tolerating my assorted shortcomings and sharing my interest in colonial America, which certainly helped to create an environment conducive to producing this latest work. Daughter Gwyneth provided invaluable assistance to a technologically challenged author attempting to cope with various software issues.

And I must acknowledge another fellow historical interpreter, Bunkie Maddock, for suggesting that I write a book in the first place. Now I've written two of them, which makes her idea twice as good or twice as bad as it was before.

Finally, homage must be paid to WCHP, the hallowed ground where I hang out. I love having the opportunity to share my interest and passion about the Revolutionary War era with people of all ages, backgrounds, and nationalities, and even more so to do it in a place that is suffused with the indelible imagery of an inspirational struggle for American independence and freedom.

INDEX

Index

Index

The following is an excerpt from David Price's book
RESCUING THE REVOLUTION: *Unsung Patriot Heroes and
the Ten Crucial Days of America's War for Independence*

EDWARD HAND

Colonel Edward Hand and the outnumbered soldiers
under his command bravely and skillfully resisted the advance
of the British and Hessian troops marching from Princeton to
Trenton on January 2, 1777, and their delaying action bought
the Continental Army enough time to successfully defend its
position on the banks of the Assunpink Creek at the Second
Battle of Trenton later that day. The clash at the creek became
the precursor to Washington's audacious overnight end run
around the enemy's left flank, followed by the next day's triumph
at Princeton in the capstone event of the "Ten Crucial Days."

According to one description, "Hand looked the part of
a soldier . . . tall, lean, and leathery, a natural leader." He was 32
years old in 1776 and a native of Ireland, where he had earned
a medical degree at Trinity College, Dublin. Hand enlisted as
a surgeon's mate in the 18th Royal Irish Regiment in 1767 and
came to America that year. In 1774, he resigned his commission
and settled in Lancaster, Pennsylvania. A strong supporter of the
Revolution, he helped organize the Lancaster County Associators
and was commissioned a lieutenant colonel in command of
a rifle company known as the 1st Pennsylvania Continental
Regiment. He was promoted to colonel a few months later, and
his regiment joined the newly established Continental Army—
camped in Cambridge out-side Boston shortly after the battle
at Bunker Hill in 1775—as the first unit to report from beyond
the boundaries of New England. According to one description,
most of the 1st Pennsylvania soldiers "were backwoodsmen—
tall, lean men who wore hunting shirts, leather leggings, and
Indian moccasins, and carried that deadly long rifle which proved
to be a thing of terror to the British and Hessians."

The skilled marksmen of Hand's outfit would become known for employing their American-made long rifles with lethal effect against the enemy. These weapons added a new dimension to the firepower of Washington's army. As described by John Ferling, "They were a backcountry tool, made mostly in Pennsylvania and used there and in the Chesapeake colonies by men who hunted for much of their fresh meat. Unlike muskets, which were a smooth bore weapon, the long barrel of a rifle was etched, or 'rifled,' [on the inside] with seven or eight grooves. Rifling made the weapon accurate at a range of about two hundred yards, perhaps even three hundred, several times the reliable reach of a musket."

The British Army had never taken to the use of rifles because they took longer to load and fire and could not accommodate a bayonet. Instead, it continued to rely on the Brown Bess musket that was also used by Continental soldiers who were not in rifle companies. Although a highly unreliable weapon that was ineffective at a range of more than 80 to 100 yards, the use of the Brown Bess allowed the British to employ their "favorite tactic"—the bayonet charge "guaranteed to have a fearsome effect on an enemy."

By December 1776, Colonel Hand and his regiment "had fought in nearly every important engagement" since joining Washington's army, having seen action at the Battle of Long Island in August and in the subsequent New York campaign and retreat across New Jersey. As part of the brigade commanded by Brigadier General Matthias Alexis de Roche Fermoy, a French recruit to the patriot cause, Hand's soldiers and the German Continental Regiment commanded by Colonel Nicholas Haussegger (the only American regiment named for the ethnic identity of its soldiers) were among the first to engage the Hessians at Trenton on December 26. Driving toward the Princeton Road lying northeast of the town, also known as the King's Highway, they assisted in cutting off what proved to be a futile attempt by Colonel Rall's troops to skirt the Americans' left flank and escape in the direction of Princeton. This maneuver by Fermoy's brigade would help to seal the fate of an enemy force that was soon to be enveloped by the onrushing Continentals.

The events that ensued during the week following the First Battle of Trenton set the stage for the exploits of Hand's riflemen on the road from Princeton to Trenton. After the victory on December 26, Washington marched his army and his prisoners back to Pennsylvania, but on the 29th and 30th, his men crossed the river once more and slogged back to Trenton. Washington learned that the Hessian troops below Trenton under Colonel von Donop had pulled back from their out-posts at Bordentown and Burlington in response to the attack on the Rall brigade, and he sought to take advantage of this development.

Once in Trenton, Washington was able to consolidate the American forces in the area, which included his brigades and the militia units led by General James Ewing and Colonel John Cadwalader that had also crossed over from Pennsylvania. He now had approximately 6,000 soldiers un-der his command, and they dug in along a three-mile stretch on the southern bank of the Assunpink Creek in lower Trenton in preparation for an enemy attack that they anticipated in response to the events of the 26th. This was a strong defensive position because it was on high ground overlooking a creek with very steep sides and, aside from a stone bridge near where the creek emptied into the Delaware River, offered very few places where an opposing army could cross.

While his men made ready, Washington delivered an impassioned plea to his soldiers whose one-year enlistments were to expire on December 31, asking them not to go home but to remain with the army for another six weeks. He persuaded a bare majority of them to do so, aided by a promise to pay each soldier ten dollars in hard coin in exchange for his continued service.

The attack that the Americans anticipated came on January 2, when General Cornwallis led some 8,000 British and Hessian troops down the Princeton Road in the direction of Trenton. An able field commander, "Cornwallis was smart, daring, and tough." He had pursued Washington's soldiers across New Jersey during their retreat to the Delaware River in November and early December but had been unable to prevent their escape to the Pennsylvania side. Now, in the wake of the upstart rebels' shocking win at Trenton, Cornwallis's orders from his superior officer, General William Howe, were straightforward—find the American army and destroy it. In short, his job was to finish the job.

The progress of Cornwallis's men toward Trenton on January 2 was slowed by muddy road conditions caused by rain the night before and unseasonably warm weather that day, but another impediment would prove to be even more problematic for his soldiers—Colonel Hand and his Pennsylvania backwoodsmen. The British and Hessian vanguard reached the village of Maiden-head at about 11:00 a.m. and halted to allow the main body to come up. To this point, they had only encountered occasional harassing fire from scattered pickets; however, two miles south of the village in the woods behind the Big Shabakunk Creek, several American regiments, including Hand's, lay in waiting. They totaled about a thousand men and were commanded by General Fermoy. As the enemy approached, Fermoy suddenly mounted his horse and galloped toward Trenton, abandoning his command and leaving Colonel Hand as the senior officer. Fortunately for the patriot cause, Hand was ready to lead, and his men were ready to follow. Those "tough and undisciplined backcountry riflemen were devoted to him" and never proved it more than on this day.

The soldiers under Hand's command included his regiment, the German Continental Regiment, and the 5th Virginia Continental Regiment led by Colonel Charles Scott, supported by two guns from Captain Thomas Forrest's Pennsylvania battery. As the flank and advance guards of Cornwallis's column approached, the Continentals unleashed a deadly fire that drove the enemy van-guard back into their main body and produced great confusion among them. Cornwallis was forced to throw the main body of his column into the fight and deploy artillery against the Continental sharpshooters hidden in the woods. The time it took their adversary to organize this effort and press their attack was crucially valuable to the American cause, for the longer it took Cornwallis to get to Trenton, the less time he would have to launch an attack against Washington before darkness interrupted his offensive.

Hand's resilient soldiers fell back in the face of superior enemy numbers but stubbornly fought a delaying action for much of the afternoon. They "waylaid their foe with a lethal fire from concealed positions in the untidy dark brown forests" and waged a series of "time-consuming fire-fights before melting away to take up new positions further down the road." Under heavy pressure and outnumbered more than six to one, the American units held off the advancing column for two hours until almost 3:00 p.m., when they began a slow retreat through the woods toward Trenton "in good order with all their equipment." They had been jousting with the British and Hessians, with varying degrees of intensity, for some five hours, and had held them as long as they could. When Hand's defenders were about half a mile from the town, Washington himself, accompanied by Generals Nathanael Greene and Henry Knox, rode up to encourage them and stress the importance of delaying the enemy until nightfall because the commander-in-chief had a plan that de-pended on holding off Cornwallis as long as possible.

By 4:00 p.m., with the shadows lengthening and the enemy force entering Trenton, Hand's men were falling back through the town. They directed a steady fire at their pursuers from behind the wooden houses that they passed while streaming toward the bridge over the Assunpink Creek that was held by

Washington's main body. Under protective fire from Colonel Daniel Hitchcock's Rhode Island Continental Regiment, as well as American artillery positioned below the creek, Hand and his contingent crossed over to the main line of defense behind the waterway and found Washington astride his horse beside the bridge, quietly watching as Cornwallis's troops pushed through the town in his direction.

It was now past 4:00 p m., and sunset would be at 4:46 that day. Hand's regiment and the other soldiers fighting alongside it had bought Washington the time he needed to fend off the enemy because there was not enough daylight left for a full-scale assault against the American troops below the Assunpink. Cornwallis launched a series of probes to try to find a weakness in the Continental lines, but each was beaten back with heavy losses. Although Washington had fewer soldiers than his adversary, he had more artillery—with some 40 pieces to Cornwallis's 28—and those guns were arrayed along the creek so as to provide overlapping fields of fire. The British and Hessian probes were met with "a storm of musketry, and the artillery joined in." The American cannon un-leashed "the heaviest fire ever delivered on any field in the Western Hemisphere up to this time."

Although there is no definitive information available with regard to casualties, it has been estimated that about 365 British and Hessian soldiers were killed, wounded, or captured on January 2 as compared with approximately 100 Americans. To that extent, it may be regarded as a "great victory" for Washington and "a model of a brilliantly managed defensive battle." When darkness fell, Cornwallis called a halt to the fighting, and that evening he convened a council of war. Tradition has it that the British commander—confident that he had the Americans trapped between the creek and the Delaware River and could finish them off the next day—told his fellow officers: "We've got the Old Fox safe now. We'll go over and bag him in the morning."

Unfortunately for Cornwallis, the fox would outfox the hunter, for under the cover of dark-ness, the Continentals slipped away from the creek during the early morning hours of January 3. They embarked on a forced march that would lead to an unexpected encounter with a small British force left behind in Princeton during the advance of Cornwallis's main body to Trenton the day before, which resulted in another victory for the Americans. To cover the movement of his forces from below the creek, Washington left behind several hundred men for part of the night with orders to keep their campfires burning "until there were several dozen veritable conflagrations blazing on the heights south of Assunpink Creek, convincing the British that the Americans were still there." He also instructed this rearguard to stay warm "by clanging picks and shovels on the frozen earth. The noise convinced British sentries that the rebels were building earthworks against tomorrow's assault."

Following up their feats of daring along the Princeton Road on the afternoon of January 2 and the contribution of their lethal firepower to the success of Washington's army during its twilight stand against the enemy at the Assunpink, Colonel Hand's soldiers again proved of service at Princeton the following day as they helped turn back the British charge against General Nathanael Greene's division at a critical moment in the battle.

After the "Ten Crucial Days" ended, Hand's service in the Continental Army continued throughout the struggle for independence, earning him a series of promotions: to brigadier general when he was assigned to command the American troops at Fort Pitt in 1777, to brigadier general in command of a brigade of light infantry in the Marquis de Lafayette's division in 1780, to adjutant general of the army in 1781, and then to brevet major general in 1783.

Hand resigned from the military in 1783 and moved back to Lancaster, where he purchased several hundred acres of land on which he built a Georgian-style brick mansion that became known as Rock Ford Plantation. He practiced medicine and occupied a variety of civic and political positions, as a member of the Congress of Confederation (1784-1785) and the Pennsylvania Assembly (1785-1786), and as a delegate to the Pennsylvania Constitutional Convention (1790). He died of cholera in September 1802 at age 57 and was buried in St. James Episcopal Cemetery in Lancaster.

The crucial role played by Edward Hand and his riflemen in contributing to the successful out-come of the Second Battle of Trenton has been celebrated in January of every year since 1962 as part of an annual event staged by Lawrence Township, New Jersey (which Hand's men would have known as Maidenhead) to highlight its role in the Revolution. The part of the indomitable colonel has been faithfully performed by township resident William Agress on each such occasion since 1981, and he is regularly joined by other re-enactors, Revolutionary War enthusiasts, members of the Boy Scouts, township officials, and local residents. After a ceremony at the municipal building, they march south along Route 206 (which Hand's men would have known as the Prince-ton Road) to Notre Dame High School, adjacent to the Shabakunk Creek where Hand led the Americans in their delaying action against the enemy on January 2, 1777. There a cannon is fired to mark the occasion. Year in and year out, the remembrance of this patriot hero and the exploits of his Pennsylvania sharpshooters has no greater friend than Mr. Agress and his fellow marchers.

If any revolutionary hero deserves such a loyal following over so many years, it is surely the stout-hearted rifle commander from Lancaster. Edward Hand was "the stuff of which the hard core" of Washington's army was made.

A NOTE ABOUT THE AUTHOR

David Price is a historical interpreter at Washington Crossing Historic Park in Pennsylvania and the author of *Rescuing the Revolution: Unsung Patriot Heroes and the Ten Crucial Days of America's War for Independence*. Under the auspices of the Friends of Washington Crossing Park, he conducts guided interpretive tours at this Registered National Historic Landmark and site of the Continental Army's crossing of the Delaware River in 1776, focusing on the "Ten Crucial Days" of the American Revolution and other historical aspects of the park. In addition, he is a historical interpreter at Princeton Battlefield State Park in New Jersey. Price holds degrees in political science from Drew University and Rutgers University—New Brunswick, and was a nonpartisan research analyst with the New Jersey Legislature for 31 years. He is a member of various national and local organizations relating to the Revolutionary War and lives in Lawrence Township, NJ, which was known as Maidenhead at the time of the Revolution.

Recommended Reading from TenCrucialDays.org

Specific to the Ten Crucial Days

1. *TEN CRUCIAL DAYS: Washington's Vision for Victory Unfolds* by Larry Kidder (Knox, 2019) The most authoritative modern narrative on the Ten Crucial Days.
2. *ROAD TO ASSUNPINK CREEK: Liberty's Desperate Hour and the Ten Crucial Days of the American Revolution* by David Price (Knox 2019). Says Patrick K. O'Donnell, "Assembling the best scholarship … Price has rightfully elevated the crucial importance of one of the least remembered battles…"
3. *VICTORY OR DEATH: The Battles of Trenton and Princeton* by Mark Maloy (Savas Beatie, 2018) Good overview and great for a self-guided tour.
4. *RESCUING THE REVOLUTION: Unsung Patriot Heroes and the Ten Crucial Days of America's War for Independence* by David Price (Knox 2016) Fascinating biographical vignettes about names clouded in history.
5. *1776* by David McCullough (Simon & Schuster, 2006)
6. *WASHINGTON'S CROSSING* by David Hackett Fischer (Oxford, 2004) Despite having included some of Stryker's challenged references this is the bestselling book on the subject.
7. *THE LONG RETREAT: The Calamitous Defense of New Jersey, 1776* by Arthur S. Lefkowitz (Rutgers, 1998)
8. *THE DAY IS OURS! An Inside View of the Battles of Trenton and Princeton, November 1776-January 1777* by William M. Dwyer (Viking, 1983) ▼Relies heavily on Stryker; written in a thrilling, journalistic style.
9. *THE WINTER SOLDIERS: The Battles for Trenton and Princeton* by Richard M. Ketchum. (Doubleday, 1973) ▼Relies heavily on Stryker. Good military history for the modern reader.
10. *THE BATTLE OF TRENTON/THE BATTLE OF PRINCETON: Two Studies* by Samuel Stelle Smith (Philip Freneau 1967) ▼
11. *THE BATTLES OF TRENTON AND PRINCETON* by William S. Stryker (Houghton Mifflin, 1898) ▼The earliest history from which many following works have been based. While detailed, there are unsourced references which are either questionable, or have since been proven inaccurate. Still, a must read for anyone interested in the Ten Crucial Days.

Overviews, Abridgments, and Essays on the Ten Crucial Days and the Revolution in New Jersey

1. *NEW JERSEY IN THE AMERICAN REVOLUTION* edited by Barbara J. Mitnick (Rutgers, 2005)
2. *TRENTON AND PRINCETON 1776-77: Washington Crosses the Delaware* by David Bonk (Osprey 2010) ▼
3. *A PEOPLE HARASSED AND EXHAUSTED: The Story of a New Jersey Militia Regiment in the American Revolution* by Larry Kidder (Kidder, 2013)
4. *THE AMERICAN REVOLUTION IN NEW JERSEY: Where the Battlefront Meets the Home Front* edited by James J. Gigantino II (Rutgers, 2015)
5. *FATAL SUNDAY: George Washington, the Monmouth Campaign, and the Politics of Battle* by Mark Edward Lender and Garry Wheeler Stone Ph.D (Univ OK 2016) Award winning narrative on the largest battle fought in the northern theater of the revolution.
6. *CROSSROADS OF THE REVOLUTION: Trenton, 1774-1783* by William L. "Larry" Kidder (Knox, 2017) Meticulously researched history of Trenton; rich background on how this important colonial town survived the revolution.

General Histories of the Revolution

1. *THE BRITISH ARE COMING* by Rick Atkinson (Holt 2019)
2. *THEATERS OF THE AMERICAN REVOLUTION* by James Kirby Martin and David L. Preston, Editors (Westholme 2017)
3. *WASHINGTON'S IMMORTALS: The Untold Story of an Elite Regiment Who Changed the Course of the Revolution* by Patrick K. O'Donnell (Grove 2017)
4. *AMERICAN REVOLUTIONS: A Continental History, 1750-1804* by Alan Taylor (WW Norton 2016)
5. *BAND OF GIANTS: The Amateur Soldiers Who Won America's Independence* by Jack Kelly (Macmillan 2014)
6. *THE MEN WHO LOST AMERICA: British Leadership, the American Revolution, and the Fate of the Empire* by Andrew Jackson O'Shaughnessy (Yale 2013)
7. *ALMOST A MIRACLE: The American Victory in the War of Independence* by John Ferling (Oxford 2007)
8. *THE GLORIOUS CAUSE: The American Revolution, 1763-1789* by Robert Middlekauff (Oxford 2007)

*Books for Young Readers about the Ten Crucial Days and the Revolution
Listed by Age Group*

1. *CROSSING THE DELAWARE: George Washington Fights the Battle of Trenton* by Arian Dean (Rosen 2004, Ages 5 – 9)
2. *WHEN WASHINGTON CROSSED THE DELAWARE* by Lynne Cheney (Simon & Schuster 2012, Ages 5 – 9)
3. *REVOLUTIONARY WAR ON WEDNESDAY: Magic Tree House #22* by Mary Pope Osborne (Random House 2000, Ages 6 – 9)
4. *THE AMERICAN REVOLUTION FOR KIDS: A History with 21 Activities* by Janis Herbert (Chicago Review 2002) (Ages 6 – 9)
5. *IF YOU WERE A KID DURING THE AMERICAN REVOLUTION* by Wil Mara (Scholastic 2016) (Ages 6 – 9)
6. *THE CROSSING: How George Washington Saved the American Revolution* by Jim Murphy (Scholastic 2016, Ages 8 – 12)
7. *CROSSING THE DELAWARE: A History in Many Voices* by Louise Peacock (Aladdin 2007, Ages 8 – 12)
8. *GEORGE WASHINGTON: The Crossing* by Jack E. Levin, Mark R. Levin (Threshold 2013, Ages 8 – 12)
9. *TIME ENOUGH FOR DRUMS* by Ann Rinaldi (Laurel Leaf 2000, Fiction, Ages 12+ -)

Television and Film

1. "Turn" - AMC - www.amc.com/shows/turn (rife with historical liberties, but a nice sense of time and place).
2. "Winter Patriots" - www.WinterPatriots.com. Produced by Mount Vernon, with support from the F. M. Kirby Foundation
3. "The Crossing" - A&E TV 2003 (rife with historical liberties, but a nice sense of time and place).

These and other fine books and educational materials are available at your local library, or wherever books are sold including the David Library of the American Revolution 215-493-6776, the gift shops at The Old Barracks Museum 609-396-1776, and Washington's Crossing Historic Park 215-493-4076. (Titles listed with a ▼ are out of print and are available at libraries or perhaps online)

Relive the
"Ten Crucial Days"
of the
American Revolution

Visit These Historic Sites:

Washington Crossing Historic Park

This Pennsylvania state park and National Historic Landmark is where General George Washington's army began its epic crossing of the Delaware River on the night of December 25-26, 1776, which may have saved our nation's quest for independence when the American Revolution appeared all but lost. This was the beginning of the "Ten Crucial Days." The park offers a visitor center and more than 500 acres of American history, natural beauty, and family fun.

Located less than a mile from the park is **The David Library of the American Revolution**. It is a specialized research library, open free of charge to the public, which is dedicated to the study of American history between 1750 and 1800. This nonprofit educational institution is a valuable and welcoming resource for anyone seeking information about virtually anything relating to America's war for independence. It also features lectures and events of interest to the historical community.

Washington Crossing State Park

This New Jersey state park lies opposite its Pennsylvania sister and is part of the same National Historic Landmark. It is the site where Washington's army landed after crossing the Delaware River to attack the Hessian brigade occupying Trenton. In addition to its historical significance, the 3,500-acre park is well known for its trails and wildlife habitat.

OLD BARRACKS MUSEUM

This museum in Trenton has a unique history dating back to 1758, when it was built to house British soldiers during the French and Indian War. It is a remnant of 18th century Trenton that helps visitors understand both the Battle of Trenton on December 26, 1776 and the Battle of Assunpink Creek (also known as the Second Battle of Trenton) on January 2, 1777. From military quarters to widow's home, from brothel to museum, the building offers visitors a fascinating look at the history of the area.

PRINCETON BATTLEFIELD

This New Jersey state park is where the Battle of Princeton was fought on January 3, 1777 - the capstone event of the "Ten Crucial Days" campaign that altered the course of the war. It is the site of what is considered to be the fiercest fight of its size during the long conflict. The 1772 Clarke House witnessed the battle and served as sanctuary for the wounded General Hugh Mercer, who died there nine days later. It contains period furniture and Revolutionary War exhibits.

Learn more about these historic sites at:

www.tencrucialdays.org

Look for more books from Knox Press Books
- E-books, paperbacks, and Limited Edition hardcovers.

The best in military history can be found at:

www.knoxpress.com

Also, look at our sister companies at:

www.wingedhussarpublishing.com

for information and upcoming publications.